ST. BERNARD
OF CLAIRVAUX

ST. BERNARD
OF CLAIRVAUX

Seen through his Selected Letters

Newly translated
and with an introduction by

Rev. Bruno Scott James

Foreword by
Thomas Merton

Chicago · HENRY REGNERY COMPANY · *1953*

NIHIL OBSTAT: EDVARDVS MAHONEY, S.T.D.

CENSOR DEPVTATVS

IMPRIMATVR: E. MORROGH BERNARD

VICARIVS GENERALIS

WESTMONASTERII: DIE XVIII DECEMBRIS MCMLÏI

FOREWORD

"It has been the ordinary rule of God's dealing with us," says Cardinal Newman, "that personal sanctity should be attendant upon high spiritual dignity of place or work. . . . The prophets have ordinarily not only gifts but graces; they are not only inspired to know and teach God's will, but inwardly converted to obey it. For surely those only can preach the truth duly who feel it personally; those only transmit it fully from God to man, who have in the transmission made it their own."

It is this "ordinary rule" that makes God so wonderful in His saints. It is the only explanation of a St. Bernard in whom, as in some of His other great saints, God is not only wonderful but also scandalous. Did not St. Paul warn all generations that the folly of the Cross would always be a scandal?

Bernard of Clairvaux was plunged deep in the mystery of the Cross, which was the mystery of God's will for his world and ours. He who had left the world to become a monk was thrown back into the world to be an apostle, a worker of miracles, a peacemaker and a warmaker, the reformer of abbeys, the monitor of Popes and a prophet sent to alarm kings.

The saint who wrote these letters became the passionate embodiment of the truths in which he believed. The words of God, which are purified by fire, burned white hot in a human frame scarcely able to contain them. The zeal for the House of God was devouring a sick man whose continued existence on earth could only be explained by miracle.

Bernard, the contemplative, was a great man of action because he was a great contemplative. And because he was a contemplative he never ceased fearing to be a mere man of action. He knew better than anyone that even the saints cannot touch pitch without being defiled by it. The natural sincerity and the supernatural zeal for divine truth that burned within him could not help showing him the faults of frailty and passion which even a saint could commit in the heat of ruthless and energetic action. Yet he refused to have mercy on his body or on his soul, and threw himself fiercely into the most difficult problems of his age. Most of these letters were hammered out of the white hot material found in conflict. They show the man as he is, and because he is so much a man, readers who forget that saints must be men may here and there be inclined to question his sanctity. That would be a great pity in an age which needs saints as badly as ours. Bernard is sent to instruct us how human a saint must be, to forge out the will of God in the heat of the affairs of men. In his Sermons on the Canticle he can be as lyrical as St. Francis. In his letters he is too busy upbraiding the bishops to have time for a sermon to the birds.

In these letters we see, more than anything else, the public facets of a manysided character. They are the facets Bernard himself liked least, and he would have been ready to admit that he did not appear at his best in some of the petty business which his letters endeavored to settle. How often do we not hear him cry out against the *necessitas*, and the *malitia diei*, the "evils of the day," the trivial and often sordid material questions that inevitably arise in human society to draw men down from God? But Bernard was more humble than his own protestations of humility would lead us to believe. He had the humility to be himself in the thick of a silly argument. He had the good grace to admit that a saint might possibly have to bicker with another saint over their respective rights to a monk who had skipped from one monastery to another without observing the proper formalities. He did not fear to display a bold and grandiose impatience with his correspondents, even were they kings. He could open a letter to the King of England with words like these: "The King of kings has for long chastised your royal majesty for he is more powerful than you." And he could do so without starting a war, because it was so evident that he knew this King of kings that he spoke of so familiarly: that he was, indeed, His spokesman, and required a respectful hearing.

Father Bruno James suggests that St. Bernard is "at his best when he is angry." I need not defend the righteous anger of St. Bernard, for only God can tell the difference between a holy indignation and the "anger of man which worketh not the justice of God" (James 1: 20). But I know that when St. Paul was angry it was Christ Who spoke in him (II Cor. 13: 2-3). I only hope that the angry Bernard, the passionate Bernard, who even in his anger and in his passion was a saint, will not blind everyone to the merciful Bernard, the gentle and longsuffering monk who could be as tender as a mother to anyone who did not give evidence of being a hardened Pharisee, and who had in his heart something of Christ's unending patience with the weak sinner and His compassion for the publican.

Some of these letters are curiously amusing, like the one which records a discussion between St. Bernard and St. Norbert, in which the letter expressed his conviction that Antichrist would appear on the scene in their "own generation." St. Bernard "did not feel compelled to agree." Most of the letters contain concise and memorable aphorisms which will bear long meditation. He tells a Cluniac monk, who has just been elected Bishop of a wicked city: "You must not only be patient so as not to be overcome by evil, you must also be peaceable so as to overcome evil by good." To another Bishop elect, whose past life offers little to recommend him for such a difficult position, St. Bernard writes drily: "It is laid down that we should love others as we love ourselves. But if you were to love others as you have hitherto loved yourself, I for one would not wish to be committed to your care." But there are other letters which show St. Bernard as a speculative mystic. The twelfth letter to the Carthusians, on the subject of "pure love" takes us at once to the heart of St. Bernard's theology. It sets forth the principle that the "immaculate law of God" is charity, and that there is no mystical liberation, no transformation in Christ, for the soul that has not been elevated, by the Spirit of God, above the law of selfishness and cupidity to the realm of divine charity.

But it is needless for me to add another introduction to St. Bernard when the translator himself has already written a good one. It only remains for me to praise his translation, which I can do in good conscience because it is easily the best English version of the Saint's Letters so far published.

Although English can never quite recapture the solidity of Latin, Father Bruno James has preserved most of the vigor and life and rhythm of the original. This is a rare translation which really sounds something like St. Bernard. I think such a success could only have been achieved by someone who had a great love for the saint and for the Cistercians of the twelfth century.

Nothing remains to be said except that whether the reader may like St. Bernard or not, whether he may understand St. Bernard or not, he can hardly fail to recognize, in perusing these letters, that he is face to face with an imposingly important personality. St. Bernard is too important to be overlooked. He belongs on the bookshelves of every educated man, along with St. Augustine, and St. Gregory, St. Anselm and St. Thomas Aquinas. The whole Bernard is not to be found in his letters alone: but the whole Bernard can never be known without them.

If we really take the trouble to know him, we will gain more than mere respect for his great gifts. We will come to admire and love him. Admiration and love mean little, without imitation. Perhaps our own century needs nothing so much as the combined anger and gentleness of another Bernard. If we lack the special grace which alone is capable of achieving such a paradox, let us at least gather from St. Bernard that letter-writing is an art which has been forgotten, but which needs to be re-learned by men.

Abbey of Gethsemani, Ky.

THOMAS MERTON

CONTENTS

THE LETTERS OF ST. BERNARD

INTRODUCTION

SAINT BERNARD of Clairvaux was born in the year 1090 at Fontaines-les-Dijon and died on August 20th, 1153, at Clairvaux. He came of a distinguished family on both sides. His father, Tescelin, held Feudal lordship over property in Burgundy and Champagne, and Aleth, his mother, was related to the Dukes of Burgundy. Highly intelligent and with the backing of his influential family, any career in Church or State would have been open to the young Bernard. But at the age of twenty-two he chose to leave everything, turn his back on the world and become a monk. Had he elected to join one of the great Abbeys there would have been nothing strange about his action, there would still have been scope for soaring ambition. The famous Abbey of Cluny had given popes to the Church. Instead he chose the Abbey of Cîteaux, a poor and insignificant monastery which few had ever heard about and none took very seriously. It had been founded a few years previously by what were probably considered a group of rather eccentric though doubtless holy men, as an escape from the pompous magnificence of the great monastic houses back to the simplicity of Saint Benedict's Rule. At first it had enjoyed a measure of fame and young men had come to try the life, but they did not persevere. The situation was unhealthy and the community was desperately poor. Undoubtedly the life was rough and austere, but we must not exaggerate the contrast between the life that Bernard had left behind him in the world and the life he followed at Cîteaux. The life of even the richest nobility in those days was intolerably rough compared to that of even the poorest people of our day. Bernard did not enter Cîteaux alone, he gave early proof of those wonderful powers of persuasion and leadership which he was to show all through his life by bringing with him no less than thirty companions. He was twenty-two years old when he knocked on the gates of the monastery, and the Abbot at that time, the man who was to have the responsibility of his spiritual formation, was an Englishman, a native of Dorset, called Stephen Harding. After this the waters closed over the head of Bernard and we hear nothing more of him until three years later when he was sent out to found a new monastery. For this venture a remote valley of evil repute, called the valley of Wormwood, was chosen, or rather given. It could not have seemed very suitable except for its remoteness from the world, but the monks were too poor to be particular. In a very few years Bernard and his sons were to earn for this valley another name, it was to become known the world over as Clairvaux, or the Valley of Light. Very soon after this Bernard was dragged from the peaceful service of God in his monastery on to the arena of world affairs. It was by no choice of his that this happened, the needs of the hour and the obedience he owed to his Bishop and the Pope compelled him to come forth. In vain he pleaded sickness, for he was always ailing; in vain he pleaded his incompetence to deal with great affairs; men would not listen to him. Honours and anything that the world could give men were prepared to load upon him, but the one thing he asked for, to be left in peace and obscurity, they denied him. He was not free to decline the burdens and troubles of his fellow men, but he could and did reject their honours and adulation. When a great schism in the papacy rent the whole of Christendom into two camps, Bernard had to heal it. When a violent quarrel broke out in far-off England over the election of the Archbishop of York, Bernard was appealed to. When a Bishop repented of the evil for which he had been deposed, he came to Bernard to implore his intercession with the Pope. When a heresy threatened the Church, Bernard had to quell it.

When the Emperor made his help to the Pope depend upon a shameful condition, Bernard was called upon to confront him and bring him to a sense of his duty. When the Saracen began to threaten the Holy Places in Palestine, Bernard was chosen to preach the Crusade. And then, on top of all this, there were the troubles of poor and humble people, the poignant troubles of the ordinary men and women of his day. They all came to Bernard for comfort and for help, and they were none of them turned away. From the seclusion of his cloister Bernard carried the whole world upon his shoulders, bowed down but not broken by the burden.

Every age has its great men. They strut across the pages of history full of sound and fury, and then they are gone. Darkness overtakes them and the dust they stir by their brief and angry progress settles into the dry records of their biographers. Great men they may be, but they are of their age and with their age they pass away. Yet some few are great enough to transcend the limitations of their age with a message for all time. Shining more with the light of God than with their own, the light they shed remains to inspire men to seek the things that are above and to guide their steps through the storms and darkness of life. Such a man, beyond all question, was Saint Bernard of Clairvaux. He was the very embodiment of all that was best in his times, yet his doctrine, his writings, his example are as vital and living for us as they were for the men and women of his day. During his life he bestrode the world like a colossus; and he has not ceased in our time to dominate the consciousness of Christians. In every age men have succumbed to his influence and paid tribute to his goodness and sincerity even when they have not been able to sympathize with his doctrine. Clearly everything we can learn of such a man will be of the utmost interest and significance. Happily there is no shortage of information. His early disciples have left us accounts of his life and actions and every

year brings to light new records. But best of all we have the
living picture he has given us of himself in his letters. Here,
in these intimate and spontaneous documents, his soul is laid
bare for all to see. His correspondence must have been enormous and only a tiny fraction of it has survived but enough
to give a glowing picture of a man great by any standard, great
enough to fill the canvas of all time. We find him correspond-
ing with Emperors, Kings, Popes, Philosophers and the ordinary men and women of his day. On one page we find him
upbraiding some great prince of the Church or State for
neglecting his duty towards his flock or for overstepping the
bounds of his authority, and on another pleading for a poor
man who has lost his pig. In one letter we find him comforting
one of his monks or consoling a dear friend in the world, and
in another writing with words of fire on the love of God to
the monks of The Grande Chartreuse. Sometimes we see him
in a light and gay mood, at other times aflame with indignation
and wrath on behalf of some poor wretch who had suffered
an injustice, and at yet other times ill and tired, worn out by
the folly and pettiness of human nature. These letters seem
to open for us a small window through which we can gaze out
upon all the life and color of the Middle Ages.

In this selection of Saint Bernard's letters I have tried to
choose those which are most revealing of their author, those
which show best his many-sided character. With two or
three notable exceptions I have avoided the longer letters as
apt to be rather tedious for the ordinary reader. In this bunch
all the grapes are ripe, but the reader is advised to take them
here and there as his mood and the circumstances of the moment dictate and not to run his teeth through the whole bunch
at one time. Above all they should be picked and "inwardly
digested" slowly and carefully. But in order properly to
understand them and savour their full flavour it should be borne
in mind that the whole of Bernard's thought, not merely his

phrases, was moulded by the sacred Scriptures all of which he knew by heart. His indignation finds its natural expression in the burning words of Jeremias, his affection in the yearning languors of the Canticle, and his fears in the forebodings of Daniel and the prophets.

This translation makes no attempt at being a crib. It does not claim to be a literal, word for word translation. It has been the endeavour of the translator to take the sense of the text and wield it into an idiom that can be understood by the ordinary men and women of today, while at the same time preserving as much as possible of the characteristics of the original. In this work much help has been received from many different quarters all of which have been carefully acknowledged in the introduction to the complete collection of the letters. The letters in the present edition, by the way, are numbered according to their order in the complete collection.

BRUNO SCOTT JAMES

THE LETTERS

To Robert, His Nephew

(About the Year 1119)

Robert of Châtillon was the son of Otho of Châtillon and, probably, Diana, the younger daughter of Robert of Montbard. He would thus be Bernard's first cousin although, because of the great disparity in their ages, he was always known as his nephew.

When he was still a child his parents promised him to Cluny. But later, when old enough to act on his own account, he joined the Cistercians, attracted, no doubt, by the fame of his kinsman. After some delay owing to his extreme youth, Robert was admitted into the novitiate at Cîteaux and, after the regular year of probation, made his vows as a Cistercian monk.

Whether he was professed at Cîteaux and then followed St. Bernard to Clairvaux, or whether he went with Bernard when he made the foundation, is not certain. But he was not long at Clairvaux before he began to find the austerities irksome and to compare the life there with the easier ways of Cluny. To support his unsettled state came the insidious doubt as to whether he was not bound to Cluny by the promise of his parents.

This is one of the most characteristic of Bernard's letters and it is interesting from an historical point of view as the first shot fired in the great controversy between the congregation of Cluny and the Cistercian reform. It is also interesting for the circumstances under which it was written. The monk William, Bernard's secretary at this time, tells us that while

Bernard was dictating in a secluded corner out of doors, where he could not be overheard, heavy rain began to fall. But when he tried to protect the letter Bernard told him to write on for it was God's work and yet, although rain fell all round, the letter remained dry 'in imbre sine imbre'.

LONG enough, perhaps too long, have I waited, dearest Robert, for the Lord that he might deign to touch your soul and mine through yours, moving you to salutary regrets for your error and me to joy for your deliverance. But seeing myself still disappointed of my hope, I can no longer hide my sorrow, restrain my anxiety, or dissemble my grief. And so, against all the laws of justice, I who have been wounded am forced to recall him who wounded me; who have been spurned, him who spurned me; who have been smitten, him who struck the blow. In short I must cast myself at the feet of him who should cast himself at mine. Sorrow is not careful to count the cost: is not ashamed; does not nicely weigh the pros and cons; is not fearful for its dignity; respects no rules; it cares only that it has what it would be without, or lacks what it would have. 'But', you will say, 'I have hurt no one, spurned no one. Rather have I, spurned and repeatedly hurt, sought only to fly my oppressor. Who can I have hurt, if I have only avoided being hurt? Is it not wiser to yield to the persecutor than to resist him? To avoid him who strikes than to strike back?' Quite so; I agree. I am not writing to dispute with you, but to remove the grounds for dispute. To fly persecution implies no fault in him who flees but in him who persecutes. I do not deny this. I shall overlook the past. I shall not ask why or how the present state of affairs came about. I shall forget old injuries. To act otherwise were better calculated to open than to heal wounds. I am concerned with what lies closer to my heart. Unhappy man that I am who have not you by me, who cannot see you, who am obliged to live without you for whom to die would be to live, and to live without whom is no better than death! So I do not ask why you left me, I only grieve that you do not return; I do not blame your going away, I only blame your not coming back. Only come and there will be peace; return and there will be satisfaction. Return, I say, return, and I shall sing in my heart, 'My brother who was dead has come to life again; was lost and is found'.

2. No doubt it may have been my fault that you left. I was too severe with a sensitive youth, I was too hard on a tender stripling. Hence your grumbles against me (as I remember) while you were here; hence your ceaseless complaints about me even now that I am absent. The fault of this will not be laid at your door. I might, perhaps, excuse myself by saying that only in this way could the passions of youth have been curbed and that, at first, a strict way of life must be hard on a raw youth. I could quote Scripture to support me saying, 'Smite thy son with a rod and thou shalt deliver his soul from hell', and 'It is where he loves that the Lord bestows correction', and 'The wounds of a friend are better than the deceitful kisses of an enemy'. It may have been my fault that you left, as I have said. We will not let arguments about who is to blame delay correction of what is blameworthy. But it will surely begin to be your fault as well if you do not spare me now that I am sorry, if you do not forgive me now that I acknowledge myself to blame because, although I have been unwise in my treatment of you, I was certainly not malicious. And if you in future distrust my wisdom, you must know that I am not the same man I was, because I do not think you are what you used to be. Having changed yourself, you will find me changed too. You may now embrace me without hesitation as a companion whom you used to fear as a master. And so if you left through my fault, as you believe and I do not deny, or through your own fault, as many believe but I do not affirm, or, as I think more probable, through the fault of both of us, from now on you alone will be to blame if you do not return. If you

would be free of all blame in the matter you must return. If you acknowledge your share of the blame, I forgive you. But you too must forgive me what I acknowledge as my share. Else if you acknowledge your share and at the same time dissemble it you will be too lenient with yourself, or if you refuse to forgive me even when I declare myself ready to make satisfaction, you will be too hard on me.

3. If you still refuse to come back you must seek another pretext to quiet your conscience because there will no longer be anything to fear from me. You need not fear that in future you will have any reason to fear me because even while you are not with me I have cast myself with my whole heart at your feet, moved thereto with all my affection. I humble myself before you, I assure you of my love: can you still be afraid? Be bold and come where humility beckons you and love draws you. Forearmed by my assurances, approach without fear. Now that I am become gentle, return to me from whom you fled when fierce. My severity frightened you away; let my tenderness draw you back. See, my son, how I long to lead you now not any more in the spirit of slavery to govern you in fear, but in the spirit of adoption whereby we cry 'Abba, Father'; you who have been the cause of so much grief to me, I shall lead not with threats but with encouragements, not by menacing but by entreating. Perhaps anyone else would try another method. And indeed who would not rather insist on your guilt and inspire you with fear; face you with your vow and propose judgement. Who else would not scold your disobedience and be angry at your desertion, that you should have left the coarse habit for soft raiment, a fare of roots for delicacies, in fine poverty for riches. But I know your heart. I know that you can be lead more easily by love than driven by fear. And what need is there to goad you again who have not kicked against the goad, why make you more fearful who are already timid enough, abase you more who are by nature bashful, you who are schooled by your own reason, whose own conscience is a rod, and whose natural

shyness is a discipline. And if it seems wonderful to anyone that a shy and timid boy should dare to desert both his vow and his monastery against the will of his brethren, the authority of his superior, the injunctions of the rule, let him wonder also that the sanctity of David was defrauded, the wisdom of Solomon deceived, the strength of Samson destroyed. What wonder if the Evil One should have been able to deceive a youth in a place of horror and a great wilderness who could deceive the first man when he was in the paradise of Eden. And this youth was not deceived by physical beauty like the old men of Babylon, nor by money like Giezi, nor by ambition like Julian the Apostate, but he was duped by sanctity, misled by religion, allured by the authority of age. Do you ask how?

4. First there came a certain Grand Prior sent by the chief of all the priors himself. Outwardly he came in sheep's clothing, but within he was a ravening wolf. Alas! The shepherds were deceived by his semblance to a sheep and admitted him alone into the fold. The smallest sheep in the fold did not fly from this wolf, he too was deceived and thought he was a sheep. What happened then? This wolf in sheep's clothing fascinated, allured, and flattered. He preached a new Gospel. He commended feasting and condemned fasting. He called voluntary poverty wretched and poured scorn upon fasts, vigils, silence, and manual labour. On the other hand he called sloth contemplation, gluttony, talkativeness, curiosity and all intemperance he commended as discretion. 'When', he asked, 'was God pleased with our sufferings; where do the Scriptures say that we should kill ourselves; what sort of religion is it to dig the soil, clear forests, and cart muck?' Does not Truth itself say, 'It is mercy that wins favour with me and not sacrifice'; and 'I do not wish for the death of a sinner but rather that he should turn from his ways and live'; and 'Blessed are the merciful for they shall obtain mercy'? Why did God make food if we may not eat it? Why did he give us bodies if we may not look after them? In fact 'Whose friend is he, that is his own enemy, and leaves his own

cheer untasted?' 'What healthy and sane man has ever hated his own flesh?'

5. By such sophistries the too credulous boy was talked round, led astray and led off by his deceiver. He was brought to Cluny and trimmed, shaved, and washed. He was taken out of his rough, threadbare, and soiled habit, and clothed with a neat and new one. Then with what honour, triumph, and respect was he received into the community! He was favoured beyond his contemporaries; a sinner in the desires of his heart, he was praised as if he were a conquering hero returned from battle. He was set up on high and, although a mere youth, was allocated to a position above many who were his seniors. He was be-friended, flattered, and congratulated by the whole fraternity. Everyone made merry over him as though they were victors dividing the booty. O good Jesu, what a lot of trouble was taken for the ruin of one poor little soul! Who would be so hard-hearted as not to soften at the sight of it! Whose soul, be it never so detached, would not be troubled by it! And who in the midst of all this would care to consult his conscience? And how could anyone amidst such vanities recognize the truth and achieve humility?

6. In the meantime representations were made at Rome. The authority of the Holy See was cajoled. And to make sure that the Pope would not refuse his assent, it was suggested to him that this youth while still a child had been oblated at Cluny by his parents.[1] There was no one present to refute this nor was it

---

1. An oblate was a young child formally offered to a monastery by his parents. St. Benedict lays down the conditions under which the offering must be made in the 59th chapter of his Rule. The hand of the child is to be wrapped in the altar cloth together with the petition of the parents. If the parents are rich they can offer land for the support of the child and retain, if they wish, the income of it for their lifetime. Poor parents simply offered their child without any gifts. But whether rich or poor the child might not under any circumstances receive anything or have the prospect of receiving anything either from the parents or from a third person. The child thus formally offered became a member of the Community and might not return to the world.

The dangers of this system were fully realized. Two successive popes,

anticipated that there would be. Judgement was pronounced on the case in the absence of the judged. Those who had done the injury were upheld, the plaintiffs lost their suit, the defendant was absolved without making satisfaction. And this far too indulgent sentence of absolution was confirmed by a cruel ordinance whereby the hesitating and doubtful youth was confirmed in an ill-advised stability and security. The gist of the rescript, the sum of the judgement, the whole significance of the suit was nothing more than that the robbers could keep their spoils and that those who lost thereby must keep silent. And withal a soul for whom Christ died must be lost to please Cluny. So another profession is made, what will not be kept is vowed, what will not be performed is proposed: and since the first sin has been made void, in the second transgression is doubled, and sinning there is sin beyond measure.

7. But he will come, he will come who will judge again the misjudgements of men, who will confute what has been unlawfully vowed, who will execute judgement for them that suffer wrong, who will judge the poor with justice and reprove with equity on behalf of the meek of the earth. He will surely come who has warned us by the Prophet in the psalm, 'When I shall choose a time, I will judge righteousness'. What will he do about unjust judgements who will judge even righteousness? It will come, I say, the day of judgement will come and then a clean heart will avail more than crafty words, and a good conscience more than a full purse. He will then be judge who can neither deceive nor be deceived by words and who cannot be bribed by

---

Clement III and Celestine III, granted a general permission for all oblates to return to the world if they wished. Guigo, Prior of the Chartreuse, forbade in his statutes the reception of oblates because of the dangers involved by the system.

St. Bernard contends in this letter that Robert was only promised and not formally oblated to Cluny. And in any case, he maintains, a vow made by parents on behalf of their child before he was old enough to know anything about it, could not weigh against a vow, especially for a higher perfection, made by the child when he was old enough to be responsible for his own actions.

gifts. To your judgement seat, Lord Jesu, I appeal; I reserve my defence for your court. To you I commit my suit, Lord God of Sabaoth, who judges justly and searches the reins and the heart, who can neither deceive nor be deceived. You know who they are that seek their own ends and who they are that seek your glory. You know with what agony of heart I waited upon the youth in his trials, how I beat upon your loving ears with my prayers for him, how for his anxieties, troubles, and vexations, I was on fire, and torn, and afflicted. And now, I fear, it has all been in vain. I believe that, so far as I know, for a youth already hot-blooded and insolent enough such foments were of little use to the body and such trials of glory of little avail to the mind. And so, Lord Jesu, be you my arbiter, let my judgement come forth from your countenance.

8. Let them see and judge which has the most force: the vow a father makes on behalf of his son, or the vow a son makes on his own behalf, especially when it is a vow of something better. Let your servant and our law-giver, Benedict, judge which is the more in order: a vow made for a child when it is too young to know anything about it, or the vow he afterwards makes for himself when he realizes and understands what he is doing, when he is of an age to speak for himself. However, there is no doubt that the boy was only promised to Cluny without any formal oblation, for the petition prescribed by the Rule was not made by his parents, nor was his hand bound in the altar cloth, and the offering made before witnesses.[1] They point out the land which, they say, was made with the child and for him. But if they received him with the land how was it they kept the land and not the child? Can it be that they prized the land more than the child? If he had been oblated what was he doing in the world? A nursling of God, why was he exposed to the maw of the wolf? You yourself, Robert, are a witness that you entered our Order from the world and not from Cluny. You implored to be admitted, you begged and besought, but, much against your will,

1. See note, p. 12.

your entrance was put off for two years on account of your tender age. When this time had been allowed patiently to pass and without evasion, at last with prayers and (as you will remember) with many tears you besought the long awaited mercy, and were granted the admission you had sought for so long. You were tried in all patience for a year according to the Rule, living perseveringly and without complaint. After the year had passed you, of your own free will, made your profession and then, for the first time, you put off the attire of the world and were clothed in the habit of Religion.

9. You foolish boy! Who has bewitched you to break the vows which adorned your lips? Will you not be justified or condemned out of your own mouth? Why then are you so anxious about the vow your parents made and yet so regardless of your own? It is out of your own mouth and not out of the mouth of your parents that you will be judged. Of your own vow, not of theirs, will you be called to render an account. Why does anyone try to bamboozle you with an Apostolic absolution, you whose own conscience is bound by a divine sentence, 'No one putting their hand to the plough and looking back is fit for the kingdom of God'? Would they persuade you that you have not looked back who say to you, 'Well done!' My son, if sinners shall entice you, consent not to them. Believe not every spirit. Be at peace with many, but let one in a thousand be your counsellor. Gird yourself, cast off your seducers, shut your ears to flatterers, search your own heart, for you know yourself best. Listen to your conscience, examine your intentions, consider the facts. Let your conscience tell you why you left your monastery, your brethren, your own place, and myself who am related to you by blood, but even more closely by spirit. If you left so as to lead a harder, higher, and more perfect life, fear not, you have not looked back, rather you can glory with the Apostle, saying, 'Forgetting what I have left behind, intent on what lies ahead, I press on with the goal in view'. But if it be otherwise, be not high minded but fearful because (you must pardon my say-

ing this) whatever you permit yourself in food, unnecessary clothes, idle words, vain and curious travel in excess of what you promised when you were with us, is without any doubt to look back, to equivocate, to apostatize.

10. And I have said this, my son, not to put you to shame, but to help you as a loving father because if you have many masters in Christ, yet you have few fathers. For, if you will allow me to say so, I begot you in Religion by word and by example. I nourished you with milk when, while yet a child, it was all you could take. And I would have given you bread if you had waited until you grew up. But alas! how soon and how early were you weaned. Now I fear that all I had cherished with kindness, strengthened with encouragement, confirmed with prayers, is even now fading and wasting away. Sadly I weep, not for my lost labour, but for the unhappy state of my lost child. Do you prefer that another should rejoice in you who has not laboured for you? My case is the same as that of the harlot Solomon judged, whose child was stealthily taken by another who had overlain and killed her own. You too were taken from my side, cut from me. My heart cannot forget you, half of it went with you, and what remains cannot but suffer.

11. But our friends who have tried to do this thing, whose sword has pierced my side, whose teeth are spears and arrows and whose tongue is a sharp sword, for what advantage of yours have they done it, for what necessity? If I have in any way offended them (and I am not conscious of having done so) they have certainly paid me back in full. I would not wonder if I have received more than my share of retaliation, if indeed they have suffered anything like what I suffer now from them. It is not a bone of my bones, flesh of my flesh that they have taken, but it is the joy out of my heart, the fruit of my spirit, the crown of my hopes, and (so it seems to me) the half of my soul. Why have they done this thing? Perhaps they were sorry for you? Perhaps they feared that because I was like a blind man leading the blind, we would both fall into the ditch. So they took you

under their leadership. Hard necessity! Grievous charity! So careful of your good that it must strike at mine. Is it not possible that you should be saved except at my cost? Ah! would that these men might save you apart from me. Would that if I die you, at least, may live! But how can this be? Does salvation rest rather in soft raiment and high living than in frugal fare and moderate clothing? If warm and comfortable furs, if fine and precious cloth, if long sleeves and ample hoods, if dainty coverlets and soft woollen shirts make a saint, why do I delay and not follow you at once? But these things are comforts for the weak, not the arms of fighting men. They who wear soft raiment are in kings' houses. Wine and white bread, honey-wine and pittances, benefit the body not the soul. The soul is not fattened out of frying pans! Many monks in Egypt served God for a long time without fish. Pepper, ginger, cummin, sage, and all the thousand other spices may please the palate, but they inflame lust. And would you make my safety depend on such things? Will you spend your youth safely among them? Salt with hunger is seasoning enough for a man living soberly and wisely. If we eat before we are hungry, then we must concoct mixtures with more and more I know not what far-fetched flavours to arouse our greed and stimulate our flagging appetites.

12. But what, you say, is to be done if one cannot live otherwise? Good. I know you are not strong, that you would now find it difficult to support a harder way of life. But what if you can act so as to make yourself able to do so? I will tell you how it could be done. Arouse yourself, gird your loins, put aside idleness, grasp the nettle, and do some hard work. If you act thus you will soon find that you only need to eat what will satisfy your hunger, not what will make your mouth water. Hard exercise will restore the flavour to food that idleness has taken away. Much that you would refuse to eat when you had nothing to do, you will be glad of after hard work. Idleness makes one dainty, hard work makes one hungry. It is wonderful how work can make food taste sweet which idleness finds

insipid. Vegetables, beans, roots, and bread and water may be poor fare for one living at his ease, but hard work soon makes them taste delicious. You have become unaccustomed to our clothes and now you dread them as too cold in winter and too hot in summer. But have you not read, 'They that fear the frost, the snow shall fall upon them'? You fear our vigils, fasts, and manual labour, but they seem nothing to anyone who considers the flames of hell. The thought of the outer darkness will soon reconcile anyone to wild solitudes. Silence does not displease when it is considered how we shall have to give an account of every idle word. With the picture before our eyes of that weeping and gnashing of teeth the difference between a rush mat and a feather bed seems small enough. If we spend well all the night enjoined by the Rule in psalmody, it will be a hard bed on which we cannot sleep. If we labour with our hands as much during the day as we are professed to do, rough indeed will be the fare we cannot eat.

13. Arise, soldier of Christ, I say arise! Shake off the dust and return to the battle. You will fight more valiantly after your flight, and you will conquer more gloriously. There are many soldiers of Christ who have begun valiantly, stood their ground well, and finished by conquering, but few who have returned to the battle after they had fled, thrown themselves once more into the thick of the danger from which they had escaped, and put to flight the foe from whom they had run. A thing is the more precious for being rare, so I rejoice that you can be one of those who are the more glorious for being so scarce. But if you are still fearful, I ask you why you should be afraid where there is no cause for fear, instead of where you have every reason to tremble. Do you think that because you have forsaken the front line the enemy has forsaken you? Far from it. He will follow you in flight more readily than he would fight you when striking back. He attacks you more willingly from behind than he would strive with you face to face. Can you sleep unarmed without anxiety in the morning hours when it was at that time

that Christ rose from the dead? Do you not know that unarmed you are both more fearful and less to be feared? A multitude of armed men surround the house, and can you still sleep? Already they are scaling the ramparts, swarming over the barriers, pouring in at the rear. Would you be safer alone or with others? Naked in bed or armed in camp? Get up, arm yourself, and fly to your fellow soldiers whom you have forsaken by running away. Let the fear that drove you away also bring you back. Is it the weight and discomfort of arms that you shun, feeble soldier? Believe me when an enemy is at hand and darts begin flying a shield seems none too heavy, and a helmet and corselet are not noticed. Everything seems hard at first to someone coming suddenly from darkness into light, from leisure to labour. But when you have got away from your former habits you will soon get used to the labour. Practice soon makes perfect. What seemed difficult at first presently becomes quite easy. Even the bravest soldiers are apt to tremble when they first hear the bugle summon to battle, but after they have closed with the enemy hope of victory and fear of defeat soon inspires courage. Surrounded by a company of single-hearted brethren, what have you to fear? What have you to fear at whose side angels stand and whom Christ leads into battle encouraging his friends with the words, 'Fear not, I have overcome the world'. If Christ is with us, who is against us? You can fight with confidence where you are sure of victory. With Christ and for Christ victory is certain. Not wounds, nor falls, nor bruises, nor (were it possible) can a thousand deaths rob us of victory, if only we do not forsake the fight. Only by desertion can we be defeated. We can lose the victory by flight but not by death. Happy are you if you die in battle for after death you will be crowned. But woe to you if by forsaking the battle, you forfeit at once both the victory and the crown. May Christ save you from this, dear son, for at the last judgement you will incur a greater penalty on account of this letter of mine if, when you have read it, you do not take its lesson to heart.

[4]

To Arnold, Abbot of Morimond

Arnold was the first Abbot of Morimond, an abbey founded from Cîteaux in the year 1115. He was the brother of Frederick, Archbishop of Cologne, and Henry, later Abbot of Riddagshausen, a Cistercian house in Brunswick.

This letter belongs to the year 1124[1] and was occasioned by a sad moral disaster to the Order. Arnold, tiring of the difficulties of his charge (apparently his lay-brothers were lazy, his monks disobedient, and his neighbours hostile), suddenly, and without consulting anyone, left his charge and with a handful of monks set out for the Holy Land 'where', says Bernard in another letter concerning the same subject, 'it is well known that soldiers to fight and not monks to sing are what is wanted'. But he died suddenly in Belgium the next year without having either accomplished his purpose or corrected his error.

As soon as the news of Arnold's death reached Bernard he set about trying to mitigate the ill-effects of his behaviour. He immediately wrote letters to persuade the fugitive monks to return and had his own prior, Walter, appointed to succeed him.

From the dates, as well as from the evidence of the following let er, it is clear that Arnold and Bernard had been at Cîteaux together and were well known to each other. As Bernard knew the l dstrong character of Arnold, so Arnold must have been fully are of the persuasiveness of Bernard for, unwilling to be turne from his purpose, he was careful to keep out of Bernard's way.

Of some passages in this letter the late Watkin Williams has said: 'They are some of the few that have come down to us revealing the tumultuous emotionalism of the Saint, an emotionalism which with him is never the master, but always the servant,

1. See *Statuta Capitulorum Generalium Ordinis Cistercienses*, Ed. D. Josephus Canivez.

deliberately controlled, disciplined to a purpose, directed to an
end as the keenest of instruments in the hand of the kindest of
surgeons. And real! . . . Bernard could safely be severe because
he loved so tenderly; and the more tenderly, the more robust'
(Journal of Theological Studies, Oct., 1939

To the Lord Abbot Arnold, the spirit of compunction and
counsel, from Brother Bernard of Clairvaux.

I WANT you to know first of all that our lord of
Cîteaux had not returned from Flanders where he had lately
gone, passing by here, when your messenger arrived. So he has
not received the letters you instructed be given him and is
still ignorant of this novel venture you ave taken upon yourself. He is happy, even if it be for only a short time, to know
nothing of the sad rumours that are going round. And by forbidding me to attempt your recall, saying it would be useless for
me to try to dissuade you by letter from what you have, as it
were, firmly settled with yourself, you have reduced me to
despair. In this matter I probably ought not in reason to obey
you and, I confess, in any case, for the very grief I feel I could
not do so; although, were I to know ow to find you, I would
come in person rather than write to you, perhaps to achieve
more by my presence than I could by letter. Confident in your
own obstinacy and sure that no force, no prayers, no efforts
whatsoever can turn you from your purpose, you probably
smile at what you will consider my futile assurance. But I trust
in the power of him who has said To him who believes all
things are possible', and I do not hesitate to apply to myself the
words 'Nothing is beyond my power thanks to the strength
God gives me'. Although I know something of the obstinacy of
your stony heart, yet I wish I were by your side to persuade you
even if I could achieve nothing. Whether it would be of any
avail I do not know, but I would lay before you the great reasons
that compel me to oppose you, I would plead with you not only

by my words but also by my tears and sorrow. I would throw myself at your feet, embrace your knees, hang upon your neck and kiss your dear head, that head which has been bowed with mine in a like purpose under the sweet yoke of Christ for so many years. I would beg and implore you with tears, with all my might, in the name of the Lord Jesus first that you should spare his cross, the cross which redeemed those whom you are doing your utmost to destroy, the cross which gathered together those whom you are scattering. I say advisedly destroy and scatter, for, whether they be those you are taking with you or those you are leaving behind, they are both in danger of an equal though different fate. And then that you should spare us your friends for whom, quite undeservedly, you have left only tears and sorrow. Were it only permitted me I would bend you by affection, if I could not convince you by reason! That steely heart of yours, so far proof even against the fear of Christ, I would soften with the touch of brotherly affection! But alas! even this opportunity you have taken from me.

2. Great support of our Order! listen, I beg you, even to an absent friend wholly opposed to your venture, yet sympathizing wholly with your difficulties and dangers. Great support of our Order, have you no fear at all that with your fall the collapse of the whole structure will soon follow? But, you say, I have not fallen. I know quite well what I am doing. My conscience is clear. Be it so; I believe what you tell me of yourself. But what about us who already groan under the heavy burden of scandal caused by your departure and who fear more to come? Can it be that you know all this and yet pretend not to? How can you suppose yourself to stand when you are causing the fall of so many? You were placed in a position of authority not for your own sake, but for the sake of others; not to promote your own interests, but to promote the interests of Jesus Christ. How, I ask, can you possibly set forth with security when by so doing you deprive of all security the flock which has been entrusted to your care? Who will be there to keep

away the prowling wolves? Who will be there to console the afflicted and counsel the tempted? Who will hold at bay the raging and roaring lion that goes about seeking whom it may devour? They will all be exposed, without any doubt, to the teeth
of the evildoer who devours the children of God as if they were
bread for the eating. Alas! what will happen to those new plan-
tations[1] of Christ set by your own hand in 'the wilderness and
fearful desert places'? Who will be there to dig them about and
dung them? Who will build a hedge round about them and
prune away their untoward growth? Either these still tender
saplings will be easily uprooted by the first storms of trouble, or
else for lack of anyone to clean the ground about them they will
be choked by the weeds that grow up with them, so that they
will bear no fruit.

3. Judge therefore for yourself what sort of good this can be
which you are seeking, or whether, involving as it does so many
evils, it can be a good at all. However great the fruit of repentance you hope to bring forth, will it not be choked for certain by these thistles? In fact, as the Scripture says, 'Even if you
offer rightly, will you not sin if you divide not rightly'. What of
this? Perhaps you will say that you have divided rightly because you have consulted the good of your own soul. But can
you say this while knowing that you have deprived of a father's
care those sons whom you have left behind and left orphans?
Unhappy and wretched are they, and all the more so for being
deprived of their father while he is still alive! You should have
some doubts, to be sure, whether it is the good of your soul that
you have consulted, seeing that you have presumed such an unheard-of thing without the advice of your brethren and brother
abbots and without the licence of your father and master. What
upsets many is that you should have taken with you only weak
boys and inexperienced youths. Either they are strong and ex-

1. The foundations of Morimond referred to here are: Bellevaux in Haute-
Saône on March 22nd, 1120; La Creste, near Chaumont, on June 30th, 1121;
Vieux-Camp, near Dusseldorf, on January 31st, 1123.

perienced men, in which case, they would be necessary for their orphaned house; or else they are, as I have said, weak and inexperienced, and therefore not fit for the long and tedious journey. But I do not think you can still wish to rule over them as their superior, since I know you to be minded to lay down your pastoral charge and henceforth to care only for your own soul. And indeed it would be most unfitting were you to presume to undertake, without being asked, in one place what in another with equal audacity you have given up against the will of your superiors. But you know all this and so I conclude by promising you in all good faith that if you but give me the chance of speaking with you, I for my part will do what I can so that this venture you have undertaken against orders and therefore with great danger to your soul, you may be able to finish with permission and without disobeying your superiors.

[8]

To the Monk Adam

Abbot Arnold had just died when this letter was written. Evidently the leadership of the party had devolved on Brother Adam, the same Brother Adam to whom Letter 6 is addressed. The implications of monastic obedience are discussed in it at great length, so that it is more a small treatise on the subject than a letter. In a manuscript referred to by D. Mabillon it is, indeed, entitled De discretione Obedientiæ.

WERE you still abiding in the charity which at one time I knew or thought abided in you, you could not but feel the condemnation of charity for the scandal you have caused to the weak. Charity would not offend charity nor scorn when she is offended; she cannot be divided against herself, nor deny her own nature. Rather is it her nature to unite again what has

been divided. If, as I have said, she abided in you and you in
her, she would not be keeping silent, she would not be resting,
or feigning ignorance, but she would be groaning, she would be
on fire within you and clamouring, 'Who is scandalized and I
am not on fire', for she is kind, and loves peace, and rejoices in
unity. It is she alone who begets unity, confirms it, binds it up,
and preserves it in the bonds of peace. Wherever charity is,
there too is peace. So, I ask you, how can you, when you have
thus wounded the mother of unity and peace, dare to hope that
your offering will be acceptable to God? The Apostle himself
believes that even martyrdom without charity 'availeth nothing'. How can you believe that you have not offended her
whose very bowels and dear pledges you have lacerated by your
brutal treatment of her? You have not spared her in the past,
nor do you spare her now, but you rend unity and break the
bonds of peace. Lay down your offering by the altar and go first
to be reconciled, not with just one brother, but with the whole
multitude of brethren who have this against you and those few
who are with you, that, as with a sword, you have wounded
their peace and unity by your desertion. They lament with the
bride in the Canticle crying, 'The sons of my mother have
fought against me', and rightly so, because being no longer
joined in unity with them you are against them. And do you
think that charity, their loving mother, can hear without grief
this just complaint of her children? She joins her tears with
theirs and says of you: 'My own sons, that I have reared and
brought to manhood, think to defy me'. Charity is God himself. Our peace is Christ, 'who hath made two nations one'. In
the Trinity itself, unity is honoured. What share, therefore, can
the enemy of charity, peace and unity have in the kingdom of
Christ and God?

2. But perhaps you will say, 'My abbot commanded me to
follow him. Would you have me disobedient?' But you surely
have not forgotten the decision we reached together when you
first told me of the scandalous project which you were even

then considering. If only you had remained firm to that it might have been said of you not inaptly, 'Blessed is the man who hath not walked in the counsel of the ungodly'. But be it so, as you say. Let us grant that as you were his sons and disciples you ought to have followed your abbot; that an abbot may lead his sons where it shall please him and teach them what he wishes— but surely not now that he is dead? Now that he is dead whose teaching you were bound to hear and in whose footsteps you were bound to follow when he was alive, why do you delay in setting right the great scandal you have caused? Who is now to prevent you hearing, I do not say myself, but God sweetly calling to you through the mouth of Jeremias: 'Shall not he that falleth rise again? And he that is turned aw y, shall he not turn again?' Does he intrude even from the grave o prevent you rising again or daring to think that you should urn again? Now that he is dead is it necessary for you to obey h n against charity and at the peril of your soul? You would allo surely, that the bond which links abbots with their disciples is t stronger than the bond which God has tied with an inviola sacrament between husband and wife, according to the word f our Saviour himself: 'What God has joined together let no n an put asunder'? Yet on the authority of the Apostle a woma is no longer tied to her husband when he is dead. Do you then i lieve yourself still bound by the command of your abbot no that he is dead, against an even holier law, the law of charity?

3. I have not said this because I think you ough to have obeyed your abbot in this matter, even when he was live; or that such yielding to him could even be called obedien . That sentence from Scripture applies to all obedience of t kind: 'Feet that stray into the snare the Lord will punish as he p ishes wrong doers'. And so that no one should contend that this oes not apply to obedience, even when it is in something evil, it ys more clearly in another place: 'The son shall not bear the n- iquity of the father, and the father shall not bear the iniquity of the son'. From this it is clearly apparent that no one is to be

obeyed when he commands evil, especially as, although we may seem to be obeying a man when we do so, yet really we are dis- obeying God who has forbidden all evil. It is extremely per- verse to profess to be obedient by disobeying the higher for the sake of the lower, or in other words by disobeying the com- mandments of God for the sake of the commands of a man. What then? Am I to turn a deaf ear to God when a man com- mands what he forbids? Not so the Apostle who cried out: 'It is better to obey God than man'. For this the Lord rebukes the Pharisees in the Gospels saying: 'Why do you transgress the commandments of God for the sake of your own traditions?' and by the prophet Isaias he says: 'In vain they worship me teaching the commandments and doctrine of men'; and again to the first man: 'Because thou hast harkened to the voice of thy wife rather than to mine, the earth is accursed in thy work'. Therefore to do evil, command it who may, is to disobey rather than to obey.

4. Now so that you may understand me you must know that there are some things wholly good and others wholly evil, and in these latter there can be no obedience due to any man. No one may forbid the former; no one may command the latter. And between these two extremes there are middling things; things neither good nor evil, but indifferent. And these things derive their character of goodness or badness from the circum- stances of manner, place, and time. It is in this sphere that the law of obedience obtains as in the tree of the knowledge of good and evil which was in the midst of Paradise. In these things we may in no wise follow our own will so as to ignore the com- mands of our superiors. Let us see now whether it is a thing such as this that I have rebuked in you, when, perhaps, on this account I should not have done so. This will be all the clearer if I give some examples of the foregoing distinctions. Faith, hope, charity, and the like are wholly good and it can never be wrong to enjoin them and never right to forbid or neglect them. Wholly evil are theft, sacrilege, adultery, and the rest, which it

can never be right to enjoin or to do and never wrong to forbid or not to do. The law of obedience is not concerned with these, since no prohibition is valid against what has been laid down, and what has been forbidden cannot be recommended by the commands of anyone. Then there are the middling things, neither good nor evil, and these can be indifferently, either well or ill, commanded or forbidden. In these things obedience is never wrong. As examples of them I give fasting, vigils, reading, and the like. But you must know that some middle things can often become either wholly good or wholly evil. Thus marriage is neither enjoined nor forbidden; but once contracted it cannot be dissolved. What, therefore, before the nuptials was clearly a middling thing, after them becomes, for the persons married, a thing wholly good. Likewise, whether a secular person should hold property or not is a matter of indifference; but for a monk it is wholly evil, for he is not permitted to hold any property at all.

5. Do you see now, brother, to which of my foregoing divisions your leaving the monastery belongs? If it can be classed as wholly good, it is praiseworthy; if as wholly bad, it is blameworthy. But if it is to be classed between the two extremes as being neither good nor evil, then the going forth might be excused on the grounds of obedience, but not the delay in returning. From what has been said already it should be quite clear to you that if your abbot commanded anything he ought not to have done, now that he is dead he is no longer to be obeyed. This should be clear enough, but, for the sake of those who unreasonably seek opportunities to object, I will try to make it still more clear, so that there can be no shadow of doubt that it was not an indifferent matter, neither good nor evil, but wholly evil that you should have obeyed and left your monastery in the way you did. But so that God shall not say of me with righteous anger, 'Men have taken away my judgement', I shall not mention your abbot. He now has God for his only judge and before his Lord he either stands or falls. I will discuss not what he did,

but what he ordered, so that we may see whether his orders had force to bind his subjects even in the teeth of the scandal they have given. But first I will say this, if there be some, as I could well believe there are, who, although they did wrong to leave their monastery, yet did it in good faith, supposing their abbot to have had the permission of the Bishop of Langres and the Abbot of Cîteaux, to both of whom he was subject, my rebuke does not touch them, providing they return to their monastery so soon as they learn the true facts of the case.

6. I speak only against those, or rather for the sake of those, who knowingly and deliberately have put their hands into the fire; who, though conscious of their audacity, yet followed the audacious one, heedless of the Apostle warning them to have nothing to do with a vagabond brother, and of the Lord himself saying: 'Who does not gather with me, scatters'. You, brothers, you, I say, take particular heed of that taunt of Jeremias which I remember with grief: 'This is a people which hath not harkened to the voice of the Lord their God'. For this is the voice of God authoritatively pointing out his enemy, as with a finger, to deter the simple from his ungodly example: 'Who is not with me', he says, 'scatters', as if to say, if you follow him when he scatters abroad what I have gathered together, you can know that you are not with me. When God himself cries out, 'Who does not gather with me, scatters', must you follow the scatterer? When God, I say, invites you to gather, ought you to obey in preference a man so as to scatter? He ignores his superiors, he betrays his subjects, he troubles his brethren, and yet you on seeing the thief ran with him! I had intended to keep silent about the dead but I am obliged, I confess, to overstep a little my limit, because the obedience cannot be blamed without showing up the command as blameworthy. Further, as both the command and the deed were united in the same man, it would appear impossible to blame the one without reflecting blame on the other. Yet it is clear that this sort of command cannot be obeyed for to do so were to disobey God. Also the ordinances

of our fathers are to be preferred to those of lesser persons, and there can be no doubt that personal commands must not be obeyed if they conflict with the common observance, for all this is the Rule of St. Benedict.

7. I might indeed bring forward the Abbot of Cîteaux as complaining that you have ignored him in favour of your own abbot. And he would have every right to complain for he is as much the superior of your abbot as a father is of his son, or the master of his disciple, or in fact an abbot of his monks. I might also cite the Bishop of Langres for whom he showed inexcusable contempt by not awaiting his permission before setting out, even when the Lord has said: 'He who despises you despises me'. But because the authority of the Roman Pontiff could be opposed and preferred to these as being more weighty, since they say that you have not omitted to fortify yourselves with his licence (this matter of licences I will deal with later), I will cite one whose authority no man may gainsay, the High Priest who, by his own blood, alone and once and for all entered into the sanctuary having obtained eternal redemption, and I will cite him crying with a great voice that no one shall dare scandalize one of his little ones. But the scandalizing of one might be forgiven you if the evil rested there, for pardon comes speedily to the fault from which no great evil arises. But now that, beyond doubt, many have been scandalized, who cannot clearly see how churlish you have been in obeying man rather than God? Who, unless he were mad, would dare to call such an action as yours good or even middling, neither good nor bad, however great the dignity of the man who commanded it? But what is not good nor ever able to be good is, without doubt, wholly evil. Consequently your journey forth from your monastery because it gave rise to the scandal of so many was, for this reason, against the command of God, and so it was not either wholly good or indifferent, but wholly evil. For what is wholly good can never be anything but good, and what is between the two, neither good nor evil, can be good.

8. Since, as it has been shown, what is wholly evil can never be justly commanded or lawfully done, how, I ask you, can the command of an abbot or the permission of the Pope render it lawful? When violation of God's law is involved the excuse of human obedience is futile. Nor do I fear your taking refuge behind that answer the Lord gave when they told him of the scandal he had given to the Pharisees, 'Let them be, they are blind leaders of the blind', as if on that account you need not worry about the scandal you have given us. There is no comparison either between the persons or the causes. Our Lord is speaking there of the scandal caused to the proud Pharisees, whereas you have given scandal to the humble poor of Christ. And in his case it was truth that caused the scandal, in yours it is frivolity. Also, to repeat what has been said already, you have preferred not only human authority to divine, but private judgement to the common life. But it should be proof enough for you that not only the whole of our Order, but also the usages and customs of every monastery cry out against your strange novelty and insolent audacity.

9. 'We have sought and obtained', you say, 'an apostolic licence.' I reply that this is just an indication that you were not easy in your mind or satisfied in your conscience. What a futile expedient! It is like the first man trying to cloak his shame with fig leaves, as if they were a remedy and not just a cover. It would have been better had you sought the counsel rather than the consent of the Pope. But why did you obtain this licence? In order that you might lawfully do what it was not lawful for you to do? But what is unlawful is evil. Therefore the intention which inclined to evil, was evil. Unless indeed you say that it was lawful for you to do with a licence what would not have been lawful otherwise. But that argument has been utterly demolished further back. When God said, 'See to it that you do not treat one of these little ones with contempt', he did not add, 'unless you have permission of the Pope'; nor did he say, 'Whoever scandalizes one of these little ones without an apostolic

licence ... '! It is clear that, except in the interests of truth, and there is no question of that in your case, it is never lawful for anyone to give scandal or to command what would give scandal. You think it necessary to obtain a licence from the Pope in order to commit this sort of evil. So that, I suppose, you may sin more impudently and therefore more perilously! What wonderful caution! What astonishing foresight! The evil you conceived in your heart you were careful not to bring forth until you had secured a licence! You conceived sorrow, but you did not bring forth iniquity until the Pope had given his consent. But what have you gained? How is the evil lessened? Does it, on account of the Pope's consent, cease to be evil or become a lesser evil? As if anyone would think it was not evil to consent unto evil! I refuse to believe the Pope did this unless you got round him by lies or overwhelmed him by importunity. How else could he have been induced to permit the sowing of scandal, the stirring up of schism, the upsetting of friends, the disturbing of peace, the disruption of unity, and the contempt of the bishop? And all this for what purpose? There is no purpose in my saying for the results are a clear enough indication. I bewailed your progression, but I have yet to see any progress.

10. You tell me that to assent to such great evils, to yield to them, to assist them, is to be obedient, modest, and meek. I tell you that you are simply cloaking the worst vices under the names of the virtues. You call the most deceitful presumption, obedience; the most outrageous frivolity, modesty; the most cruel discord, meekness. By doing this you merely foul the holy names of the virtues. This is not the sort of obedience I would want for myself; such modesty, I should say molestation, would not be for me; may such meekness be far from me! Such obedience is worse than any haughtiness; such modesty exceeds all mode. Shall I say it is beyond measure or not up to measure? It would be perhaps more true and more pertinent to say that it is completely outside any measure. What sort of meekness is this of which the very mention exasperates everyone? Nevertheless

I wish you would show a little meekness to me. As you are so patient that you allow yourself to be dragged without complaining even where you ought not to go, permit me, I beg you, to be a little more bold with you, or else, if I alone am singled out for the object of your wrath, I have indeed deserved ill of you.

11. I invoke your conscience. Did you set out from your monastery because you wanted to or unwillingly? If because you wanted to, then it was not from obedience. If unwillingly, then it would seem that you were doubtful about the order to which compliance was such a burden. But when an order is in doubt, there should be inquiry. Yet so that you might put your patience to the proof, or give a proof of your patience, without any inquiry whatsoever, you suffered yourself to be dragged off not only unwillingly, but even against your conscience. Who would not be impatient with such patience! I cannot help, I confess, being angry with such headstrong patience. You saw your abbot scattering the flock and you followed with him; you saw him ordering scandal, and you obeyed him. It is the nature of true patience to suffer and act against self-will, but not in excess of what is lawful. I wonder how you heard the whispers of a man when you were deaf to the voice of God proclaiming in tones of thunder: 'Woe to the man through whom scandals come!' Not only the voice of the Lord, but also his blood cries aloud with a terrible voice for even the deaf to hear. The pouring of it forth is its cry. It was poured forth for the scattered children of God that they might be gathered together in one fold, and justly it raises its voice against the man who would scatter again. Concerned only to gather together, it abhors the man who scatters. With a great and mighty cry it awakes the dead in their tombs and summons souls from below. It is the voice of a trumpet calling heaven and earth together to give peace to both. The sound of it has gone out to the ends of the earth, but it has not pierced your deafness. That voice of power, that voice of glory, was powerless to pierce your deafness! And

what does it say? 'Let God arise, and let his enemies be scattered'; and again: 'Scatter them by thy power; and bring them down, O Lord, my protector'. It is the blood of Christ, Brother Adam, it is the blood of Christ which raises its voice for the faithful gathered together, against the impious one who would scatter them abroad. The blood which was poured forth to gather together those who had been scattered, threatens to scatter what it has gathered together. If you do not hear its voice, he hears it from whose side it flowed. And how could he not hear the voice of his own blood, who heard the voice of the blood of Abel?

12. 'But what is all this to me?' you say. 'He should have looked to it who gave me the order. It was not for me to contradict my abbot. The disciple is not above his master. I clove to him in order to be taught, not to teach. I was the disciple and it was for me to follow, not to lead, my master.' So you are another simple Paul![1] If only your abbot had been another Anthony, so that there would have been no need for you to inquire into anything he said, but simply to obey without question the slightest word that fell from his lips! What an obedient monk you are, you do not suffer one jot or one tittle of your senior's words to escape you: it is enough for you that a thing should be commanded that without pausing to question the command...[2] And this is the true obedience without delay. But if this sort of obedience were proper, then it would be useless to read in Church: 'Prove all things; hold fast that which is good'. Were this sort of obedience becoming, then we should delete the words of Scripture, 'You must be prudent as serpents', for it would be enough to have said ' . . . as simple as doves'. I do not say that subjects should question the orders of their superiors when it is clear that they do not conflict with the divine ordi-

1. The Paul here mentioned was the disciple of St. Anthony in Egypt about the year 300. St. Anthony was called by St. Athanasius, who wrote his life, the model for monks and the founder of asceticism. His disciple Paul was well known for his docility and childlike simplicity.

2. The MS. is here defective.

nances, but I say that prudence is necessary in order to understand whether they do conflict, and freedom too in order can-
didly to ignore them if they do. But you reply that it does not
concern you to question the orders of your superiors; that they
are responsible for their orders. Tell me then, I beg you, were
your abbot to place a sword in your hand and command you to
cut his throat, or were he to tell you to push him headlong into
the fire, would you obey? Would you not say that it would be
murder even not to hinder such a thing? Come then and see to
it that you have not co-operated in an even graver matter, under
pretext of obedience. You know who said (in case you do not
believe me), 'If anyone scandalizes one of these little ones that
believe in me, he had better be drowned in the depths of the
sea'. Why did he say this if not to indicate that torments so great
beyond the grave await those who give such scandal that in
comparison temporal death seems a blessing rather than a punishment? Why then did you co-operate in the scandal by obeying and following your abbot? Would it not have been better
for him that he should have been drowned in the depths of the
sea with a millstone about his neck? What then? O most obedient monk, so obedient that rather than part with your abbot for
one second or by a palm's breadth, you followed him into the
pit, not blindly but, like Balaam, with your eyes fully open; do
you believe that you were acting for his good by showing such
obedience, an obedience that was for him more grievous than
death? Now indeed I understand the truth of those words: 'A
man's enemies are of his own household'. If you see and understand this, do you not groan and tremble for what you have
done? According to the judgement, not of myself, but of
Truth, your obedience has been worse than murder.

13. If you know this, how can you not fear? And if you are
afraid, how is it you do not mend your ways? Otherwise what
sort of conscience will you bring before the dire judgement of
God? Then the judge will not want for a witness, then truth
itself will search the intentions, then the scrutiny of faults will

reach into the most hidden places of the heart, then the eye of God will search the most remote secrets of the mind. Then the corners of the heart will expand under the sudden brightness of the sun of Justice and pour forth the good and bad which they were hiding. Then, Brother Adam, those who have done evil and those who have consented to evil will receive a like penalty. Then both thieves and their partners in guilt will await the same punishment. Then both those who entice to sin and those who have allowed themselves to be enticed will receive a like judgement. Go ahead then, Brother Adam, and say: I have touched pitch and yet I am not black, I have held fire to my bosom, and yet I am not burned. Say that you have taken your portion with adulterers, and yet it is no business of yours. Isaias thought differently. He blamed himself not only for being unclean, but for keeping company with the unclean, saying: 'Woe is me because I am a man of unclean lips and I dwell in the midst of a people with unclean lips'. He blamed himself, I should have said, not because he lived with evil men, but because he did not blame the evils, for he says: 'Woe is me because I have held my peace'. But where do we hear that he yielded to the evil which he blamed himself for not blaming in others? And what about David? Did he not believe that he could be infected with the sins of others when he said: 'Not mine to take part with wrong doers, not mine to mingle with the company they keep'? And then he prays: 'From my secret sins cleanse me, O Lord, and from those of others spare thy servant'. It is also clear that he declined the company of those whose evil he did not wish to share, for he says: 'I have not sat with the council of vanity, neither will I go in with the doers of iniquity'; and to this verse he adds: 'I have hated the assembly of the malignant, and with the wicked I will not sit'. Finally Wisdom counsels us: 'If sinners entice thee, consent not to them'.

14. Did you really think that you ought to have obeyed anyone in the face of these and many other testimonies of truth? What hateful perversity! Obedience which has hitherto always

been the ally of truth, you have armed against it. I should call happy the disobedience of Brother Henry. He soon repented of his error and returned to his monastery without experiencing such obedience as yours. How much more sweet and desirable is the fruit that he plucks of his disobedience and even now is tasting with a good conscience because, while his other companions are breaking the hearts of their brethren with the scandal they are causing, he is living peacefully among his brothers faithful to his Order and profession. Had I to choose I would rather have his inactive disobedience with his good conscience than the zealous obedience of the others with the scandal. I consider he does better thus preserving unity in the bonds of peace, disobedient to his abbot yet not to charity, than those others who for the sake of obedience to one man endanger the unity of all. I would add with all assurance that it is better to endanger obedience, than to jeopardize all the benefits of piety and the vows of our profession.

15. Not to mention anything else there are two things handed down to us who dwell in monasteries for especial observance. One is submission to the abbot, the other is stability in our monastery. And these two are so to be observed that there is no conflict between them. That is to say, we should not be led by our stability to disdain subjection to the abbot, or by our subjection to the abbot, to lose stability. Further, if you abominate one who although persevering in stability yet ignores the commands of his abbot, can you wonder if I censure the obedience you adduce as the cause or occasion of your losing stability by leaving your monastery? Especially as in our regular profession while stability is explicitly promised there is no mention at all of it being subject to the abbot.

16. But perhaps you will ask how I reconcile the stability I confirmed at Cîteaux with living elsewhere. I answer that while it is true I was professed a monk of Cîteaux in that place and was sent by the abbot to live where I do, yet I was sent in peace, without any scandal or discord, according to the customs and

common observance of our Order. Therefore so long as I persevere in the same peace and concord wherein I was sent, so long
as I stand fast in unity, I am not preferring my private judgment
to the common observance. I am remaining quietly and obedi-
ently where I was put. I say my conscience is at peace because
I have not broken the bond of unity, because I have not left the
firm ground of peace. And if under obedience I am absent in
body from Cîteaux, yet by a fellow devotion, by a life in all
things the same, I am always there in spirit. But the day on which
I begin to live by other rules (which may God forbid!) and
other habits, to keep other observances, to introduce new things
and follow different customs, on that day I shall no longer believe I keep my promise of stability. I say, therefore, that the
abbot is to be obeyed in all things, but according to the tenor of
our profession. You, who were professed according to the Rule
of St. Benedict, when you promised obedience, you promised
as well stability. So if you should be obedient, but not stable, by
offending in one, you offend in all, and if in all, then also in
obedience.

17. Do you now see the force of your vow of obedience?
That it cannot, in fact, suffice to excuse the transgression of stability, not even having the force to support itself. We make our
professions solemnly and according to Rule in the presence of
the abbot, but only in his presence, not at his pleasure. The
abbot witnesses, but does not dictate the profession. He is there
to help, not to hinder, its fulfillment. He is there to punish, not
instigate, infringement. What then? Do I leave in his hands what
I have confirmed by my mouth and hand before God and his
saints, knowing from the Rule if I ever act otherwise I will be
condemned by him whom I mock? If my abbot, or even an
angel from heaven, should command what is contrary to this, I
shall boldly excuse myself from an obedience that I know would
render me a transgressor of my vow and a perjurer before God.
I know from Scripture that out of my own mouth I shall be
justified or condemned because 'the mouth that lies killeth the

soul' and because we chant before God, 'Thou wilt destroy all that speak a lie', and because 'Everyone shall bear his own burden' and 'Everyone of us shall render an account of himself to God'. Were it otherwise how could I dare to sing before God: 'I will render unto thee the vows my lips have uttered'? It is the duty of my abbot to consider how he may best follow the explicit direction of the Rule that 'he should maintain the present rule in every particular'. In the same way it is also laid down in the Rule as a general principle from which no one may be excused: 'Let all follow the Rule as their guide, and from it let no man rashly turn aside'. And I have so determined to follow my abbot always and everywhere providing that he never by his teaching departs from the Rule which, in his presence, I have vowed and determined to keep.

18. Let me now meet another question that might be raised, but briefly so as to bring this letter, which is already too long, to a close. It seems at first that by receiving and keeping monks that come to me from other monasteries I act contrary to my own teaching. It could be asked why I receive monks who break their vows of stability and ignore the commands of their seniors by coming to me when I condemn those who leave their monasteries not only with permission of their abbot but even by his order. To this there is a short answer, but a perilous one. I fear that what I am to say will displease some people. But I think I would have more to fear for myself if, by not telling the truth, I could no longer sing from my heart: 'I have not hid my righteousness within my heart: my talk has been of thy truth and thy salvation'. Therefore I will say that I received them for the reason that I did not think they were wrong in leaving their monasteries, if they could not observe there the vows their lips have uttered, and coming to where they may be better able to render them to God who is everywhere, repairing the harm they have done by breaking their vow of stability by an exact observance of the others. If there is anyone whom this does not please, and who murmurs against a man for seeking his own

salvation, the author of all salvation shall answer him with the words: 'Is thine eye evil because his is good?' O whoever you are who envies another his salvation, spare at least your own. Have you not read: 'By the envy of the devil, death entered the world'? Take heed for yourself. If death and envy go together, you cannot envy and live. Why trouble your brother if he tries to honour the vows his lips have uttered? What do you lose by a man seeking how and where he may best fulfill what he has promised to God? Perhaps if he owed you a little money you would oblige him to encompass sea and land until the whole debt had been repaid even to the last farthing. What then has your God deserved of you that you should not wish him too to receive his due? In fact by envying one you have offended two. While you deprive the Lord of his servant's service, you also deprive the servant of the grace of his Lord. Why do you not imitate him by also paying what you owe? Do you think that your debt too will not be required of you? In fact you impiously anger God even more by saying: 'He will not require it of me'.

19. 'What', you say, 'do you condemn all those who do not follow these monks into your Order?' No, I do nothing of the sort. But listen to what I have to say of them and do not make futile accusations. Why do you try to make me hateful in the eyes of many thousands of holy men, who live under the same vows as I but not in the same manner, yet who live holy lives and make holy deaths? I know quite well that God has left to himself seven thousand men who have not bowed the knee to Baal. Listen and attend to what I have to say, envious and calumnious man. I have already told you why I believe that those who come to us from other monasteries are to be received. Does it not follow that I condemn those who do not come? I have excused those who do come but I have not accused those who do not. I only do not excuse the envious, for I cannot. Leaving aside these, if there should be any who wish to change to the purity of the Rule but dare not for fear of scandal, or

cannot on account of some bodily weakness, I think they do not sin providing they live where they are soberly, honestly, and piously. If by the customs of their monastery they cannot live so strictly as the Rule would seem to require, they will probably be excused either on account of their charity which holds them back from hastening to something better for fear of giving scandal, according to the words of Scripture, 'Charity covers a multitude of sins', or else on account of their humility by which they are conscious of their own infirmity and deem themselves imperfect on that account, and of such it has been written: 'God gives grace to the humble'.

20. I have said much to you, beloved, without there being any need for many words in your case, for I know well how quick you are to understand and how prompt you are to follow good advice. But although I have addressed myself to you especially, I have not written at such great length especially for you, but for those who need it. But I do warn you, as one who has been now for long well known to me, with few words and the fullest confidence, not to keep the souls who need you in any longer suspense, to the fearful peril of your own soul. You hold in your hand the fates of yourself and, unless I am deceived, of those who are with you. I believe they will follow you in whatever you do or wish to be done. Otherwise do not hesitate to proclaim to them the sentence of excommunication, which none can ignore, passed on them by all the abbots in Chapter: 'Who return shall live, who refuse shall die'.[1]

1. This was the Chapter held in 1124, when St. Bernard was instructed to recall the fugitives. See *Statuta Capitulorum Generalium Ordinis Cisterciensis*, ed. D. Josephus Canivez, Louvain, a work of superb erudition and interest.

[9]

To Bruno, Archbishop-Elect of Cologne

In spite of the doubts of St. Bernard, Bruno accepted the Arch-bishopric of Cologne. He was consecrated in the year 1132 and died in Italy four years later. He left a reputation for great learning.

YOU ask my advice, most illustrious Bruno, whether you should yield to those who would raise you to the episcopate. But what mortal would venture to decide such a matter? Perhaps God calls you, and then who would dare to dissuade you? Perhaps he does not call you, and then who would dare to persuade you? But whether or not he does call you, who can tell save the Spirit, who can search even the hidden things of God, or one to whom God himself might perhaps reveal it? The humble but terrible confession you make in your letter, accusing your past life so gravely yet not, I believe, untruly, renders advice on the matter even more doubtful. It cannot be denied that the sort of life of which you accuse yourself is not worthy of the sacred ministry. But again you are afraid, and not without reason, for I also fear the same thing, that you might do wrong if you did not trade with the talent of knowledge which has been committed to you, because you feel unworthy; unless there is some other sphere in which you could use it, less fruitfully perhaps, but also with less peril. I confess (for I must tell you what I feel in the matter) that I tremble for you when I consider from what depths you are being called to such heights, especially as there is no time for you to prepare yourself by penance for the perilous transition. And indeed right order requires that you should learn to look after yourself before you undertake care of others. It is written that the first step in piety is to 'have pity on your own soul, pleasing God'. And from this an orderly charity proceeds on right lines to the pity of others, inasmuch as it is laid down that we should love others as we love ourselves. But were you to love others as you have hitherto loved yourself, I for one would not wish to be committed to your care. Learn first to love yourself, and then you can love me.

2. But what if God were to hasten his graces and multiply his mercies so that your innocence is restored to you more effectively by his prompt compassion than it would be by years of penance, according to the words: 'Blessed is the man to whom the Lord hath not imputed his sin'. Who shall indict the elect of God? Who is he that condemns if God justifies? The good thief took this short way to salvation. On one and the same day he confessed his sin and was brought to glory, satisfied to use the cross as a short bridge from the state of otherness[1] into the land of the living, from the filth of this life to the paradise of delights. And the sinful Magdalen was also blessed with this same prompt remedy of piety, when grace began immediately to abound in her soul where iniquity had superabounded. Without any great labour of penance many sins were forgiven her because she had loved much, and in a short time she deserved to receive the abundance of charity which covers a multitude of sins. And the paralytic in the Gospels immediately experienced the double favour of being cured first in his soul and then in his body.

3. But it is one thing to obtain immediate forgiveness of sins and quite another to step immediately from enormities into the bishop's throne. I see Matthew raised immediately from the seat of custom to the dignity of an Apostle, but what disturbs me here is that he did not immediately hear with the other Apostles: 'Go ye into the whole world and preach the Gospel to every creature'. Before hearing this he had first to do penance by enduring with the Lord in his trials and by following him for a

1. *De regione dissimilitudinis.* This is almost a technical phrase with St. Bernard. Created by God in his own likeness, man has become disfigured by sin and so exiled from the land of Likeness to God to the land of Unlikeness . . . *Regio dissimilitudinis.* Actually the phrase is taken from St. Augustine (*Confessions*, Book vii, ch. 10), but St. Bernard makes a very personal use of the expression. See St. Bernard, *Sermo 'de diversis'*, XLII.

long time and with great labour withersoever he went. If Ambrose occurs as an example of one who was raised immediately from the secular tribunals to the dignity of the priesthood, it is no comfort because from boyhood he had lived in the world but not of the world and, deeming himself unworthy of the dignity, he tried to avoid it by flight, by hiding himself, and by other ruses. If Saul becoming immediately Paul the vessel of election and Doctor of the Gentiles is cited, the example lacks force because although he sinned, he did so, as he himself tells us, in ignorance and firm incredulity. Although there may be other good and excellent instances of what the Scriptures call 'the change of the right hand of the Most High', they are to be regarded more as miracles of grace than examples to be followed.

4. For the time being you must be satisfied with this provisional answer. I cannot give you a certain answer because I am myself uncertain about the matter. And unless a Prophet is consulted this must always be the case. Clear water cannot be drawn from a muddy pond. But there is one thing we can always do for a friend without any danger and with great advantage, and that is to offer him such help as our prayers to God can achieve. Leaving therefore to God his hidden counsels, of which I am ignorant, I pray him with humble devotion and devout humility to bring to pass in you and for you what most becomes his glory and your good. You have Father Norbert[1] to consult quite near you. As he lives closer to God he would be better able to know his hidden mysteries.

[10]

To Bruno, now Archbishop of Cologen

I HAVE received with devotion the letter of your Grace and I have been careful to do what you asked. It will be

1. This is St. Norbert, the founder of the Premonstratensian Order.

for your Grace to judge how far I have been successful. But enough of this. I am writing what follows in the same spirit of charity. If it is certain that all who are called to the ministry are also called to the Kingdom of heaven, then the Archbishop of Cologne has nothing to fear. But if it is true that Saul was called to the kingship and Judas to the priesthood by no other than God himself; and the evidence of Scripture cannot be gainsaid; then the Archbishop of Cologne has every reason to fear. And if, as is indeed true, the sentence of Scripture still holds good for to-day, that not many noble, not many mighty, not many wise according to the flesh are chosen, has not the Archbishop of Cologne a threefold cause to fear? Let us in high places have a care that we become not high minded, but walk with the humble, and fear. 'Have they made you ruler?' says Scripture. 'Be among them as one of them'. And again: 'The greater thou art, humble thyself the more in all things'. Very wise is this counsel and not other than the words of Wisdom himself saying: 'He that is greater among you, let him become as the younger'. Otherwise 'a most severe judgment shall be for them that rule', so let the powerful fear. And the servant who knows the will of the Lord but does it not, shall be beaten with many stripes; so let the man of letters fear. And let the noble also fear, for the judge of all is no respecter of persons. This three-strand rope of necessary fear is difficult to break. Does it seem hard that I do not flatter you, but incite you to fear, that for my friend I wish the beginning of wisdom? It is my wont ever thus to favour my friends, inciting them with wholesome fear rather than with deceitful flattery, and to this I am urged by the words, 'Blessed is the man that is always fearful', and I am recalled to it by him who says: 'O my people, they that call thee blessed, the same deceive thee'.

[12]

To the Prior Guy and other Religious of the Grande Chartreuse

Guy was the fifth Prior of the Chartreuse (1109-1136) and became the organizer of the Order. He codified the observances of his House in a book of customs for the benefit of other foundations. The Scale of the Cloisters *and a book of* Meditations *are also attributed to him. He died in 1137, leaving a reputation for great sanctity. Saint Bernard always maintained the most cordial relations with the Carthusian monks. There is even a tradition that he was for a short time a Carthusian Postulant, and although there is no truth in this, it is undoubtedly true that he was full of admiration for the eremetical life of the Carthusians and took every occasion for visiting them.*

To the most reverend of fathers and most dear of friends, Guy, Prior of the Grande Chartreuse, and the other saints who are with him, eternal life, from Brother Bernard of Clairvaux.

I RECEIVED the letters of your Holiness with a delight equalled only by my longing eagerness for them. I have read them and mused upon them and they have fired my heart like so many sparks from the fire which the Lord came to spread over the earth. How great must have been the fire burning in your meditations to have sent out such sparks as these! Your burning and kindling greeting seemed to me, I confess, to have come, not from man, but from him who 'sent word to Jacob'. It was no ordinary greeting such as one gives in passing on the road, or from habit; I could feel it came from the heart, a welcome and unexpected benison. May the Lord bless you for troubling to meet me, your child, with such a blessing in your letter to me that you have given me the courage to write back to you, after I had for so long wanted to, but not dared. For I was loath to harass your holy peace in the Lord, to disturb even for one moment your unbroken silence from the world, the whispers of your heavenly converse, by my uncalled-for scribbling; or to distract with my own affairs your ears absorbed in celestial praises. I feared lest by so doing I should be as one disturbing Moses on the mountain, or Elias in the desert, or Samuel watching in the temple. When Samuel cries, 'Speak, Lord, for thy servant heareth', should I dare to push myself forward? I feared lest I should be as one troubling David when he was taking to himself the wings of a dove to fly away far off, and hear the angry words: 'Let me be. I cannot hear you. I would sooner listen to what I can hear with greater pleasure: "I will hear what the Lord will speak in me; for he will speak peace unto his people and unto those whose hearts are turned towards him". Or even: "Depart from me, ye malignant; and I will search the commandments of my God" '. What? Should I be rash enough to wake the bride sleeping gently in the embraces of the Bridegroom for so long as she wishes? I think I would thereupon hear from her the words, 'Do not trouble me. "My beloved to me and I to him who feedeth among the lilies." '

2. But what I do not dare, charity does. She knocks confidently on the door of a friend, knowing that she is the mother of friendships and will not be repulsed. Sweet as your leisure is, she does not fear to disturb it a little on her business. She it is who, whenever she wishes, can draw you away from your contemplation of God for her own sake; and it was she who, when she wished, made you attentive to me, so that you have not thought it at all beneath you, not only to bear with me when I am speaking, but moreover kindly to encourage me to speak when I am silent. I embrace your goodness, I admire your condescension, I praise and venerate the purity of your intention which leads you to rejoice in the Lord for what you consider my progress. I glory in the testimony you have given me of

your good will, in your spontaneous friendliness. It is now my joy, my glory, and the delight of my heart that I have not lifted my eyes in vain to the hills from which I have already received so much help. From these hills a sweet dew has come down: may it still come until our valleys are filled with corn. It will ever be for me a day of joy and a day worthy of lasting remembrance on which I was honoured to see and welcome that worthy man through whom I was received into your affections. Although it is clear from your letters that you had received me into your affections even before this, yet now I understand it will be with an even closer and more intimate affection, since he has told you certain favourable things about me which he doubtless believed, although without sufficient cause. Far be it from such a religious and good man to have said anything but what he believed to be true. So I have now found out for myself the truth of those words of our Saviour: 'He who gives a just man the welcome due to a just man, shall receive the reward due to a just man'. The reward due to a just man is to be thought just, for no other reason than that he has received a just man. If he has said anything else about me then he was judging me, not according to the facts, but according to his own goodness. You have listened to him, you have believed him, you have rejoiced in what he said, you have written to me, and thereby you have gladdened me not a little, not only because I have won a place and no small place in your affections, but also because you have shown me something of the purity of your own soul. In a few words you have shown me for certain of what spirit you are.

3. I rejoice on my own account and on yours; I congratulate you on your charity, and myself on the profit my soul has derived from it. For that is a true and sincere charity to be attributed entirely to a pure heart and unfeigned faith which leads us to love our neighbors' good as well as our own. The man who loves his own good in preference to his neighbours' good or

who loves only his own good proves, by the very fact that his love is not disinterested, that he does not love the good with a chaste love. Such a one could not obey the Prophet when he says: 'Praise the Lord because he is good'. He may praise the Lord because he is good to himself, but not because he is Goodness itself. And he should know that the same Prophet is casting a reproach at him for this when he says: 'He will praise thee when thou do well to him'. There are those who praise the Lord because he is powerful, and these are slaves and fearful for themselves; there are those who praise him because he is good to them, and these are hirelings seeking themselves; and there are those who praise him because he is Goodness itself, and these are sons doing homage to their father. Both those who fear for themselves and those who seek themselves are acting only for themselves; only the love of a son seeks not itself. On this account, I think that the words 'The Law of God is unspotted' refer to charity, because it alone can turn the heart from love of self and the world, and direct it to God alone. Neither fear nor love of self can turn the soul to God; they may sometimes change the aspect or influence the actions of a man, but they will never change his heart. Even the slave sometimes does God's work, but because he does not do it willingly he proves that his heart is still hard. And the hireling too will sometimes do God's work, but because he only does it for reward, he is known to be attracted only by his greed. Where there is self-seeking, there too is self-esteem; where there is self-esteem, there too is private interest; and where private interest makes a corner for itself there rust and filth will collect.[1] Let fear itself be the law of a slave, by it he is bound; let greed be for the hireling his law, by it he also is confined when by it he is led off and enticed away. Neither of these two laws is unspotted, neither can turn

1. *Porro ubi proprietas, ibi singularitas; ubi autem singularitas, ibi angulus; ubi vero angulus, ibi sine dubio sordes sive rubigo.* Literally: 'Where there is proprietorship, there is singularity; where there is singularity, there is a corner; where there is a corner, there without doubt is filth or rust'.

the soul to God; only charity can do this, because she alone can render a soul disinterested.

4. I would call his charity unspotted who never keeps anything of his own for himself. When a man keeps nothing of his own for himself, everything he has is God's, and what is God's cannot be unclean. Therefore the unspotted law of God is charity, which seeks not what may benefit itself, but what may benefit many. Charity is called the law of the Lord, either because the Lord himself lives by it or else because none may have it except by his gift. Let it not seem absurd that I should have said even God lives by law, for I have also said that the law is nothing else but charity. What else but charity preserves that supreme and unspeakable unity in the blessed Trinity? Charity is therefore a law, and it is the law of the Lord holding together, as it were, the Trinity and binding it in the bonds of peace. Yet let no one think that I speak of charity here as if it were a quality or something accidental to the Godhead, as if I were saying (may it be far from me to say any such thing!) that there was something in God which is not God; but I say that charity is the divine substance itself. And there is nothing new or strange about this, for St. John himself has said, 'God is charity'. It follows that charity can be correctly said to be both God and the gift of God; that charity gives charity; the substance of charity, the quality of charity. When we speak of the giver we mean the substance; when we speak of the gift we mean the quality. This is the eternal law, the creator and ruler of the Universe, since through it all things were made in weight, measure, and number. Nothing is left without law, since even the law of all things is not without a law, yet a law not other than itself for, although it did not create itself, it nevertheless rules itself.

5. The slave and the hireling also have a law, a law not from God, but which they make for themselves; the one by not loving God and the other by loving something more than God. They have, I say, a law, but a law of their own, not of God, yet

a law which is, nevertheless, subject to the law of God. Any-one can make a law for himself, but he cannot withdraw it from the immutable order of the eternal law. But anyone who thus makes a law for himself is perversely trying to imitate his Creator by ruling himself, and making his own self-will a law for himself, just as God is his own law and subject only to him-self. Alas! what a heavy and insupportable burden is this on the children of Adam; we are bowed down and bent under it, so that our lives are dragged down nigh to hell. 'Unhappy man that I am, who will deliver me from the body of this death', by which I am so oppressed that unless the Lord had helped me, I would almost have dwelt in hell. He too was groaning under this burden who said: 'Why hast thou set me opposite to thee, and I am become burdensome to myself'. When he says, 'I am become burdensome to myself', he shows that he has been a law unto himself, and that no other than he himself had done this. But when, speaking of God, he says, 'Why hast thou set me opposite to thee', he shows that he has not scaped from the law of God. It is the property of the eternal law of God that he who will not be ruled sweetly by him, shall be ruled as a punishment by himself; that he who, of his own will, throws off the sweet and light yoke of charity shall unwillingly suffer the insup-portable burden of his own self-will.

6. And so in a wonderful way the eternal law keeps the rene-gade both 'opposite itself' and yet subject to itself, so that he is neither able to evade the law of justice nor to rest in the peace and light of God. He remains subject to the power of God and yet far removed from happiness. O Lord, my God, why dost thou not take away my sin, why dost thou not remove my in-iquity, so that I may cast off the burden of my self-will, and breathe again under the light yoke of charity, no longer forced by servile fear nor enticed by the hireling's lust for gain? Why am I not led by thy spirit, the spirit of liberty, the spirit which leads thy sons, and which bears witness to my spirit that while

thy law is also mine, I too am one of thy sons; and as thou art, so also may I be in this world. For it is certain that those who fulfill the words of the Apostles and 'owe no man anything except to love him' are in this world even as God; not hirelings nor yet slaves but sons. Therefore neither are the sons of God free from law, unless anyone should think differently on account of the words, 'The law is not made for the just'. But it should be understood that the law promulgated in fear by the spirit of slavery is one thing, and the law given graciously by the spirit of liberty is quite another. Sons are not bound by the former, but neither are they suffered to live without the latter. Listen to why the law is not made for the just, 'because', says Scripture, 'you have not received the spirit of bondage again in fear'. Listen also to why the just are under the law of charity: 'You have received the spirit of the adoption of sons'. And now hear the just man admitting that he is at once not under the law and not without law: 'I became to those that are under the law, as if I were under the law (whereas myself I am not under the law), that I might gain them that were under the law. To them that are without the law, I became as if I were without the law, whereas I was not without the law, but was in the law of Christ'. Hence, 'The law is not made for the just' does not mean that the just are without law, but that the law is freely and lovingly accepted by them from him who graciously inspired it and not imposed on them against their wills. Wherefore the Lord has beautifully said, 'Take my yoke upon you', meaning that he does not impose it on us against our will, but that we can take it on ourselves if we wish, and if we do not we shall find labour and not peace for our souls.

7. Good and sweet is the law of charity, not only light to bear, but also an easement of the law of slaves and hirelings. For it does not destroy these laws, it brings them to perfection, according to Our Lord's words: 'I have not come to set aside the law, but to bring it to perfection'. Tempering the one and

controlling the other, it eases both. Charity will never be without fear, but a chaste fear; nor ever without self-interest, but an ordered self-interest. It brings the law of the slave to perfection by inspiring it with devotion; and also the law of the hireling, by controlling self-interest. When devotion is mixed with fear it does not nullify it, but amends it; it takes from it the anguish which it never lacks when it is servile, and renders it chaste and filial. The words 'Perfect charity casteth out fear' must be understood as meaning that it removes the anguish which, as I have said, is never lacking to fear so long as it is servile. It is a common mode of speech, putting the cause for the effect. And the self-interest inherent in the law of the hireling is controlled by charity, so that it entirely rejects what is evil, prefers what is better to what is good, and what is good only for the sake of what is better. And, when this is fully effected in the soul by the grace of God, the body and all created good are only loved for the sake of the soul, and the soul only for the sake of God, and God for his own sake.

8. Because we are flesh and blood born of the desire of the flesh, our desire or love must start in the flesh, and it will then, if properly directed, progress under grace by certain stages until it is fulfilled in the spirit for 'that was not first which is spiritual, but that which is natural; afterwards that which is spiritual', and we must first bear the image which is earthly and afterwards that which is heavenly. At first a man loves himself for his own sake. He is flesh and is able only to know himself. But when he sees that he cannot subsist of himself, then he begins by faith to seek and love God as necessary for himself. And so in the second stage he loves God, not yet for God's sake, but for his own sake. However when, on account of his own necessity, he begins to meditate, read, pray, and obey, he becomes accustomed little by little to know God and consequently to delight in him. When he has tasted and found how sweet is the Lord he passes to the third stage wherein he loves God for God's

sake and not for his own. And here he remains, for I doubt whether the fourth stage has ever been fully reached in this life by any man, the stage, that is, wherein a man loves himself only for God's sake. Let those say who have experienced it; I confess that to me it seems impossible. It will come about, doubtless, when the good and faithful servant shall have been brought into the joy of his Lord and become inebriated with the fulness of the house of God. For he will then be wholly lost in God as one inebriated and henceforth cleave to him as if one in spirit with him, forgetful, in a wonderful manner, of himself and, as it were, completely out of himself.

9. I consider the prophet to have felt this when he said: 'I will enter into the powers of the Lord; O Lord, I will be mindful of thy justice alone'. He certainly knew that when he would enter the spiritual powers of the Lord, he would leave behind him all the frailties of the flesh, so that he would no longer have to think any more of them but would be wholly occupied with the justice of God. Then each of Christ's members will be able to say for himself what St. Paul said of their head: 'We have known Christ according to the flesh, but now we know him so no longer'. For no one will know himself there according to the flesh because 'flesh and blood cannot possess the kingdom of God'. I do not say that the substance of the flesh will not be there, but that every carnal need will be absent, that the love of the flesh will be absorbed in the love of the spirit, and that what are now weak human affections will be transformed into divine powers. When charity shall pull up on to the shore of eternity the net which she is now drawing through this vast and great sea so as to bring in without ceasing every sort of fish, she will then cast aside the bad and keep only the good. For in this life her net keeps every sort of fish within its ample folds and she accommodates herself to all making, in a sense, her own all the good and evil fortunes of everyone, not only so as to rejoice with the glad but also to weep with the afflicted. When

she shall have come to shore everything that she has hitherto borne with sorrow she will cast aside as evil fish, retaining only what gives her pleasure and happiness. Will St. Paul, for example, then become weak with the weak or on fire for the scandalized, when all scandals and all weaknesses are done away? Or will he weep for those who have not repented where it is certain that as there will be no one who sins, so there will be no one to repent? Far be it from him to mourn for those who are condemned to eternal flames with the devil and his angels, in the city of God 'which the stream of the river maketh glad' and the 'gates of which God loves above all the tents of Jacob'. Because, although there may sometimes be rejoicing over victory in tents, yet there is also the labour of battle and often danger to life. But in that home-land no adversity or sorrow is admitted according to those words which are sung of it: 'All the world rejoicing finds its dwelling place in thee' and 'Everlasting joy shall be unto them'. And then how can there be any recollection of mercy where only the justice of God is remembered? Where there will be no place for misery or time for mercy, there can be no feeling of compassion.

10. I feel myself driven to compose a long discourse by my insatiable desire to speak to you, my most dear brothers, but there are three things which indicate that it is time for me to finish. The first is that I fear more than anything to become a burden to you. The second is that I am ashamed of my wordiness. The third is that I am hard pressed by the cares of my household. Finally I beg you to have pity on me. If you have rejoiced over the good you have only heard about me, have compassion on the evils that are real. Perhaps the good man who told you such favourable things about me saw certain small things and made of them something great. And you, in the goodness of your heart, found no difficulty in believing what you were so glad to hear. I give thanks for your charity which 'believeth all things'; but I am abased to the dust for the truth

which knows all things. I want you to believe what I, rather than another, who sees only the surface, say of myself: 'No man knoweth the things of a man, but the spirit of a man that is in him'. I tell you, therefore, who speak of myself from experience and not from conjecture, that I am not as I am believed or said to be. I say this with an assurance supported by the proof of experience, so that I would prefer to obtain nothing more by your special prayers than to be such as your letters make me out to be.

[22]

To Matthew, the Legate

The following letter is addressed to Matthew du Remois, Cardinal Bishop of Albano. It was evidently written in reply to a summons from the Legate to attend the Council of Troyes over which Matthew presided in the year 1128. In this letter Bernard tries to excuse himself from attendance on the grounds of ill health, but at the end he indicates that he is willing to obey the summons in spite of his illness. In fact he was present, and it was under his influence that the Knights Templar received the formal sanction of the Church at the Council. This letter is typical of the many letters the Saint wrote imploring to be excused from the burden of external activities.

MY heart was ready to obey your summons, but not so my body. My weak flesh, parched by the heat of a raging fever and exhausted by constant sweating, was not able to satisfy the demands of my willing spirit. And so, although I wanted to come, my weakling body impeded my ready will. Whether or not this is a sufficient reason for not coming, those friends of

mine must judge who, regardless of my protests, are always
trying to drag me, enmeshed in the net of obedience, from the
cloister to the cities. They must know that this is not a mere
pretext, but a grievous affliction, and so they will learn that
there is no evading the will of God. They would certainly have
been indignant with me if I had said to them: 'I have put off
my garment, how shall I put it on? I have washed my feet, how
shall I soil them?' But now they must either be angry with the
providence of God or submit to it, for it is not my fault that I
cannot come when I am ready to do so.

2. They tell me that the matter is important and the necessity
grave. If this is so then they must find someone suitable. If they
think I am he, then I assure them not only that I believe they are
mistaken, but that I am quite certain they are. Be the matters
weighty or trivial which they press upon me, they are no concern of mine. If these matters in which you try so hard to in-
volve your friend at the cost of his peace and silence are simple,
then they can be settled without me; if they are difficult then
they cannot be settled by me. Unless of course I am considered
a person of such consequence that great and difficult matters
must be reserved for me because there is no one else to settle
them. If this is so then only in my case have the designs of God
been frustrated. Why has he put me under a bushel when I
could give light from a candlestick or, to speak more clearly,
why, if I am necessary to the world, a man without whose aid
the bishops cannot settle their own affairs, has God called me
to be a monk and 'hidden me in his tabernacle in the day of evil
things'? As it is, all that my friends have done for me is to make
me feel troubled when I speak to one whom, hitherto, I have
never thought of without serenity and joy. But you know, and
it is to you I speak, my father, that 'I am ready and not troubled
that I may keep your commands'. But I beg you, of your kindness, to spare me whenever you can.

[25]

To the Universal Doctor, Gilbert, Bishop of London

Gilbert was Bishop of London from 1128 to 1135. It is therefore probable that this letter was written about the year 1130. He was called the 'Universal Doctor' because he excelled in all branches of learning. St. Bernard congratulates him in his letter for overcoming avarice by living as a poor man while Bishop of London. Henry of Huntingdon, however, attributes the spartan life of the bishop to miserliness.

THE fame of your life has spread far and wide, and it has been as a most sweet odour for all unto whom it has come. Your avarice has been stifled: who would not delight in this? Charity rules in its stead: who does not relish this? All men know you to be wise because you have crushed the chief enemy of wisdom. This is something worthy of your priesthood and your great name. The witness of your life well becomes your philosophy; it is a fitting crown of your studies. Yours has been the true wisdom which scorns filthy lucre and refuses to consort with the service of idols. For you it was no great thing to be a bishop, but to be a bishop of London and yet to live as a poor man, this is something clearly magnificent. The dignity of high office could have added little to the lustre of your fame, but the humility of your poverty has added much. To bear poverty with resignation argues great patience; to seek it of one's own free will is the highest wisdom. The Scriptures acclaim and praise the man who does not set his heart on riches, but you have deserved even higher praise by scorning them. Unless cold reason can see nothing wonderful in a wise man acting wisely. And without any doubt you are a wise man, taking your pleasure in all the books and studies of the wise men of the world, and studying all the divine Scriptures so as to give life to their meaning and apply it to the present day. For have you not 'dispersed and given to the poor'? But it is money you have given. And what is money in comparison with the justice for which you have exchanged it? 'His justice remaineth for ever and ever'. Can the same be said of money? It is certainly a desirable and worthy sort of commerce to exchange what passes for what lasts for ever. O admirable and praiseworthy Master, may you always be able to do business in this way! It only remains for you to finish the good work you have begun, so that the tail of the victim may be joined to the head.[1] I gladly accept your blessing, especially as it comes recommended by the joy I take in your high perfection. Although the bearer of this letter is a most worthy person in himself, yet I wish him to be acceptable to you for my sake as well, because he is very dear to me by reason of his integrity and piety.

[26]

To Hugh, Archbishop of Rouen

Hugh was elected Archbishop of Rouen in the year 1130. Before his election he had been a monk of Cluny and then Abbot of Reading.

THE evils of our time may grow worse every day, but they cannot prevail. They may disturb us, but they should not dismay us. 'Wonderful is the surging of the waves', but more wonderful is the Lord on high. If you are frank with yourself you must admit that God has been very good to you. The care of Providence has seen to it that you were not put in charge of sinners before you had associated with good people, so that in

1. This is a favourite metaphor of St. Bernard, taken from *Lev.* 3-7, to signify perseverance.

their company and by their example you might become good
enough to lead a good life among evil people. We save our souls
by living a good life amongst good people, but we deserve praise
as well by living a good life amongst evil people. The first is safe
and easy, the second all the more virtuous for being more difficult. It is as difficult to do this as it is to touch pitch without
being sullied, to put one's hand into the fire without being
burned, to live in darkness without losing the light. There was
once darkness over the land of Egypt so thick that it might be
felt, but 'wheresoever the children of Israel dwelt there was
light'. David was a true Israelite and therefore he was careful to
say that he did not live in Cedar, but 'with the inhabitants of
Cedar', as if to imply that although the dwelling place of his
body was with the people of Cedar, yet he dwelt always in the
light. And he rebuked some who were not true Israelites because
'they mingled with the heathen and were a stumbling-block to
them'.

2. So I say to you that according to the words, 'With the
innocent man thou wilt be innocent', it was enough for you
when you were at Cluny to have kept yourself innocent, but
now that you live amongst the people of Rouen you must also
have patience according to the words of the Apostle: 'The
servant of God must not wrangle, he must be mild to all men,
ready to teach them, and be patient'. And you must not only be
patient so as not to be overcome by evil, you must also be
peaceable so as to overcome evil by good. By being patient you
will bear with evil people, by being peaceable you will heal
them of their evil. In your patience you will possess your soul,
but you must also be peaceable so as to possess the souls committed to your care. What is more glorious than to be able to
say: 'With them that hated peace, I was peaceable'? So be patient because you are with evil people; and be peaceable too
because you have to rule over them. By all means let your
charity be zealous, but for the time moderate your severity.
You must never condone evil, but sometimes it is well to defer

rebuking it. Justice should always be eager, but never hasty. All that pleases is not lawful, so all that is lawful is not always expedient at the moment. But you know all this better than I, so I will forbear from saying any more. Pray for me without ceasing, for I am ceaselessly sinning.

[33]

To Jorannus, Abbot of Saint Nicasius
of Rheims

With the réclame of the new Cistercian movement difficulties were always arising through monks of the old observance wishing to leave their monasteries for the Cistercians. Naturally it would nearly always have been the best and most fervent subjects of the old monasteries who wished to do this. The following letter is written to comfort Abbot Jorannus on the loss of one of his monks, a certain Brother Drogo, to the Cistercians. If it is read with the two following letters which are also concerned with the same brother, St. Bernard is shown in a very human light.

Apparently Drogo did not persevere with the Cistercians, but returned to St. Nicasius before his profession.

Later on Abbot Jorannus himself left the Benedictines to become a Carthusian.

Mabillon ascribes this letter to the year 1120.

HE WHO bore in his body all our griefs knows how deeply I sympathize with you. I would willingly counsel you if I knew what to say, and help you if I knew what to do, even as I hope for the counsel and help of him who knows all things and to whom all things are possible. I would certainly never have advised Brother Drogo to leave you, if he had consulted me on the matter; I would certainly never have received him here, if he had come to me after leaving you.[1] But, as you know, I have done what I could by immediately writing to the abbot who received him. What, my father, can I do more than this now? As regards yourself, you know as well as I do that perfect men are 'confident not only in their hope of attaining glory as sons of God, but are confident even over their afflictions', being consoled by those sayings from the Scriptures: 'Pottery is tested in the furnace, man in the crucible of suffering. Though a hundred trials beset the innocent, the Lord will bring them safely through them all. We cannot enter the kingdom of heaven without many trials. All those who are resolved to lead a holy life in Jesus Christ will meet with persecution.' But this is not to say that we are not to commiserate with our friends when they are in trouble, for we do not know what the outcome of it will be, and there is the chance that they may fall away. With the saints and elect trouble makes for endurance, endurance gives proof of their faith, and a proved faith gives ground for hope. But with the damned and reprobate on the contrary trouble makes for faint-heartedness, faint-heartedness for worry, worry for despair, and that is the finish.

2. So that you may not be drowned in this horrid storm, so that you may not be swallowed up in the depths, so that the mouth of the insatiable pit may not close over you, do you in humble prudence take care that you are not overcome by evil, but rather overcome evil by good. And overcome you will if you put your hope in God and patiently await the issue. If Brother Drogo[2] should be brought to his senses either by his fear of you or by the difficulty of what he has undertaken, well and good; but if not, then for your own good you must 'bow down under the strong hand of God' and not kick against the ruling of heaven, because what is of God cannot be undone.

1. Cf. the following two letters.
2. Apparently this brother was sometimes known as 'Hugo-Drogo', because he was held in such high esteem by Hugo, Abbot of Pontigny.

You should try to control your stirrings of anger, however justified they may be, by remembering that saying of one of the saints who, when some of the brethren were provoking and reproaching him for not recalling a brother who had gone to another monastery in defiance of him, replied: 'Not at all. Wherever he is, if he is good, he is still mine.'

3. My advice to you would not be sincere if I did not follow it myself. When one of my own monks, not only a professed religious but also a relation of mine, was received and kept at Cluny against my will, I was sorry certainly, but I held my peace and prayed to God for those who had taken him away that they might return him, and for him too that he might come back of his own free will. But I left my vengeance to God 'who redresses wrongs' and 'who rights the wrongs of the defenceless'.[1] Through your mouth my spirit warns Brother Hugh of Lausanne 'not to believe every spirit' nor hastily to leave a certain good for one that is uncertain. Let him understand that the devil always attacks perseverance because he knows that it is the only virtue which wins the crown. I warn him that it would be safer for him to persevere with simplicity in the vocation to which he has been called, than under the pretext of seeking supposedly higher good to abandon what he has begun only perhaps to find that he is not equal to what he has presumed to undertake.

[34]

To Hugh, Abbot of Pontigny

To his most beloved Lord, Abbot Hugh, all that he could wish for himself, from Brother Bernard of Clairvaux.

AS far as I can gather from your letter it appears that either I have worded myself less clearly than I had wished or else that you have not understood me in the way I had intended

1. See Letter 1.

you to do. The warning I gave you of the consequences of receiving that monk was quite genuine, I really did fear them and I still do, even as I wrote to you. But I had no intention of trying to persuade or advise you, still less did I mean, as you said I did, that the monk ought to be returned to his monastery. As I have known his wish to join us for a long time, I ought rather to congratulate him than urge his return. But when I was implored by his abbot,[1] with whom I am very intimate, and by the Archbishop of Rheims, to write to you and ask for his return, I tried so far as I could both to clear myself of any suspicion of complicity in the affair and to warn you of the abuse you might incur by your action, while at the same time satisfying them. Knowing your shrewdness I thought you would read between the lines and see this, or that at any rate you would gather what I meant from what I put at the end of the letter, if you read it in the spirit in which it was written. For when I had warned you of the consequences which I feared, and not without cause, might come of your receiving this monk, I added, if I remember right: 'Should you prefer to endure all this rather than lose the man, that is your affair and you must see to it'. These, or very nearly these, were my words. I had intended by saying this at the end of the letter to give you a covert hint that I had written what I did under pressure to satisfy, not to say hood-wink, others.

2. What you say about my insinuating to this monk by means of the messenger, that if he came to me I would obtain secretly a dispensation from Rome is, I assure you by the very Truth, quite untrue. Is it likely that I would boast or even hope that I could receive a monk from a monastery which is well known to me, whom I do not think even you can keep without giving great offence? But even were this so, even if I did envy you the monk and try to attract him to myself, hoping or pretending I could engineer his dispensation from Rome, is it likely that I would reveal to the messenger of all people that I

1. See previous letter.

was plotting against his own monastery? I must tell you, so that you may not think the affection you have had for me hitherto has been misplaced, that I shall consider it my duty to continue to work for your interests as I see them as hard as I do for my own, or even harder, and this, not so that the harmony between us may be further strengthened, as I have done hitherto, but that it may not now be altogether broken. What more can I say? Only that I could never have believed you capable of such an action as you, on the sole grounds of mere suspicion, attribute to me.

It remains for me to tell you that Count Theobald has now received the letter I wrote on behalf of Humbert, but has not yet replied to it. What more you can do about it your own pity will suggest if you consider the misery of a man who has been exiled unjustly.

[35]

To the Monk Drogo

This letter should be read with the two preceding. It is to the monk with whom those letters are concerned.

IT is now quite clear, my dearest Drogo, that my affection for you has not been misplaced. Even before this I saw that you were a very lovable person, and I perceived that there was something about you, I know not what, apart from what I saw and heard of you, entitling you to respect as well as to affection. Perhaps even then you had heard the voice of the Bridegroom, in whose pure arms you are now closely held, whispering to your soul, as to a shy dove: 'Fair in every part, my true love, no fault at all in thy fashioning'. Who would have believed what you have done! The whole city was talking of your holiness and exact observance, so that it was hard to believe that there could be any improvement possible in you. And now you have left your monastery, as a secular would leave the world, and, although already bent under the burden of Christ, you have not considered it beneath you to submit yourself again to the observances of a new discipline. In you, brother, the truth of that saying of Scripture is proved once more: 'Reach thou to the end of thy reckoning, thou must needs begin again'. That you should have now begun again, is an indication that you had reached the end of your reckoning; that you should have considered you had not yet finished, indicates that you had already done so. No one is perfect who does not wish to be still more perfect; the more perfect a man is, the more he reaches out to an even higher perfection.

2. But, dearest friend, he whose envy brought death into the world is not asleep, even now 'his bow is bent in readiness'. He has no power within you because you have turned him out of your heart, but outside he rages as much as he can. To speak more clearly: do you not know that the Pharisees are scandalized at what you have done? But remember that there are some scandals that we do not need greatly to trouble about, according to the answer our Blessed Lord gave under similar circumstances: 'Let them be, they are blind leaders of the blind'. It is better that there should be scandal than that the truth should be denied. Remember who it was who was born for the rise and fall of many and do not wonder that for some you should be 'a life giving perfume' and for others 'a deadly fume'. If they should threaten you with curses, if they should hurl the darts of their anathemas at you, harken to Isaac answering them for you: 'A curse on those who curse, a blessing on those who bless thee'. And do you, protected by the impregnable wall of your conscience, answer them from within: 'Though a whole host were arrayed against me, my heart would be undaunted: though an armed onset should threaten me, still I would not lose confidence'. You will not be overcome if you answer them

thus at the door. I am confident in the Lord that if you stand up firmly to the first blows and do not give way either to threats or to blandishments, you will quickly crush satan under your feet, and 'honest men will rejoice to witness it, and malice will stand dumb with confusion'.

[51]

To Cardinal Haimeric, Chancellor of the Holy See

It is clear from this very instructive letter that someone had been making mischief in Rome about St. Bernard. There is nothing new or surprising in this. It was indeed inevitable that a man like St. Bernard should have been the victim of petty jealousy and even the quite sincere distrust of men with narrow horizons. It is not always wicked people who stone the prophets, more often it is the perfectly sincere formalists.

To the illustrious Haimeric, Chancellor of the Holy Roman See, salvation in eternity, from Brother Bernard, styled Abbot of Clairvaux.

CANNOT wretchedness escape envy? Must truth breed hatred even for the poor and needy? Should I be glad or should I deplore that I am treated as an enemy? Is it because I spoke the truth or because I did right? This is for your brothers in Curia to decide who 'speak evil of the deaf' against the law and who, regardless of the Prophet's curse, 'call evil good and good evil'. What have I done that displeases them? Is it because at Châlons a man discredited on all sides was removed from his stewardship for squandering the goods of the Lord in the Church of Verdun over which he had been placed?[1] Or because at Cambrai Fulbert, who was manifestly wrecking his monastery, was forced to withdraw in favour of Parvin whom everyone considered a wise and prudent servant? Or because at Laon his sanctuary was restored to the Lord after being a brothel of Venus?[2] For which of these things do you, I do not say stone me, for I would not set myself in the place of my Lord, but tear me to pieces? This is what I might have answered you rightly and with pride if I could have claimed for myself any credit for these things. But why am I blamed for the actions of others? Or supposing they were mine, why am I blamed for them as though they were evil? No one could be so imprudent as to doubt or so impudent as to deny that these things were well and justly done. You can choose between either denying or admitting that I am the author of them. If I am, then I am wrongfully rebuked and deserve praise for doing what was praiseworthy. If I am not, then I am no more worthy of blame than I am of praise. This is a new sort of detraction, not dissimilar to what Balaam did who covered the people with blessings when he had been summoned to curse them. For what could be more just and pleasing than that while intending to rebuke me you should have only commended me the more, so as to have

1. Henry, Bishop of Verdun, was suspected of corrupt administration of the funds of the Church. He consulted St. Bernard on the matter and St. Bernard advised him to resign, so as to avoid public scandal. His resignation was accepted by the Pope's Legate, Matthew, Bishop of Albano, at a Council held at Châlons-sur-Marne in 1129.

2. The Abbey of St. John at Laon is referred to here. The lax and scandalous life of the nuns there had for long been a cause of grave anxiety to the bishop, Bartholomew le Vir. A council was held at Arras in 1128, attended by the king (for the abbey was a royal foundation), the Archbishop of Rheims, the Bishops of Laon, Arras, and Soissons, as well as several abbots, including St. Bernard. The reform of the abbey was decreed and confirmed by the Pope through his Legate, Matthew, Bishop of Albano. This time the king made no objections, probably, as Williams in his *Life of St. Bernard* says, because the state of affairs was too scandalous to admit of any doubt as to the correct procedure.

used all unknowingly praises instead of insults; than that while intending to disparage me, you should have praised me unwittingly? It is as if your brothers in Curia were reproaching me or rather crediting me with other people's good deeds, because they could not find any evil that I had done.

2. I am not disturbed by undeserved blame nor do I accept unmerited praise. I am not greatly concerned about things for which I am not responsible. Let them praise, if they wish, or blame, if they dare, for the first my lord of Albano, for the second my lord of Rheims, and for the third the same archbishop together with the bishop of Laon, the king, and many other reverend persons. None of them will deny responsibility for these affairs or that they were the chief persons concerned. If they have done well it does not concern me any more than if they have done ill. Is it my whole and only fault that I was present on those occasions, I who am only fit to live hidden away, I who am my own judge, accuser, and witness of my life, to see that my actions become my profession and that the name I bear of monk is justified by my solitary existence? I was present, I do not deny it. But I was summoned and dragged there. If this does not please my friends in Curia, it pleases me just as little. I wish that I had not gone there, I wish that I need never go on similar occasions. I wish that I had not lately been where I saw with shame a violent tyrant armed against the Church by the Apostolic authority, as if he were not raging enough without such help. When a sudden load was placed upon my shoulders by the indisputable authority of the Apostolic rescript, then I felt, in the words of the Prophet, my tongue cleave to the roof of my mouth. 'I was dumb and patient so that I would not speak even to good purpose', when I saw the innocent suddenly covered with ignominy by that rescript and wicked men rejoice the more in their wickedness and delight exceedingly in their vile deeds, and my sorrow was renewed within me. The ungodly was shown mercy so that, according to the words of the

Prophet, he should not learn his lesson. He who in the land of the righteous worked iniquity was freed of the most just interdict under which his domains were held.

3. For reasons of this sort, even were there no others, I am vexed at having been embroiled in these disputes, especially as I knew that I was not concerned personally in them. I am vexed, but I am dragged into them none the less. But by whom can I better hope to be relieved of all this than by you, the best of men? You do not lack the power to do this, and I see that you do not lack the will. I am delighted to know that you are displeased that I should have been concerned in these affairs. It is most just and friendly of you. May it please you to bestir yourself in the matter, and because you understand that it is expedient for your friend and becoming for a monk, see that what we both want is speedily effected for the sake of justice and for the salvation of my soul. May it please you to bid the noisy and importunate frogs to keep their holes and remain contented with their ponds. See that they are heard no more in the councils of the mighty or seen in the palaces of the great, that no necessity and no authority may have the power to drag them into public affairs and embroil them in disputes. In this way perhaps your friend can avoid the stigma of presumption. Indeed I do not know how I was able to incur it, for I know that it was my purpose and determination never, except on the business of my Order, to leave my monastery unless the Legate of the Apostolic See or my own bishop bade me do so. As you know very well, a person in my humble state may not refuse the command of such authorities, except by the privilege of some higher authority. So if I can ever achieve this through your good offices, then without any doubt I shall have peace at home and leave others at peace. But I do not think that because I am hidden away and keeping silent the troubles of the Church will cease so long as the Roman Curia continues to pass judgements to the prejudice of the absent in order to please those who are at hand. Farewell.

To Geoffrey, Bishop of Chartres

The Dom Norbert mentioned in this letter was Saint Norbert, founder of the Premonstratensian Canons. It is interesting for showing Bernard's opinion of Norbert's prophesy.

I DO not know whether Dom Norbert is going to Jerusalem or not. When I last saw him a few days ago and was deemed worthy to drink in his heavenly wisdom, he never mentioned the matter to me. He spoke of the coming of Antichrist and, on my asking him when he thought this would be, he declared himself quite certain that it would be during this present generation. But when I heard the reasons he had for his certainty, I did not feel compelled to agree with him. He concluded by saying that he would live to see a general persecution of the Church.

2. May I remind you of that poor and exiled man, Humbert? He twice begged you, when you were at Troyes, to intercede for him with Count Theobald who has dispossessed him. And now I join my prayers with his to implore your aid in the matter. I myself have written to the Count but, not finding favour, I achieved nothing.

3. And now I must tell you something which you will be very glad to hear. Your Stephen is 'not running his course like a man in doubt of his goal; or fighting his battle like a man who wastes his blows upon the air'. Pray that he may so run as to reach the goal, so fight as to conquer.

[67]

To Alexander, Bishop of Lincoln

This letter concerns a young canon named Philip who, on his way to Jerusalem, turned aside to pause at Clairvaux, and was blessed to find there his vocation, even as St. Stephen Harding on his way to Rome found it at Molesme. Alexander was Bishop of Lincoln from 1123-1147, and was known as Alexander the Magnificent. Saint Bernard was an artist in words and in the first paragraph of this letter we see him at his most eloquent. Perhaps there has never been written a more compelling invitation to the mystical life than this short paragraph.

To the honourable Lord Alexander, by the grace of God Bishop of Lincoln, that he may desire honour in Christ rather than in the world, from Bernard, Abbot of Clairvaux.

   I WRITE to tell you that your Philip has found a short cut to Jerusalem and has arrived there very quickly. He crossed 'the vast ocean stretching wide on every hand' with a favourable wind in a very short time, and he has now cast anchor on the shores for which he was making. Even now he stands in the courts of Jerusalem and 'whom he had heard tidings of in Ephrata he has found in the woodland plains, and gladly reverences in the place where he has halted in his journey'. He has entered the holy city and has chosen his heritage with them of whom it has been deservedly said: 'You are no longer exiles or aliens; the saints are your fellow citizens, you belong to God's household'. His going and coming is in their company and he has become one of them, glorifying God and saying with them: 'We find our true home in heaven'. He is no longer an inquisitive onlooker, but a devout inhabitant and an enrolled citizen of Jerusalem; but not of that earthly Jerusalem to which Mount Sinai in Arabia is joined, and which is in bondage with her children, but of that free Jerusalem which is above and the mother of us all.

2. And this, if you want to know, is Clairvaux. She is the Jerusalem united to the one in heaven by whole-hearted devotion, by conformity of life, and by a certain spiritual affinity. Here, so Philip promises himself, will be his rest for ever and ever. He has chosen to dwell here because he has found, not yet to be sure the fulness of vision, but certainly the hope of that true peace, 'the peace of God which surpasses all our thinking'. But this blessing, although he has received it from on high, he wishes to have, and is indeed quite sure that he does have, with your good will, because 'a wise son maketh the father glad'. He begs you of your fatherly love, and I unite my prayers with his, that the arrangement he has made for his creditors to have his prebend, may be allowed to stand, so that he may not become (God forbid) a defaulter and breaker of his covenant, and his daily sacrifice of a contrite heart be unacceptable because a brother has something against him. He also begs that the house which he has built for his mother on Church lands with the ground which he has assigned to it, may remain hers so long as she lives. So much for Philip.

3. And now I turn to yourself. I feel impelled and even inspired by the Charity of God to exhort you not to regard the passing glory of the world as if it would never pass away, and so lose the glory that endures for ever; not to love your possessions more than your self or only for your own sake, and so lose both your possessions and your self; not to allow the flattery of present prosperity to hide from you the inevitable end, so that when it comes it will bring endless adversity; not to allow the pleasures of this world to beget for you and conceal from you the endless woe which they beget by concealing, so that when you think death is far off, it may come upon you unawares, and while you are counting on a long life, life itself may suddenly leave you ill prepared, according to what has been written: 'It

is just when men are saying, All quiet, all safe, that doom will fall upon them suddenly, like the pangs that come to a woman in travail, and there will be no escape from it'.

[70]

To the Monks of Flay

The Cistercian life and the dynamic character of St. Bernard were constantly attracting monks from other houses, especially from the Black Benedictines. It was the main source of rancour between the two Orders. The Rule of St. Benedict is quite explicit on the point[1]: a monk coming from an unknown monastery may be received and, if he seems a desirable acquisition, he may even be persuaded to stay, but a monk from a monastery which is known may on no account be accepted.

This letter concerns yet another trouble occasioned by a monk leaving his monastery to live at Clairvaux.

To Dom H.,[2] superior of the church of Flay, and to the brothers who are with him, greetings from the brothers who are at Clairvaux.

WE understand from your letters that you are upset by our having received one of your monks here. We are sorry that you should be sad about this for we are not sure that your sadness is that 'sadness according to God' or supernatural sadness, spoken of by the Apostle Paul. If it were this sort of sadness we do not think you would have reproached us so bitterly without knowing anything about us although, indeed, we are your brothers and could be, if you wished it, your friends; or without ever having met us or held any communication with us

1. *Rule of St. Benedict*, Chap. 61.
2. This appears to be Abbot Hildegard.

either by letter or word of mouth. You say that you are amazed that we should have received Brother Benedict and you threaten us with the consequences if we do not return him to you at once. Taking it for granted that your monastery is well known, you cite the Rule forbidding the reception of monks from a known monastery. Your monastery may be well known, but not to us. Even though the fame of your religious observance may have reached Rome, as you say it has, it does not follow it has reached us who are, in fact, some way from Rome! It may seem to you surprising, but it is none the less a fact, that we have not the slightest knowledge of any one of you, abbot or monks, or even of your neighbourhood, and we have never heard of your religious observance or way of life. And this is nothing to be wondered at seeing that we are separated by great distances, different provinces, and another language. We have not the same bishop nor even the same archbishop. So we do not consider that the passage you quote from the Holy Rule to the effect that a monk may not be received from a known monastery is particularly relevant to the case in dispute, for if it meant that a monk could not be received from any monastery that was known to anyone then, as there is no monastery that is not known to someone, there would be no monastery left from which we could lawfully receive anyone. And how could one reconcile this with that other injunction of Blessed Benedict which lays it down or at any rate allows that a stranger monk should be received not only into the guest house for as long as he likes, but that, if he is suitable, he should even be persuaded to join the community.

2. However, we acted very differently in the case of Brother Benedict. When he came and begged us to receive him we turned him away and advised him to go back to his monastery. He would not listen to us and betook himself to a hermitage near by and lived there quite quietly, without any trouble, for nearly seven months. But he did not think it safe for himself to live alone any longer and so he was not ashamed to ask again

for what had already been refused him once. We again advised him to return to his own monastery and asked him why he had ever left it. Then he told us that his abbot used him not as a monk but as a doctor[1]; that he forced him to serve or rather used him to serve not God but the world; that in order to curry favour with the princes of this world he was made to attend tyrants, robbers, and excommunicated persons. And he told us that when he suggested to his abbot both in private and publicly that all this was a source of danger to his soul, no attention was paid to him, so that finally, with the advice of experienced men, he left, not so much his monastery as the occasions of sin, not so much his holy religion as his unholy way of life. When he had told us all this he once more begged us to open to his knocking and admit him for the safety of his soul. And when we saw his constancy and heard the reasons for his leaving the monastery and could discover nothing against him, we granted him admission, proved and approved him, admitted him to profession, and now regard him as one of ourselves. We did not compel him to enter and we will not force him to leave. He says that if we should drive him out he would not come back to you but would go still farther away. So stop, we beg you, reviling us with unmerited abuse for we have done you no harm, and cease troubling us with your useless letters. Even your accumulated insults cannot force us to reply to you save as respect demands, nor can your threats scare us for we are quite confident that we have acted lawfully in receiving your monk.

1. It was the custom in those days for monks to work as doctors. It was eventually forbidden by Canon Law.

To the same, and concerning the same subject

The greetings of Brother Bernard to the reverend brothers of
Flay, to the Abbot H(ildegard) and all the other brothers.

IT would have been more becoming, dear brothers, if
you had been content with my last reply to your complaints
and ceased from your uncalled-for invectives. But as to your
former charges you have now added worse ones and tried once
more to give me grounds for quarrelling with you (may the
grounds you have given be no more fertile than formerly). I
shall truthfully answer a second time the accusations you impudently throw at my head, lest if I say nothing my silence may
be interpreted as an acknowledgement of guilt. As far as I can
make out, the great injury I have done you, my whole fault,
amounts to nothing more than this, that I have opened the doors
of my monastery to a lonely, strange, poor, and unhappy monk
who, fleeing from danger to his soul and seeking his salvation,
knocked and implored to be admitted; and that I refuse to turn
out again without sufficient reason the man I have received
under these circumstances, 'to put myself in the wrong by
pulling down what I have built up'. On these grounds alone you
accuse me of breaking the Rule, of transgressing the Canons, of
violating the natural law. You angrily reproach me for doing
to others what I would not tolerate others doing to myself, by
receiving into my monastery one of your own monks whom
you have excommunicated. What can I say about this excommunication when you yourself know the answer, namely that
he was not excommunicated by you before he was received by
me. And, as he had been already received and lawfully received
by me, it follows that you excommunicated, not one of your
own subjects, but one of mine. Whether this is as it should be is
your affair!

2. The only grounds for enquiry between us, the only thing that remains to be discovered, is whether he was rightly received by me. You for your part, as you cannot deny that a monk may be lawfully received from an unknown monastery,[1] contend that you are not unknown to me. I deny this, but you will not believe me. And so, as you will not believe my simple word, I affirm it again by oath. By the very Truth, which is God, I assure you that I have not known you and do not know you. Your letters are from persons quite unknown to me, and my letters to you are to unknown persons. I have experienced vexation and worry from you, but I have had no experience of you who vex and worry me. So as to prove me guilty of feigned ignorance you bring forward the irrefutable argument that I must know you because I have inscribed the name of your abbot and monastery upon my letters,[2] as if to know the name of a thing were the same as to know the thing itself. By this reasoning it would be a great thing for me to know the names of the angels Michael, Gabriel, and Raphael because by the very sound of the words I would be blessed with a knowledge of the blessed spirits. By this reasoning I must have profited not a little by hearing the names of Paradise and the third heaven from the Apostle, because, although I have not been rapt there with him, from the very names themselves I should be able to know the secrets of heaven, and words unspeakable which it is not lawful for men to utter. And how foolish I must be, for although I know the name of God yet I continue to groan and sigh with the Prophet, saying, 'I long, Lord, for thy presence', and 'When shall I come and stand in the presence of my God?' and 'Smile upon us, O God, and we shall find deliverance'.

3. And what is it that I have done to you which I would not tolerate others doing to myself? You believe it is that I would

1. *Vide Holy Rule*, Chap. 61.

2. Clearly the difference between knowing something and knowing *of* something. The Monks of Flay must have thought that the relevant passage in the Rule referred to monasteries the abbot knew *of*, but did not necessarily know.

not want a monk who had left my monastery to be received into another. I can only say that I wish all those committed to my care could be received by you and saved without me! If one of my monks should come to you for the sake of greater perfection or a stricter way of life, not only would I not complain if you were to minister to his desire, but I should beg you to do so. And so far from considering myself offended I would admit that I had been greatly helped by you. Finally you deny the truth of what I have heard of you, namely that by your command or consent Brother B was obliged to turn his medical skill to secular uses while he was with you, and you accuse him of falsehood who has said this. Whether he has lied or not I do not know, that is his affair, but this much I do know: whether he did this of his own will, as you say, or of your will, as he says, he nevertheless did it at great risk to his soul. And who would be so inhuman as not to help, if he could, a soul in such peril, or who would not at least advise him if he could not help him? But if, as you say, he was drawn by his cupidity and curiosity to run around here and there selling his art, what was his reason for leaving you? Was it because a stricter application of pastoral discipline made such wandering no longer possible? If so why when he had already come to us did you try to entice him back by promising that he would be left in peace in the cloister, if you did not know that he wanted this and did not remember that he had asked for it? But now that he has found among strangers the peace and seclusion he could not find among his own, he is not willing to leave what is certain for the sake of what is doubtful. He holds on to what he has and scorns to accept what is offered too late.

4. Cease therefore, brothers, cease worrying your brother about whom you have no cause to worry, unless indeed (and may such a thing be very far from you!) it is your own interests and not the glory of God you are seeking, your own satisfaction in your brother's return and not the salvation of his soul. As you say he was always a rolling stone with you and,

contrary to his state and the commands of his abbot, spending the money he made from the practice of his art upon himself, if you love him you ought to rejoice now that by the mercy of God he is cured. For I bear witness that never now does he wander abroad but, peacefully persevering in the monastery, he lives without complaint among poor men the life of a poor man. So far from having betrayed the faith he first pledged with you, he has now ratified it; together with obedience and conversion of manners,[1] without which he is deceived who trusts in his stability, he now keeps that faith whole and entire. So I beg you, brothers, calm your anger and stop worrying me. But if you will not, then do what you like, write what you like, abuse me as much as you like, charity suffers all things, beareth all things. And for my part, I am determined that from henceforth I shall love you with a pure love, treat you reverently, and regard you as friends.

[72]

To Guy, Abbot of Trois-Fontaines

A letter of advice and consolation to Guy who is in great distress because when he came to the Communion at Mass, he discovered that through an oversight of the server there was no wine in the chalice. In the twelfth century the chalice was prepared by the servers before Mass. It has been suggested that water instead of wine had been put into the chalice. This is a mistake that can be very easily made by the half light of candles in the early dawn when a white wine is used. It is true that there is nothing in the letter to suggest that this is how the mistake happened, but it would explain what would otherwise be

1. Monks, as distinct from Friars and Clerks Regular and post-Tridentine Orders, explicitly vow only obedience, stability, and conversion of manners.

a very extraordinary carelessness of the server who prepared the chalice, and also why Guy did not notice the mistake at the fraction of the Host.

The Guy to whom this letter is addressed is the same person as the Guy mentioned in Letter 66. He succeeded Roger as Abbot of Trois-Fontaines in 1129, and was elected Abbot of Cîteaux in 1134, but was deposed some months later by the General Chapter. The abbey of Trois-Fontaines was founded from Clairvaux in the year 1118 and is to be distinguished from the other abbey near Rome called Tre Fontane and dedicated to SS. Vincent and Anastasius.

I SYMPATHIZE with your sorrow, my dear friend, because I know the cause of it; but only if it is not excessive. Unless I am mistaken it is that supernatural sorrow or sorrow 'according to God' spoken of by the Apostle. There can be no doubt at all that such sorrow will be one day turned to joy. And so, dear friend, 'do not let anger betray you into sin', as the Psalmist says. On an occasion like this you would sin just as much by being too angry with yourself as by not being angry at all. Not to be angry with oneself when one should be is complacency, but to be more angry than one should be is to add sin unto sin. If complacency in sin is wrong, how could it not be wrong to accumulate one sin on the top of another? If guilt is made to depend on the matter of our actions, your sorrow, even were it immense, would not be to blame, because it would be sorrow for an immense fault. For the fault would be great in proportion as the matter concerned was sacred. But now in judging what you have done you should, according to my opinion, consider rather your own intention than the dignity of the sacred matter because the motive not the matter, the intention and not the results of the action constitute its moral character, according to those words of our Blessed Lord: 'If thy eye is clear, the whole of thy body will be full of light; if thy eye is diseased, the whole of thy body will be in darkness'.

My prior and I after having thought a great deal about it by ourselves and discussed it at length between ourselves, can see in it ignorance on your part and carelessness on the part of the servers, but certainly no malice. You surely know very well that as there is no good but what springs from the will, so there can hardly be any great evil in a matter which is clearly involuntary. Otherwise were involuntary good actions to merit no reward and involuntary evil actions to deserve heavy punishment, for one and the same cause evil would be reckoned but good not recognized. Let him who believes this say if he wish, not that 'wisdom has overcome evil', but that evil has overcome wisdom.

2. But so as to ease your unquiet conscience and in case what has happened should be a warning of some more grave evil lurking in the monastery, I give you as penance the seven penitential psalms to be said with seven prostrations every day until Easter and seven disciplines. And let him who served your Mass make similar satisfaction. As for him who prepared the chalice before Mass and forgot to pour in the wine, he seems to me to be the one most at fault so, if you agree, I leave him to your judgement. And if word of this thing should have got out among the brethren let each of them receive the discipline once so that it shall be fulfilled what is written: 'Bear ye one another's burdens'. And now as regards your action when you had discovered what had happened, in pouring wine on to the particle of the sacred Host in the chalice; I commend it and in such a difficulty I do not think you could have done better. Although of course the wine would not have been turned into the blood of Christ by its proper consecration, yet it would have become holy from contact with the sacred body.[1] They

1. During the Canon of the Mass the priest breaks the sacred Host into three pieces . . . two large and one very small piece. The small piece he drops into the chalice. Therefore if the chalice was empty, Guy would have found at the Communion that only the particle of the sacred Host was there. If there was water in the chalice, as some think, the particle would have been in the water.

say that some writer or other has thought differently, namely that the presence together of all three elements, bread, wine, and water, is necessary for the Sacrifice, so that the lack of one would invalidate the whole. But this is a matter on which each one must believe as seems best to himself.

3. If the same thing had happened to myself, in my own poor opinion there is one of two things I should have done to remedy the situation: either I should have acted as you did, or else I should have repeated the consecration prayer from the words *Simili modo postquam cœnatum est . . .* [1] and so have completed the Sacrifice. I would have no doubts in this case about the validity of the consecration of the bread, for by her very rites the Church teaches me what she has herself received from the Lord, namely that although bread and wine are both consecrated together, they are not both consecrated together at the same time. Therefore since first the bread is consecrated, so as to become Christ's body and then the wine so as to become his blood, if through forgetfulness the wine is presented later, I cannot see that the delay would annul the preceding consecration of the bread. And I think that if it had pleased the Lord to have postponed a little the consecration of the wine or to have omitted it completely after the bread had been consecrated, so as to have become his body, his body would have nevertheless remained and what had not yet been done would have in no way affected what had already been accomplished. I do not deny that bread and wine mixed with water ought to be presented together, on the contrary I maintain that this ought to be done; but I say it is one thing to blame negligence if this is not done, and quite another to deny the validity of the sacrament. It is one thing to discuss whether a thing was well done, and quite another to deny that it was done at all. This is all I have to say on the matter at present, and I have said it without any prejudice to what you or others wiser than myself may think.

1. 'In like manner after he had supped . . .'.

[73]

To the same

To the Lord Abbot Guy, a spirit of knowledge and of pity, from Brother Bernard.

    I AM certainly moved to pity when I consider the piti-ful condition of this poor wretch, but I rather fear it will be in vain. And yet my pity does not seem to me to be wasted, even though it benefit only myself without helping the wretched object of it. Yet I was not moved to it by any thought of self-interest, it was the sight of a neighbour's wretchedness, a brother's misery, which smote my breast. Pity is an emotion that moves tender hearts irresistibly to compassion for suffer-ing, but it cannot be induced by the will and it is not subject to the reason. Reason and will, although they can prevent emo-tion from having any effect on a man's actions, yet they can-not stifle it. And so as long as he for whom I pour forth my prayer remains unconverted let them keep away from me who would console me by saying that 'my prayer shall return to my own bosom'. As long as the wicked man remains in his wickedness, I will not listen to those who would flatter me by saying: 'Good will befall the good'. I will not, I say, be con-soled, while I witness my brother's misery. So if, dearest son, your kind heart is moved to pity or, I should say, because it cannot be otherwise moved but by pity, although the poor man seems to you to have made a habit of his wretched com-ings and goings from the monastery, yet because he thinks he has a grievance, you should listen to what he has to say, not only patiently, but even willingly. I think we ought to take every reasonable opportunity to save a man in such desperate circumstances, a thing which (as we both know from experi-ence) will be difficult enough in the Order, but far more so out-side. So I advise you to call all the brethren together in council and not to be ashamed to withdraw any previous sentences you may have given against him, so that his obstinate pride may be healed by your humility and some means be found for receiving him back without violating the Rule. Do not fear that by so doing, by thus preferring mercy to justice, you will displease the merciful and just God.

2. I will tell you, for an example, of a similar thing that I remember happening to myself. One day I commanded, with angry voice and threatening looks, a brother who had upset me to leave the monastery. He immediately betook himself to one of our granges and remained there. When I found out where he was I wanted to recall him, but he said that he would not come back unless he was first reinstated in his old position, and not put in the last place as if he had been a runaway; for he had been turned out of the monastery, so he said, without consideration and without his case being heard, and that as he had not been given a fair trial when he was turned out, he ought not to be made to submit to judgement when he came back. As I could not trust my own judgement in the matter owing to my natural feelings about it, I submitted it to the consideration of the brethren. And they, when I was absent, ruled that the brother should not be subjected to the discipline of the Rule on being received back, as his expulsion had not been according to the Rule. If therefore such kindly consideration was shown to a monk who had only once left the monastery, how much more ought it not to be shown to a monk in such desperate circumstances as yours. Farewell.[1]

---

1. The candour with which St. Bernard tells this story seems to us wholly in keeping with his saintly character. But others have thought differently and from early times, through a mistaken idea of the nature of sanctity and a greater zeal for edification than for truth, on purely *a priori* grounds suspecion has been cast on the authenticity of this passage. Even Mabillon relegated it to the notes of his edition of the letters averring that it was out of keeping with the character of the saint, and found in only five out of the eight MSS. But now a recent discovery in the library of the Abbey of Runa of a manuscript of the thirteenth century (No. 13) containing the complete text establishes the authenticity of the passage beyond all possibility of cavil.

[75]

To Rainald, Abbot of Foigny

Foigny was in the diocese of Laon and was founded from Clairvaux in 1121, soon after which year this letter must have been written, for Rainald was the first Abbot, and it is clear from the context that he was still home-sick for Clairvaux and St. Bernard.

To his dearest Rainald, all that one devoted brother and faithful fellow-servant could wish for another, from Bernard, his brother and fellow-servant, not his father and lord.

DO not be surprised if I am frightened at the titles of honour you give me when I do not feel worthy of the honours themselves. It may indeed be becoming that you should give them to me, but it is not fitting that I should agree to them. If you think you are bound by those words of the Apostle, 'Be eager to give one another precedence', and 'As you stand in awe of Christ, submit to each other's rights', I reply that in both cases the respect mentioned is supposed to be mutual, so unless this means nothing they apply equally to myself. And if you believe that you must observe that command of the Rule which bids juniors honour their seniors,[1] there immediately occur to me certain other sayings from the rule of Truth: 'They shall be first who were last, and they shall be last who were first'; 'No difference is to be made, among you, between the greatest and youngest of all, between him who commands and him who serves'; 'The greater thou art, the more in all things abase thyself'; 'Not that we would domineer over your faith; rather, we would help you to achieve happiness'; 'You are not to claim the title of *Rabbi* . . . nor are you to call any man on

1. *Rule of St. Benedict*, Chap. 63.

earth your father'. And so the more you extol me by your praises, the more I am weighed down by these texts and have cause to lament and not sing with the Psalmist, 'I have been lifted up only to be cast down and left bewildered' and, 'So low hast thou brought me who didst lift me up so high'. But perhaps I would be describing more truthfully what I feel were I to say that he who extols me, humiliates me; he who humiliates me, extols me. You by vaunting me on high, let me down; by making too much of me, belittle me. But although you humble me by your praises you do not altogether crush me for these and the like words of Truth do comfort and, in a wonderful way, exalt me even while they abase me; instruct me, even while they humiliate me, so that by the very same words that I am abashed I am also 'lifted up joyfully singing with my whole heart': 'It was in mercy that thou didst humble me, schooling me to thy obedience. Is not the law thou hast given dearer to me than rich store of gold and silver'. This wonder is done by 'the living and effectual word of God' working sweetly and powerfully, that very word by which all things were made; in fine, it is the work of Christ's sweet yoke, of his light burden.

2. It is pleasant to admire the lightness of the burden of Truth. And it is indeed really light, for not only is it no burden for the man who carries it, but it even carries him! And what can be lighter than a burden which not only does not burden, but even carries him on whom it is laid? This is the burden which the Virgin bore and by which she was borne and not burdened.[1] This is the burden which supported the very arms of the old Simeon who bore it in his arms. And this is what snatched Paul up to the third heaven, even when he was weighed down by the corruptible body. When I look for an

1. *Hoc onus potuit uterum gravidare Virgineum, gravare non potuit.* During the whole of this section, St. Bernard is playing upon words in a graceful, but almost untranslatable, manner. Eales translates this sentence: 'This weight was able to render fruitful the Virgin's womb, but not to burden it'.

example among created things to illustrate this disburdening burden, nothing occurs to me more apt than the wings of a bird, for they, in an extraordinary way, render the body both greater and yet more nimble. What a wonderful achievement of nature that a body should be rendered lighter by its very increase in size, so that the more it increases in bulk the more it decreases in weight. Here certainly we have a clear illustration of the sweet burden of Christ which carries those who carry it. And a chariot occurs to me too, for this also increases a burden which could not be carried by a horse alone, while at the same time rendering it more portable. One burden is added to another with the result that the whole is less burdensome! Thus when the four-in-hand chariot of the Gospels is yoked to the heavy burden of the law, it at once increases the perfection of it and reduces its difficulty. 'How swiftly runs his word', says the Psalm, and his word which at first could not extend beyond the confines of Judea, because it was so oppressive that it weighed down even the hands of Moses, when lightened by the touch of grace and yoked to the four-wheeled chariot of the Gospels swiftly went out into the whole world, and was quickly carried to the ends of the earth. But I am wandering from the point.

3. And so do you, dearest friend, stop smothering rather than applauding me with undeserved titles, otherwise you will be siding with my enemies, although with the best of intentions. Of them I am in the habit of complaining to God alone in the words of the Psalmist: 'And they that flattered me did curse me'. And to this complaint of mine I soon hear the answering words of God, 'And they that called you blessed have led you into error', to which I again reply, 'Let them therefore go their way baffled, they that rejoice over my misfortune; slink away in confusion that crowed over me so loud'. But lest it should be thought that I ever launch curses and imprecations against my enemies, I ought to explain how I understand these words. I pray, then, that those who believe me to be better

than they see or hear me to be, may go their way baffled, that is to say withdraw from ignorantly praising me whom they do not know, and go on their way. How will this happen? It will happen when they know better the man they have excessively praised, so that they go their way baffled by their own error and by the discovery they have made of their friend's futility. In this manner both kinds of those people who injure me go their way baffled: the first kind who bear ill-will towards me, and flatter me with adulation; the others who are indeed quite sincere, yet injure me just as much by their well-meaning but extravagant praises. And so against both these kinds of people who praise me I am in the habit of protecting myself with these two verses as with two shields. Against the first sort who praise me malevolently, I say: 'Baffled let them go their way that rejoice in my misfortune'; and against the second sort: 'May they slink away in confusion that crowed over me so loud'.

4. But to return to yourself. As I ought, after the example of the Apostle, not to dominate over you, but only to rejoice with you, and as, according to the words of our Lord, we are all brothers having one father in heaven, it is not improper for me to turn off from myself with the shield of truth the high names of lord and father with which you think to honour and not burden me, and more appropriately call myself brother and fellow-servant as we share the same Father and the same condition. Were I to arrogate to myself what belongs to God, I might hear the words: 'If I am your master, where is the reverence due to me; and if your father, where the honour?' That I have a father's affection for you, I do not deny, but I refuse the authority of a father; nor, I think, is the affection with which I embrace you less than the affection of a father for a son. Now enough on the matter of titles.

5. To answer the rest of your letter. I could make just as well the same complaint about your absence as you do about mine, unless (which you yourself will not deny) the will of God must be preferred to our own feelings and needs. How, were it

not for Christ's sake, could I suffer you to be so far away from me, you who are my dearest and most necessary companion, because always obedient in all you do; most helpful in conference; most zealous in learning, most prompt in remembering. Blessed shall we be if we can thus persevere until the end, always and everywhere seeking the glory of Jesus Christ and not our own interests.

[76]

To the same

To his dear son Rainald, Abbot of Foigny, the spirit of fortitude.

WHEN you wring your hands, dearest Rainald, over your many troubles I too am moved to tears by your affectionate complaints.[1] When you are sorrowful, I cannot but be sorry; nor can I hear of your worries and troubles without being myself worried and troubled. But as I foresaw and warned you of the very ills which you declare have befallen you, you should have been forearmed against what was foreknown so as to have endured them with a lighter heart and, if possible, spared me the vexation of hearing all about them. As it is I suffer more than enough by not having you by me, by not being able to see anything of you and enjoy the comfort of your company, so that I am at times tempted to regret having sent you away. True it was at the behest of charity that I did so, yet whatever the need might have been, because I cannot see you, I mourn for you as lost to me. And so, when on the top of all this you who should be a staff to support me use your faintheartedness as a staff with which to belabour me, you are piling sadness upon sadness, one

1. *Piis querimoniis.* Eales translates, perhaps more literally, 'pious complaints'.

cross upon another. Although it is a mark of your affection for me that you hide none of your troubles from me, it is nevertheless unfeeling of you not to spare me, who feel as I do towards you, any details of your sufferings.[1] Why should you make me, who am anxious enough about you, even more anxious? Why should my heart, already torn by the absence of my son, be wounded still more by having to hear every detail of the trials he is enduring? I have shared my burdens with you, as with a son and an indispensable and faithful helper. But is this the way you help me to carry them? You are not helping to carry them at all, but adding to their weight, and by so doing you are making things more difficult for me without helping yourself.

2. This is the burden of souls which are sick, for those which are well do not need to be carried and so are no burden. You must understand that you are especially abbot of the sad, fainthearted, and discontented among your flock. It is by consoling, encouraging, and admonishing that you do your duty and carry your burden and, by carrying your burden, heal those you carry. If there is anyone so spiritually healthy that he rather helps you than is helped by you, you are not so much his father as his equal, not so much his abbot as his fellow. Why then do you complain that you find the company of some of those who are with you more of a burden than a comfort? You were given to them as abbot not to be comforted but to comfort, because you were the strongest of them all and, by God's grace, able to comfort them all without needing to be comforted by any. The greater your burden, the greater will be your gain; the easier your lot, the less your reward. Choose whom you want, either those who by burdening you help you or those who by

1. *Si mihi pium est nullas tuas angustias dissimulare, tibi tamen durum est sic affecto cunctas indicare.* I have translated this sentence in the same way as Eales who renders it: 'If it is a mark of your filial affection towards me that you do not hide any of your difficulties from me, yet it is hard to add trouble to one already burdened'. I cannot help feeling, however, that the contrast is meant to be between *mihi* and *tibi*, and so should perhaps be rendered: Although it belongs to my fatherly affection towards you to ignore none of your troubles, yet it is unfeeling of you. . . .

helping you burden you. The former win merit for you, the latter bilk you of merit. Without any doubt those who share your labours will also share your reward. You should know that you have been sent not to be helped but to help, and realize that you hold the place of him who came not to be served but to serve. I wanted to write you a longer letter for your consolation, but there is no need. What need is there to fill dry pages with words, when the living voice is there? I think that when you have seen the prior you will find that I have said enough, and that your spirit will revive in his presence, that you will be so refreshed by his words as to have no need to be consoled by a letter. Do not have any doubt that I send to you in him and through him that spirit of mine which you begged me in your letter to send you if I could. As you know we are of one mind and one will.

[77]

To the same

I HAD hoped, dearest son, to find a remedy for my worrying over you in not being told of your difficulties. I remember I wrote to you in a former letter that although it was a mark of your affection towards me that you should hide none of your troubles from me, it was nevertheless unfeeling of you not to spare me, feeling towards you as I do, anything of the details. But now I confess I feel my anxiety for you increased by the very thing that I had hoped would relieve it. Hitherto I have only feared or grieved over what you told me about, but now there is hardly an evil that could happen which I do not fear for you. In fact, as your favourite Ovid says: *Quando ego non timui graviora pericula veris?*[1]

1. *Quando, etc.* 'When have I not by fear made the dangers greater than they really were?' (*Ovid*, Ep. I, verse 11).

Uncertain about everything and therefore anxious about everything, I experience real sorrow for imaginary evils. He who is once fond of anyone, is hardly master over himself any longer. He fears, he does not know what; he is sorrowful when there is no cause for sorrow; he worries more than he wishes, and about what he does not wish, feeling compassion unwillingly and ruth in spite of himself. And so you see, my son, that neither my careful precautions nor your loving care has availed me at all in this matter, and I beg you no longer to hide from me all that is happening to you, lest your very efforts to spare me make me more uneasy. Please return as soon as you can those books of mine which you borrowed.

[80]

To Suger, Abbot of St. Denis

Suger was born in the year 1081 and succeeded Adam as abbot of the royal abbey of St. Denis in the year 1121-1122. Very soon after this he was appointed chief minister by the King of France, Louis 'le Gros', earning by the services he rendered in this capacity the title 'Father of his Country'. It is remarkable that Louis should have given him this appointment, for he had already intervened against his king's interests in the battle over investitures. His first direct contact with St. Bernard may have been when he secretly sought his help in this affair. Suger was typical of the great ecclesiastical statesmen of his time and is in many ways not unlike his redoubtable and rather attractive English contemporary, Henry de Blois, Bishop of Winchester, with whom Bernard came into conflict over the vexed affair of the York election. No abbot lived in greater magnificence than Suger and no abbey stood in greater need of reform than St. Denis. It had become little more than a centre for the transaction of the great affairs of state. Probably St. Bernard had the

abbot and monastery of St. Denis in mind when he wrote the
Apologia, and without doubt his diatribes caused Suger much
searching of heart. It is a striking indication of the influence of
the Cistercian reform and of St. Bernard that the Abbot of St.
Denis should have been moved to reform, not only his own life,
but also the lives of the monks under him, so as to call forth the
following letter.

THE good news of what God has done in your soul
has gone forth in our land encouraging all the good people who
hear it. To be sure all those who fear God and have heard of it
are amazed and full of joy at this great and sudden change of
the right arm of the Most High. Everywhere 'your soul is
praised in the Lord and the meek hear and rejoice'. Even those
who have not known you, but have only heard how great has
been the change from what you were to what you are, marvel
and praise God in you. But what increases both the wonder and
the joy alike is that you should have fulfilled what is written
in the Scriptures, 'Let everyone who hears this say: Come', and,
'What I have said to you under cover of darkness you are to
utter in the light of day; what has been whispered in your ears
you are to proclaim on the house-tops', by endeavouring to
spread amongst your monks the counsel of salvation which
possesses your soul. In this you have acted like a resolute soldier, or rather like a devoted and strong captain who, when he
sees his men in flight and slaughtered on all sides by the swords
of the enemy, would be ashamed to survive them and scorn to
save his own life by flight, even if he could. He stands fast in
battle, he fights stoutly, and he runs hither and thither beween
the lines amongst the blood-stained swords trying with sword
and voice to dishearten the enemy and encourage his own men.
He is always on the spot where he discovers the enemy are
breaking through and his men being hewn down. Where anyone is being hard-pressed and overcome he is always there to
assist him, being all the more ready to die for each one in that

he despairs of saving all. And, while he is trying little by little to stem and stop the advance of the enemy, it often happens that by his valour he snatches a victory for his own men from the confusion of the enemy, all the more welcome for being unexpected. They in their turn now put to flight those from whom they fled, and overcome those whom hitherto they have barely been able to stave off from vanquishing them, so that those who were lately all but victims now exult as victors.

2. But why should I compare such a religious and mighty achievement with secular things, as if religion itself did not provide many examples? Was not Moses fully confident in God's promise that if the whole people of whom he was the leader were to perish he would not only not perish with them but would on the contrary be put at the head of a great nation? And yet with what affection and zeal and with what devotion did he not help them when they were troublesome and try to meet them when they were rebellious! In the end he offered himself in satisfaction for their defection, praying God to pardon them or else blot out his own name from his record. He was a faithful advocate who easily obtained what he asked for, because he was not seeking his own interests. He was also a devoted leader united by love to his people, as the head is united to the body, so that he would rather perish with them than be saved without them. Jeremias too, although he did not sympathize with the truculence of his people, was inseparably bound to them by the bonds of compassion for their infirmity and preferred to suffer exile and slavery with them rather than to enjoy his native soil and liberty by himself. When the whole people were led off he was free to remain at home, but he chose to share their captivity because he knew they would need him. And Paul was doubtless inspired by the same spirit when he wished to be doomed to separation from Christ for the sake of his kinsmen, knowing from personal experience the truth of those words: 'Not death itself is so strong as love, not the grave itself so cruel as love unrequited'. So you see whom you have

proved yourself to be like! But I must add someone else whom I had almost forgotten. I mean the holy king David, who when he saw the slaughter of his people, was sad and made haste to stand before the angel who was smiting them and implore that the punishment might be transferred unto himself and his father's house.

3. Who suggested this perfection to you? I must confess that although I much desired to hear such things of you, yet I hardly dared hope that I ever would. Who would have believed that with one jump, so to speak, you would attain the summits of virtue, the pinnacle of merit? But God forbid that I should measure the immensity of God's love by the narrow limits of my own capacity for faith and hope. He can do whatsoever he wills. He can hasten the working of his grace and lighten the burden of his commands. It was your fault, not those of your monks, that good and zealous people censured. It was against you and not against the whole community that they murmured. In fact, it was you whom they held responsible. If you had corrected yourself, there would have been nothing left to criticize. If you, I say, had changed your ways, soon all the tumult would have died down, all the talk would have subsided. As for myself, the whole and only thing that upset me was the pomp and splendour with which you travelled. This seemed to me to savour of arrogance. If you had been content to put off your haughtiness and put away your splendid attire, the resentment of everyone would easily have died down. But you have done more than satisfy your critics, you have earned their praise, although this sudden change of so many great things should be deemed more the work of God than of yourself. In heaven the conversion of one sinner arouses great joy, but what about the conversion of a whole community, and a community such as yours?

4. From early times yours was a noble abbey of royal dignity. It served the palace and the armies of the king. Without any deception or delay it rendered to Casear his dues, but not with

equal enthusiasm what was due to God. I speak of what I have heard, not of what I have seen. They say the cloister of the monastery was often crowded with soldiers, that business was done there, that it echoed to the sound of men wrangling, and that sometimes women were to be found there. In all this hubbub how could anyone have attended to heavenly, divine, and spiritual things? But now everything is very different. God is invoked there, continence is cultivated, discipline maintained, spiritual reading encouraged, for the silence is now unbroken, and the hush from all the din of secular affairs invites the mind to heavenly thoughts. Furthermore the labour of continence, the rigour of discipline, is relieved by the sweet tones of hymns and psalms. Shame for the past encourages the austerity of this new way of life. The men who pluck the fruit of a good conscience are inspired by a desire which shall not be frustrated, and a hope which shall not be confounded. Fear of future judgement gives place to a loving practice of brotherly charity, for 'Love has no room for fear'. The variety of holy observances keeps at bay tedium and *acidie*.[1] I have recalled all this for the honour and glory of God, who is the author of it all, but not without yourself as his collaborator in all things. He could have done it all without you, but he preferred that you should share in his work, so that you might also share the glory. Our Saviour rebuked certain persons for making his house a den of thieves. And so without any doubt he will commend one who applies himself to saving a holy thing from dogs, and pearls from swine; whose efforts and zeal have restored what was little better than a workshop of Vulcan to being a sanctuary of prayer and spiritual pursuits, what was a synagogue of Satan to its former use.

5. I have certainly not recalled all these past evils so as to taunt or shame anyone, but so as to make the new glories appear all the more important and comely by comparing them to the old infamy. Recent good things show up to all the better advan-

1. A traditional term for a state of spiritual aridity.

tage when compared with former evils. We recognize like things by comparing them with like, but contrary things compared either please or displease the more. Join black things to white and the comparison will show up each colour the better. When ugly things are set against beautiful things, the beautiful seem more beautiful and the ugly seem more ugly. But so as to avoid any occasion for confusion or offence let me repeat to you also what the Apostle said: 'This is what you were once, but now you have been washed clean, now you have been sanctified'. The house of God is no longer open to seculars, the merely curious find no admittance to the holy places. There is no longer any idle gossiping, and the usual chatter of boys and girls is no longer heard there. According to the words, 'Here stand I and these children the Lord has given me', the place is free and open only to the children of Christ and is kept with becoming care and reverence only for the divine praises and sacred functions. How the martyrs, a great number of whom ennoble the place with their relics, must hear with joy the songs of these children, to whom they will reply with no less affectionate exuberance, 'Praise the Lord, ye children, praise ye the name of the Lord'; and again, 'A psalm, a psalm for our God, a psalm, a psalm for our king'.

6. Now the vaults of the great abbey that once resounded to the hubbub of secular business echo only to spiritual canticles. Now breasts are bruised by the hands that beat upon them, and knees by the stones on which they kneel, and from the altars ascend vows and devout prayers. Now one can see cheeks furrowed with tears of repentance and hear the murmur of weeping and sighs. What can better please the citizens of heaven than this, what sight can be more welcome to the King of heaven than this sacrifice of praise with which he is now honoured here? Oh if only we could have our eyes opened to see what Eliseus by his prayers revealed to his servant! Without doubt we would see 'how before us go chieftains, and minstrels with them'. We would see with what attention and with what

elation they assist in our singing, stand by us when we pray, join with us when we meditate, watch over us when we rest, and guide those of us who preside over and care for others. The powers of heaven know who are their fellow citizens, they earnestly delight over, comfort, instruct, protect, and care for in everything those who take the heritage of salvation. Although, being absent, I cannot see with my own eyes these things which you have done, yet I count myself happy even to have heard of them. But you, my brethren, I esteem still more happy, for to you it has been given to perform them. And more blessed than all is he whom the Author of all good has deigned to give the leadership in these things. On this great privilege I especially congratulate you, my dear friend, for it is due to you that all these wonderful things have happened.

7. Perhaps you are embarrassed by my praises? You should not be. What I have said has nothing in common with the flattery of those who 'call good evil and evil good', so that they betray whomsoever they praise. Theirs is a smooth but treacherous praise by which 'the sinner is praised in the desires of his soul'. Whatever kind of favour mine may be, it certainly proceeds from charity and, so far as I can see, it does not exceed the bounds of truth. He is safely applauded who is only applauded in the Lord, that is to say in truth. I have not called evil good, on the contrary I have called evil what was evil. I am all the more bound to lift up my voice and praise the good when I see it for having boldly denounced former evils or else, were I to cry out against what is evil and say nothing about what is good, I would prove myself a mere backbiter and not a reformer, one who would rather carp at evil than remedy it. The righteous man admonishes lovingly, the sinner praises wickedly. The former admonishes evil that he may remedy it, the latter praises that he may conceal what calls for remedy. You need have no anxiety that your head will be anointed with the oil of sinners as it used to be, by those who fear the Lord. I praise you because I consider you have done what is deserv-

ing of praise. I certainly do not flatter you; I am only fulfilling what you sing in the psalm: 'They that fear thee shall see me, and shall be glad, because I have greatly hoped in thy works'; and again: 'This wisdom of his shall be praised on all sides'. How many who used to abhor your folly now praise your wisdom!

8. I wish you to delight in the approbation of those who fear vice no less than they love virtue. The praises of such men are true for they praise only what is good and do not know how to pander to evil. But there are others whose praise is not true, but false, who really disparage when they seem to praise, and of these we read in the Scriptures that they are 'Vain men, light weight sons of Adam as false coins in the scales, vain in all their conspiracies to deceive'. Clearly these are men to be avoided, according to the advice of the Wise Man: 'Turn a deaf ear, my son, to the blandishments of evildoers that would make thee of their company'. Therefore sinners do not lack either wine or oil, delicious certainly, but poisonous and deadly. 'His words', that is the words of the flatterer, 'are so gentle, they soothed like oil, but in truth they are weapons of destruction.' And the righteous man also has his oil, but it is an oil of mercy, sancti- fying and full of spiritual joy. And he has his wine that he pours into the inflamed wounds of the soul. With the oil of mercy he comforts the sadness of those who are sorrowful and whose heart he sees to be contrite. When he admonishes he uses his wine; when he comforts, his oil. But his wine is without rancour and his oil is without guile. Not all praise is flattery, just as not all rebuke comes from spite. Blessed is he who can say: 'In love some just man will chastise me, reprove me; never shall the sinner sleek this head with the oil of his flattery'. By rejecting the oil of the sinners' flattery you have proved your- self worthy of the oil and milk of holy men.

9. Let these charming but savage mothers seek among the children of Babylon those whom they can feed with the milk of death, whom they may caress with their alluring favours,

and nourish with everlasting fires.[1] But when the nursling of
the Church has fed from the breasts of wisdom and has tasted
the sweetness of a better milk, already growing in grace, already satisfied with what he has received, he will say from the
bottom of his heart: 'The milk from thy breasts is better than
wine, the fragrance of rare perfumes cannot match it for
delight'. This is what he says to his mother the Church. But
when he has in a like manner tasted and seen how sweet is the
Lord he addresses him as a very dear father and says: 'What
treasures of loving kindness, Lord, dost thou store up for the
men who fear thee'. Now my desires for you are satisfied.
When in the past I sadly watched you greedily suck from the
lips of flatterers the food of death, the fuel of sin, I used to say
to myself, sighing: 'Would that you were my brother nursed
at my own mother's breasts'. May they keep far away from
you who would feed you with their alluring but treacherous
milk of flattery, who expose you to the reproaches and mockery of everyone, while they are calling you blessed to your
face! Their applause was a byword the world over or rather
made you a byword everywhere. If even now they still mutter
in your ears, say to them in the words of the Apostle: 'If I were
still courting your favour, I should not be the slave of Christ'.
Those people whom we used to please with bad things we
cannot please equally well with good, unless perhaps they too
have changed and have begun to hate what we were and
esteem what we are now.

10. Two unheard-of and detestable improprieties have
arisen in the Church lately. If you will pardon my saying so,
one of these was the arrogance of your way of life. But this, by
the grace of God, is now mended to the glory of his name, to
your everlasting reward, and to the edification of all of us. God

---

1. *Quærant sibi jam in parvulis Babylonis dulces, sed truces matres, quibus
lac mortis emulgeant, quos blandis mulceant favoribus, ac flammis nutriant
sempiternis.* Eales translates: 'Let the children of Babylon seek for themselves
pleasant mothers, but pitiless, who will feed them with poisoned milk, and
soothe them with caresses which will make them fit for everlasting flames'.

can also bring it about that we will soon be consoled by the mending of this other matter. I fear to mention this hateful novelty in public, but I am loath to let it pass in silence. My grief urges me to speak, but fear binds my tongue. My fear is only lest I offend anyone by speaking openly of what is disturbing me, for the truth can sometimes breed hatred. But I hear the truth that breeds this sort of hatred comforting me with the words, 'It must needs be that scandals come', and I do not consider that what follows applies to me at all: 'But woe to the man through whom it comes'. When scandal comes through vices being denounced, it comes through those who do what is blameworthy and not through those who blame it. And I do not set myself up as being more circumspect or more discreet than he who said: 'It is better that there should be a scandal than that truth should be compromised'.[1] Although I do not know what good it would do if I did keep silent about what all the world is talking, if I alone were to try and cover up that foul thing the stench of which is in everyone's nostrils. I dare not hold my own nose against such a bad smell.

11. And who would not be indignant, who would not deplore, even if only in secret, that a man should against the Gospel both serve God as a deacon and Mammon as a minister of state, that he should be so loaded with ecclesiastical honours as to seem hardly inferior to the bishops, while being at the same time so involved in military affairs as to take precedence over the commanders of the army?[2] I ask you what sort of monster is this[3] that being a cleric wishes to be thought a soldier as well,

1. St. Gregory, *Hom.* 7 *in Ezech.*

2. This is the notorious Stephen of Garlande. His family was very friendly with Louis 'le Gros'. Stephen came to court as a young man and succeeded his brother as seneschal of the royal palace. He was very active in affairs but became so swollen-headed that, after he had made himself objectionable to Queen Adela, he was deprived of his honours and banished from court. Besides seneschal, he was not only a deacon, but Archdeacon of Notre-Dame and Dean of Orleans.

3. It is very tempting to see here a reminiscence of the first verses of Horace's *De Arte Poetica*.

and succeeds in being neither? It is an abuse of both conditions that a deacon should serve the table of a king and that a servant of the king should minister at the holy mysteries of the altar. Who would not be astonished, or rather disgusted, that one and the same person should, arrayed in armour, lead soldiers into battle and, clothed in alb and stole, pronounce the Gospel in the church, should at one time give the signal for battle on the bugle and at another inform the people of the commands of the bishop. Unless perhaps something worse is true, namely that the man is ashamed of the Gospel in which the Vessel of Election gloried, is embarrassed at being seen as a cleric, and thinks it more honourable to be thought a soldier, preferring the court to the church, the table of the king to the altar of Christ, the cup of demons to the chalice of the Lord. This seems to be the more probable, in that although he holds many preferments from the Church, despite the unwilling toleration of the canons for such a number of offices being held by one man, yet they say he is more proud of the one name by which he is known in the palace than of all his other titles. Although he is archdeacon, deacon, and provost in many churches yet none of these titles gives him so much pleasure as Seneschal to his Majesty the King. What a novel and odious perversity it is that a man should think it more becoming to be known as a retainer of another man than a servant of God and consider it more dignified to be called an official of a king of this world than of the King of heaven. A man that puts the army before his clerical state, secular business before the Church, certainly proves that he prefers human things to divine and earthly to heavenly things. Is it more dignified to be called Seneschal than Deacon or Archdeacon? It is, but for a layman not for a deacon.

12. What a strange and blind sort of ambition this man has! He prefers the depths to the heights, a dung-hill to the pleasant places in which his lot has been cast, and he pours scorn on the desirable land. He completely confuses two different states of life, that of a minister of God and that of a minister of the king;

and he abuses with great nicety both of them by choosing the honours, but not the labour of the army in the one, and the revenues, but not the service of religion in the other. Who cannot understand that the kingdom, just as much as religion, is disgraced by this, for it is just as unbecoming to the majesty of the king that hardy men should be commanded by a cleric, as it is to the state of a deacon that he should take the king's money to fight. What king would choose to have an unwarlike cleric at the head of his army rather than one of his most intrepid soldiers? And what cleric would consider it anything but unworthy of his state to be under obedience to a layman? His very tonsure more becomes the kingly state than the condition of a retainer, and on the other hand it is not on psalms so much as arms that the throne depends. Certainly if perhaps, as sometimes happens, the one gains where the other loses so that, namely, the abasement of the king makes for the honour of the cleric or the derogation of the cleric adds something to the honour of the king, as for instance when some noble woman by marrying a man of humble birth lessens her dignity while raising his; if, I say, this is the case and from such a state of affairs either the king or the cleric gains something, the evil of it might somehow be tolerated. But as it is the loss of both has been to the advantage of neither, the dignity of both has suffered since it ill becomes a cleric to be called to be the seneschal of the king, just as much as it ill becomes the king to have in that position of government anyone but a strong and brave man. It is indeed very strange that either power should allow such a state of affairs, that the Church should not reject the military deacon and that the court should not expel its clerical chief.

13. I had intended and probably ought to have denounced this state of affairs more sharply than I have done, but the limits of a letter indicate an end. And I have spared a man whom report speaks of as your friend chiefly because I fear to offend you. I would not have a man your friend who is not true. If you persist in regarding him as your friend, prove yourself a true

friend to him by doing what you can to make him a friend of the truth. True friendship is only possible between two who are united in the love of truth. And, if he will not yield to you in this, do you hold fast to what you have got and join the head to the tail of the offering.[1] By the grace of God you have received a robe of many colours, see that it covers you for it is no use beginning a work if you do not persevere to the end. Let my letter end with this warning to you to make a good end of what you have begun.

[84]

To the Abbot of St. John of Chartres

This would probably be Stephen, who after being Abbot of the Augustinian house of St. John of Chartres became Patriarch of Jerusalem in succession to Germundus in the year 1128.

AT first I did not intend to answer your query about those matters on which you troubled to consult me, not so much because I was doubtful about what to answer as because it seemed impudent and superfluous to offer my counsel to a man of counsel like yourself. But when I considered that many or, I should say, almost all wise men, while they can easily solve the difficulties of others are apt to be doubtful and anxious about their own and place far greater confidence in the judgement of others, I decided (not unreasonably, I hope) to break my resolution and to tell you quite simply what I think, always providing that I do not thereby prejudice the judgement of those wiser than myself. Unless I am deceived you have informed me by that religious man Ursus,[2] Abbot of St. Denis,

1. This means to join the end to the beginning of the work. It is an allusion to *Exodus* xxix, which commands the offering at the same time of the head and the tail of the victim.

2. The fifth abbot of the Canons Regular of St. Denis at Rheims.

that you are thinking of leaving your country, home, and those over whom it has pleased God that you should have charge, and of setting out for Jerusalem to live there to God alone and make your own soul. I agree that it may be a good thing for a man who strives for perfection to leave his own country, according to those words: 'Go forth out of thy country and from thy kinsfolk'. But I do not see how it follows that you are justified in deserting those who have been entrusted to your care. Why do you want to do so? Are you attracted by the prospect of being free from the burden of responsibility? But charity seeketh not its own. Does the pleasant prospect of peace and leisure beckon you? But you would be obtaining it at the cost of others. For my part I would gladly forgo the prospect of any spiritual advantage whatsoever if it could only be obtained at the price of giving scandal to others. Undoubtedly charity suffers when there is scandal, and I very much wonder what sort of spiritual advantage could be obtained at the cost of charity. How can anyone who prefers his own quiet to the common good possibly say with truth: 'For me life means Christ and death is a prize to win'; and where would those words of the Apostle come in: 'None of us lives as his own master, none of us dies as his own master'; and: 'This is my rule, to satisfy all alike, studying the general welfare before my own'; and: 'Christ died for us all, so that being alive should no longer mean living with our own life, but with his life who died for us and has risen again'.

2. Perhaps you will ask, 'If this is so, whence comes my great desire?' Pardon me if I say quite frankly what I think. No one who has any experience of the wiles of Satan can have any doubt that it is his angel under the guise of an angel of light that is trying to instil into your thirsty soul the false sweetness of 'stolen waters', a sweetness which in truth is far more bitter than wormwood. In fact who else would suggest scandal, stir up dissension, and trouble unity and peace, if not the ancient enemy of the human race, the enemy of the cross of Christ, the

devil? He by whose envy death entered the world is even now envious of all the good he sees you are doing and, since he has been a liar from the beginning, he is lying now by promising you better things which he knows are not there. How could Truth suggest anything contrary to those most trustworthy words, 'Are you yoked to a wife? Then do not go about to free yourself.' And when has charity, which we know is on fire at every scandal, ever been known to instigate scandal? No, I tell you that it is the evil one, he whose envy makes him an enemy of charity, whose lies render him always hostile to truth, it is he who is now lying to you, mixing a false honey with a true gall, by promising what is doubtful as if it were certain, and by giving out what is true as if it were false, not so as to give you what you are vainly hoping for, but so as to rob you of what you are holding with such benefit. He is going about seeking how he may snatch from your flock the care of their shepherd, so that it may perish as, without anyone to save it, it undoubtedly will. And at the same time he is trying to make the shepherd subject to that terrifying curse: 'Woe to him through whom scandal comes'. But I trust that your God-given wisdom will prevent you from being led astray or deceived by any cunning ruse of the evil one to make you desert a certain good, and incur a certain evil for the sake of a good that is not certain.

[85]

To Simon, Abbot of St. Nicolas

A letter of consolation and advice to Abbot Simon on account of the persecution he was enduring. Mabillon tells us that the persecutions came from his monks because Abbot Simon insisted on giving up certain parishes belonging to the monastery on account of a suspicion of simony attaching to them. Indeed we know that because he could not get his community to agree

*with him on this matter Abbot Simon resigned his office for a
time. But the context of this letter gives the impression that his
troubles arose from a well-meaning attempt to introduce into
his monastery a stricter way of life. Abbot Simon became Abbot of St. Nicolas-aux-Bois in the diocese of Laon after being
a monk of St. Nicasius at Rheims.*

I COULD not but feel for you when I read in your letter of the persecutions you are obliged to endure for the sake
of justice. Although Christ's promise of a kingdom should be
enough for you, yet I will for my part faithfully offer you such
consolation as I can and such advice as I deem wholesome. For
who could watch without anxiety Peter amidst the waves holding out his hands for help; or hear without sorrow the dove of
Christ no longer cooing but sighing, as if to say: 'How can we
sing the songs of the Lord in a strange land'? Who, I ask, could
see without tears the tears of Christ himself, as he even now
lifts up his eyes to the hills whence comes his help? Although
to be sure I, to whom in your humility you say you look for
help, am on no hill, but am still labouring with great efforts in
this vale of tears against the insidious stratagems of the relent-
less enemy and the violent malice of the world, so that with
you I cry out: 'Our help is in the Lord who has made heaven
and earth'.

2. 'All who will live devoutly in Christ Jesus, shall suffer
persecution', so that even though they may never cease to have
holy desires yet they are often unable to accomplish them. The
multitude of wicked who make it their business to oppose the
holy resolutions of good people is so great that there is nothing
wrong in leaving them sometimes unaccomplished. So Aaron
against his will gave in to the wretched demands of the turbulent people. So Samuel unwillingly anointed Saul to satisfy the
same people, because they insisted on having a king. So David
when he wanted to build the temple was prevented from ac-
complishing his pious design because he was a man of war

obliged to wage constant war against the enemies who infested his frontiers. Just in the same way, venerable father, do I counsel you (yet not so as to prejudice the advice of those wiser than I) to moderate the full rigour of your purpose and of those who side with you, so as not to ignore the welfare of weaker souls. Those in the Order of Cluny over whom you have consented to rule should be invited and not forced to a stricter way of life. And those of them who wish to live more strictly should be persuaded to accommodate themselves, so far as they can without sin, to the weaker brethren or, if it can be done without scandal to either party, they should be permitted to live their own life where they are, or else they might be allowed to go free from the congregation so as to find a community where they can live as they wish.

[87]

To William of St. Thierry

William of St. Thierry was born at Liège in the last quarter of the eleventh century. At some unknown date he became a monk at the Abbey of St. Nicasius, and afterwards, about the year 1120, Abbot of St. Thierry in the diocese of Rheims. He was early drawn into the orbit of St. Bernard and became one of his closest friends. It was at his instigation that the saint composed his Apology *and the two important treatises on Grace and Free Will and on the Errors of Abelard. He was also the biographer of St. Bernard.*

William is an interesting character of whom we would like to know more, but his flame was eclipsed by the brighter light of his friend. He was certainly a man of God and also something of a scholar. He was the author of several treatises among them the very beautiful Golden Epistle *to the Carthusians of Mont Dieu which has been translated into English by Walter*

Shewring. Much against the wishes and advice of his friend he resigned his abbacy and became a simple Cistercian monk at the Abbey of Signy in the diocese of Rheims. We are told that the severity of the life nearly broke his resolution, which is not surprising considering that he must have been nearly fifty years old at the time and not strong physically. But he persevered and died a very saintly monk 'in great sweetness of spirit, in purity of body and soul, perfect in all the virtues'. The life of William of St. Thierry would be a fruitful matter for research.

To the Lord Abbot William, the charity of a pure heart, a good conscience, and unfeigned faith, from Brother Bernard.

NO one knows what is in man save the spirit of a man that is in him; man sees only on the surface and God alone can search the heart; yet you have been able to weigh and mutually to compare our affection for each other, so as to deliver a verdict not only on the state of your own heart, but even on that of another. I wonder how or on what grounds you have been able to do this, and I cannot wonder enough. It is an error to which the human mind is ever prone not only to consider good to be evil, what is true to be false, and what is false to be true, but also to be doubtful about what is certain, and certain about what is doubtful. You may be right when you say that my affection for you is less than yours is for me, but I am certainly certain that you cannot be certain. How can you know for certain what it is certain you cannot be certain about?[1] Paul himself mistrusted his own judgement and declared that he did not judge himself. Peter regretted that he was deceived by his own presumption when he said, 'Even though I should have to die with thee, yet I would not deny thee'. In the matter of our Lord's betrayal the disciples had no confidence in themselves, but each asked, 'Is it I, Lord?' David confessed his own ignor-

---

1. . . . *sed certe certum sum, certum non esse tibi. Quomodo ergo pro certo affirmas, de quo certum est, quia certus minime sis?*

ance and begged the Lord to overlook it. But wonderful to say, you have been able to assert, with I know not what grounds for your confidence: 'My affection for you is greater than yours is for me'.[1]

2. These are your very words, and I could wish they were not, for I do not know if they are true. If you know, how do you know? What proof have you that my affection for you is less than yours is for me? Is it, as you aver in the postscript of your letter, that the messengers from here who pass to and fro by you never bring any token of my good will or affection? What sort of token, what sort of proof do you expect? Are you worried because I have not yet once answered your many letters to me? How could I possibly suppose your mature wisdom would be satisfied with my ignorant scribbling? I have not forgotten those words, 'Little children, let us love not in word, nor in tongue, but in deed and truth', and when have you ever needed my help and not received it? O Lord, who searchest the hearts of men! O Sun of Justice, whose rays enlighten the hearts of men with divers graces! Thou knowest and I feel that by thy gift I love this man for the sake of his goodness. But how much I love him, that I cannot tell, thou knowest. It is thou, Lord, who givest the power to love, it is thou who knowest how much thou hast given him to love me and me to love him. Without thy telling him, how could any man say, 'I love more than I am loved', unless he be one who has already seen his light in thy light, seen by the light of thy truth how much he burns with the fire of charity?

3. But, O Lord, I am for the time satisfied to see my own darkness in thy light, so long as thou dost visit those who sit in darkness and the shadow of death. In thy light the thoughts of men, the hidden places of the dark are made manifest. When the shadows are dispelled, then by thy light only the light is seen. By thy favour I feel that I love this man, but I have not yet the light to see whether I love him enough. I do not know

1. *ut plus amans, inquiens, minus diligar.*

whether I have yet achieved that love, greater than which no man can have, whereby I would be enabled to lay down my life for my friends. Who shall boast that he has a clean heart, much less a perfect heart? O Lord, who dost enlighten the lamp by which I see and hate my own darkness, enlighten, I pray thee, my very darkness that I may behold within myself and be glad, an ordered charity which knows and loves only what is worthy of love and in the measure that it is worthy of love and for the reasons that it is worthy of love, and be myself unwilling to be loved save in thee and in the measure that I deserve. Woe is me, if (as I greatly fear) I am either loved by this man more than I deserve or love him less than he deserves. If the better a man is the more he should be loved, but they are the better who love the more, what else can I say than that I must love him more than myself, because I have no doubt that he is better than myself, but less than I should, because I am capable of less?

4. But (it is you I now address, my father) that your charity is greater than mine is all the more reason why you should not despise my smaller capacity, because, although you love more than I do, you do not love more than you are able. And I too, although I love you less than I should, yet I love you as much as I can according to the power that has been given me. Draw me after you that I may reach you and with you receive more fully whence comes the power to love. Why do you try to reach me and complain that you are not able? You could reach me if you but considered what I am; and you can reach me still whenever you wish, if you are content to find me as I am and not as you wish me to be. I cannot think what else you see in me besides what I am, what it is you are chasing which is not me. You do not overtake it, because it is not me, because I am not able to be what you would like me to be and, to use your own words, I do not fail you, it is God in me who fails you. And now if all this trifling pleases you, tell me and I will give you more, for, in obeying you, I shall not fear the reproach of pre-

sumption. That little preface[1] which you ask to be sent you, I have not got by me at the moment. I have not yet had it copied, because I did not think it worth while. May he who gives you the desire grant you the power to accomplish whatever you rightly wish for yourself or for your friends, most reverend father, worthy of all the affection I can bestow.

[88]

To the same

To his friend all that a friend could wish, from Brother Bernard of Clairvaux.

IT was you who gave me this formula of greeting when you wrote 'To his friend all that a friend could wish'. Receive back what is your own, and in doing so realize that my soul is not far from one with whom I share a common language. Now, briefly and as I have the time, I must answer your letter. It came on the feast of Our Lady's Nativity and all my attention was absorbed in observing the festival, so that I could think of nothing else. But your messenger was so anxious to take to his feet again that he could scarcely wait until the next day, so that I should be more free to answer you something. As for that fugitive monk, after I had given him a harsh scolding suited to his hard heart I could do nothing else than send him back whence he came for our customs forbid me to keep any monk here without the consent of his abbot. You also should scold him sharply and incite him to make humble satisfaction, then comfort him with a letter to his abbot on his behalf.

2. With regard to the state of my health, I can only answer your kind enquiries by saying that I have been sick and still am sick, but not much more than usual nor much less. The reason

1. This refers to the letter which precedes the *Apology*.

why I have not sent that man as I intended is because I fear more the scandal of many souls than the danger of one body.[1] And now, so as not to pass over completely without mention the matter you wrote to me about, I come to yourself. You say you wish to hear what I, as one who knows you well, think of your plan.[2] If I am to say what I think, I must tell you that, unless I am mistaken, it is something I could not advise you to attempt and you could not carry out. Indeed I wish for you what it has for long been no secret to me that you wish for yourself. But putting aside what both of us wish, as it is right we should, it is safer for me and more advantageous for you if I advise you as I think God wishes. Therefore I say hold on to what you have got, remain where you are, and try to benefit those over whom you rule. Do not try to escape the responsibility of your office while you are still able to discharge it for the benefit of your subjects. Woe to you if you rule them and do not benefit them, but far greater woe to you if you refuse to benefit them because you shirk the burden of ruling them.

[90]

To Oger, a Canon Regular

Oger was a Canon Regular of Mont-Saint-Éloi near Arras. He had a great reputation for learning, and it is evident that he was on intimate terms with St. Bernard. The saint submitted to him for approval his Apology *before even William of St. Thierry had seen it.*

In the year 1125 he was chosen by the Bishop of Noyon to introduce the Canons Regular into the parish of St. Médard in Tournai, and the foundation of Saint-Nicolas-des-Prés is large-

1. *Quod vero non misi quem missurus eram, causa est, plus me animarum scandalum, quan unius corporis periculum timuisse.*

2. William wanted to resign his abbacy and become a monk at Clairvaux under St. Bernard. See introductory note to Letter 87.

ly his work. He ruled this house as superior for fourteen years. It was his resignation that elicited this vehement letter of reproach from St. Bernard.

Mabillon dates this letter about the year 1126, *but it was clearly written after Oger had resigned from being the superior of Saint-Nicolas-des-Prés, and would therefore belong to about the year* 1139, *the year in which the Lateran Council met in Rome and St. Malachy on his way there stopped at Clairvaux. According to Vacandard[1] this letter and the three which follow are set in an order diametrically reverse to the chronological, so that Letter* 93 *should come first, followed by* 92 *and* 91, *all written before the foundation of Saint-Nicolas-des-Prés, with the following letter last as written after Oger's resignation. Oger is also referred to in Letter* 96, *written about the year* 1133.

To Brother Oger, that he may walk worthily before God unto the end of his days, from Brother Bernard, monk but sinner, who loves him dearly.

IF I have seemed dilatory in answering your letter the reason is that I have lacked a messenger. I beg you to believe that this letter which you now read was written some time ago but, as I have said, for want of anyone to take it, time was lost before it was sent, although not before it was written. I gather from your letter that you found your pastoral charge irksome and have relinquished it after having not so much asked for your bishop's permission as exacted it by your insistence, and that even then you only obtained it on condition that, though dwelling elsewhere but in his diocese, you should not withdraw yourself from his authority, but that as this did not please you, you had recourse to a higher authority in the person of the archbishop, and then returned to your first home and to your abbot supported by his sanction. Now you implore me to in-

1. Vacandard, *Vie de Saint Bernard*, vol. I, p. 196, n. (1927 edn.).

struct you how you should live after all this. Fine sort of doctor, incomparable teacher that I am, who when I begin to teach
what I do not know may then be expected to realize at last that
I know nothing at all! A sheep might as well come to a goat for
wool, a mill to a furnace for water, a wise man to a fool for
knowledge, as you to me for guidance. Furthermore in all your
letters you exalt me above myself, interlarding everything you
say with praises of myself, praises which, as I am conscious I
do not deserve them, I must ascribe to your good will and overlook your ignorance of the facts. You see only on the surface,
God searches the heart. If I carefully examine myself under his
awful gaze, it is certain that I will know myself better than
you know me for the reason that I am closer to myself. And so
I put greater faith in what I see when I examine myself than I
do in your praises, who believe you see in me what I know is
not there!

2. You apologize to me for not having taken my advice
when I counselled and encouraged you not to give way to
despondency but to be of good heart and carry patiently the
burden imposed on you, which once undertaken cannot be put
aside. I accept your apology, as you ask. I am fully aware of
the aridity of my own wisdom and I always suspect my rash
stupidity. As I always hope that people will act more judicious-
ly than I have been able to instruct them, I have no right, I do
not dare to be annoyed when the course I have advocated is not
followed. Whenever my advice is followed, I confess that I
always feel oppressed with a great burden of responsibility, and
I can never be confident and always await the outcome with
anxiety. But it is your responsibility, if advisedly you have not
followed my counsel in the matter. It is also the responsibility
of those whose more wholesome advice you have followed in
preference to mine, if indeed you have taken any advice at all,
whether you have acted reasonably or not. Let them see to it
whether, when Christ was obedient to his Father unto death, it
is permissible for a Christian to free himself before death of the

yoke which obedience has laid upon him. You say you asked
the bishop for his permission and obtained it. Well and good,
but you asked for it in a way that you should not have done, so
that you cannot be said to have received it so much as exacted
it. A permission that has been extorted is no permission at all
but an exaction.[1] What the bishop unwillingly did when he was
overborne by your insistence was not to absolve you, but to
cut you off.

3. I congratulate you on having disburdened yourself, but I
very much fear that in doing so you have dishonoured God.[2]
Without doubt you have, so far as you could, opposed his designs by casting yourself down from the post to which he had
promoted you. If, by way of excuse, you allege the necessity
of poverty, I reply that necessity wins a crown;[3] if you allege
the difficulty or impossibility of your position, I reply that all
things are possible to one who believes. Better tell the truth and
admit that your own quiet pleased you more than labouring for
the benefit of others. I don't wonder at it, I admit that I feel the
same way myself, but it should not please you too much. And
it is too much, if a thing good in itself pleases no matter how it
is obtained, even if it is obtained unlawfully, for nothing can
be right to have, if it cannot be had rightly, as it is written: 'If
you rightly offer and do not rightly divide, you have sinned'.
Either you should not have undertaken at all the care of souls
or, having undertaken it, you should on no account have relinquished it, according to those words: 'Are you married to a
wife? Then do not go about to be free of her.'

4. What is the point of all these arguments of mine? Am I
trying to persuade you to take up again the burden of your office, when it is clear that there is no place open to you? Or do
I despair of you, as if you had saddled yourself with a sin you
could not get rid of? Such is very far from my intention. But I

1. *extorta seu coacta licentia, licentia non est, sed violentia.*
2. *quod sis exoneratus . . . exhoneratus sit Deus.*
3. *Rule of St. Benedict,* Chap. 7.

do not want you to regard what you have done as if it were a trifling matter. I want you always to fear for it, always to be sorry for it, and never to regard yourself as safe, according to those words of Scripture: 'Blessed evermore is the timorous conscience'. You see what sort of fear it is with which I am trying to smite you? Not the sort that will lead you into the pit of despair, but the sort that will win you hope of eternal life. For there is a fruitless fear which is cruel and sad and which never obtains pardon because it never tries to; and there is a loving, humble, and fruitful fear which easily obtains mercy for anyone however great his sin. Such a fear begets, fosters, and preserves humility, and also gentleness, patience, and meekness. Who would not be delighted with such a fair progeny? But the other sort of fear begets a sorry brood: obstinacy, immoderate sadness, hatred, terror, scorn, and desperation. So I would not have you regard your fault with the sort of fear that begets desperation, but with the sort that engenders hope, fearful lest you do not fear or do not fear enough.

5. There is another thing which I fear even more for you, it is that, like those of whom it is written, 'Sin and shame is all their liking', you may be deceived not only into thinking that you have done no wrong, but even into congratulating yourself on having done something which very few are wont to do, in scorning high office and preferring to place yourself under another's rule when you were freed from ruling others yourself. This is a false humility which foments real pride in the heart that thinks such things; for what could be more proud than to attribute to a spontaneous and free act of the will what was really due to the force of necessity or the infirmity of faintheartedness. And even if you had done it voluntarily and not because you had been overcome by work or compelled by necessity, there still could be nothing more proud than to plume yourself on it; for you have preferred your own will to the designs of God, choosing quiet for yourself rather than the work for which he had selected you. If therefore having

scorned God you make matters worse by congratulating yourself on it, your self-congratulation is hardly a good thing!
Avoid all self-congratulation, put away all complacency, so
that you may always be profitably anxious about yourself, always humbly fearful for yourself, but, as I have said already,
with the fear that mitigates and does not provoke wrath.

6. If this horrible fear should ever besiege your heart, silent-
ly suggesting that your worship of God is not acceptable and
that your repentance is fruitless because you cannot correct the
matter in which you have offended him, do not for one moment give way to it, but answer it faithfully by saying to yourself: I have done evil, but it is done and cannot be undone.
Who can tell whether God has not foreseen that it would profit
me, that he who is good has not wished that good should accrue
to me out of the evil I have done? May he punish me for what
I have done amiss, but let the good which he has provided for
me remain. The goodness of God knows how to use our dis-
ordered wishes and actions, often lovingly turning them to our
advantage while always preserving the beauty of his order.
What loving care the divine goodness has for the sons of
Adam! Never does it cease to pour forth its blessings, not only
where it can see nothing to deserve them, but often where it
sees everything to the contrary! But to return to yourself:
according to the two kinds of fear which I have distinguished
above, I wish you to fear and not to fear; to presume and not
to presume. To fear, in order that you may repent; not to fear,
in order that you may presume; to presume so that you do not
lose heart, not to presume so that you become slothful.

7. Behold how great is my confidence in you! I have scolded
you sharply, and I have not hesitated to judge your conduct
before knowing all the facts so that, for all I can tell, you have
better reasons for it than I am aware of. You might not have
wished to put in your letter all the reasons that would have
excused you, either from humility, or for the sake of brevity.
So I leave the verdict undecided, for it is clear I know nothing

about the matter. There is however one thing you have done for which I have nothing but praise. I refer to the way that, when you had put off the yoke of office, without any thought of keeping your freedom you without hesitation immediately put yourself again under the discipline you loved, not ashamed to become once more a disciple after you had been a master. When you had been freed of your pastoral duties you could have remained your own master, since a religious is dispensed from obedience to his former superior when once he becomes an abbot. Yet you did not take advantage of this privilege, but as you had refused to rule others so you feared to rule yourself; believing yourself incapable of ruling others, you had no confidence in yourself and scorned to become your own master, deservedly so because he becomes the disciple of a fool who sets up to be his own teacher. What the experience of others may be I do not know, but my own experience is that I can far more easily command and far more safely rule others than I can myself. You were prudently humble and humbly prudent when you did not at all believe that you were sufficient to your own salvation and decided henceforth to live under the authority of another.

8. I praise you also that you did not seek out a new master, but returned to the familiar cloister from which you had set out and to the father whom you had left. It would not have been fitting that a strange house should have profited by the loss of your mother house in which you were brought up, but which sent you out at the behest of fraternal charity. Yet I do not want you to think it a trivial matter that you have not received the permission of your bishop to return. Hasten therefore to make what satisfaction you can, either in person or through another. After you have done this, try to live simply amongst your brethren, seeking God, submissive to your superior, obedient to your seniors, friendly with your juniors, pleasing to the angels, profitable in speech, humble of heart, kind to all. Beware of thinking that because you were once in a place of

honour, you should still be honoured above others, rather show yourself all the more humble, and more humble than any. It would be a shocking thing were you to exact honour when you have refused the labour.

9. There is another danger that can arise from this against which I would have you forewarned and forearmed. We are all of us so unstable that what we wanted yesterday we often do not want to-day, and what we reject to-day to-morrow we want. And so it can sometimes happen, at the suggestion of the devil, that the desire for honours that we remember will knock on the door of the soul, even so that what we were men enough to scorn we are childish enough to begin again to want. All that the soul once found bitter—high position, care of the house, arrangement of affairs, salutes of servants, freedom of action, power over others—all this it begins to find sweet after all, so that sorrow is felt for what it was once irksome to have. If you for one moment assent to this vile temptation (may it be very far from you to do any such thing!) your life will suffer no little harm.

10. Now you have all the wisdom of your wise and eloquent doctor whom you asked from so far away to teach you. This is the long desired and expected praise you so much wanted to hear. Or do you still expect something wonderful? You have it all. What more do you want? The spring is exhausted, and do you still expect water from a fountain that has run dry? Like the widow in the Gospels, of my poverty I have given you all I have got. Why so bashful? Why hang your head? You forced me. You asked for a discourse and now you have got it. A discourse long enough in all conscience, but saying nothing much; full of words and wind, but empty of sense. Not one calculated to order charity within you[1] as you asked for, but one which will exhibit my lack of knowledge. How can such ignorance as mine be now excused? Perhaps I might

---

1. *Non quo, ut petieras, in corde tuo cavitas ordinetur.* Eales translates: 'Such is the discourse which ought to be received by you with charity'.

say that I have been suffering from fever or that I was preoccupied with the cares of office when I dictated it, since we are told that 'The wisdom of the learned man is the fruit of leisure'. All this might have been some excuse, if I had composed something great and important, but for such a little thing as this these excuses cannot be adduced with any confidence at all. No, my only excuse is, as I have already said so often, the meagreness of my knowledge.

11. But in my confusion I have one consolation. Although I may have disappointed you by not sending what you expected, you can see by what I have sent you that I have tried. When ability is lacking the will must supply for the deed. Although what I have written may be of no use to you, it will certainly profit my humility. 'While he holds his peace, a fool may pass for a wise man', for his silence is attributed to humility and not to lack of understanding. And so by holding my peace I could have passed for a wise man. But as it is some will laugh at my stupidity, others will mock at me as a fool, and yet others will be indignant at my presumption. All this will be of no small help to my sanctification,[1] because humiliations lead to humility and humility is the foundation of the spiritual life. Humiliation is the only way to humility, just as patience is the only way to peace, and reading to knowledge. If you want the virtue of humility you must not shun humiliations. If you will not suffer yourself to be humbled, you can never achieve humility. It is an advantage for me that my foolishness should be made public, that I whose lot it has often been to receive undeserved praise from those who do not know me, should now be discomforted by those who have found me out. The Apostle alarms me when, fearful for himself, he says: 'But I restrain myself, lest any man should think of me above that which he seeth in me, or anything he heareth from me'. How aptly he has said: 'I restrain myself'! The arrogant man does not restrain himself, the proud man does not restrain himself, the vain man does

1. *religionis emolumentum.*

not restrain himself, nor does the boasting man, who either lies about himself or credits himself with what is not his own, restrain himself. Only the truly humble man can be said to restrain himself, sparing his own soul, because he prefers to conceal what he is, so that no one should believe him to be what he is not.[1]

12. It is very dangerous for anyone to hear himself spoken of above what he knows he deserves. I pray that I may be humbled before men for the truth, just as much as it has been my lot to be undeservedly praised for what is not true. I rightly apply to myself those words of the Prophet: 'I have been lifted up only to be cast down and discomforted'; and again: 'Play the mountebank I will and humble myself in my own esteem', for I shall play the mountebank that I may be mocked. A good sort of playing this, a playing calculated to enrage Michol and please God. A good sort of playing which is ridiculous to men, but a very beautiful sight to the angels. I say it is a good sort of playing by which we become an object of reproach to the rich and of ridicule to the proud. In fact what else do seculars think we are doing but playing when what they desire most on earth, we fly from; and what they fly from, we desire? Like acrobats and jugglers, who with heads down and feet up, stand or walk on their hands, and thus draw all eyes to themselves. But this is not a game for children or the theatre where lust is excited by the effeminate and indecent contortions of the actors, it is a joyous game, decent, grave, and admirable, delighting the gaze of the heavenly onlookers. This pure and holy game he plays who says: 'We are become a spectacle to angels and men'. And we too play this game that we may be ridiculed, discomforted, humbled, until he comes who puts down the mighty from their seat and exalts the humble. May he gladden us, exalt us, and glorify us for ever.

---

1. The whole sentence is a play on St. Paul's use of the word *Parco*.

[91]

To the same

I WILL pass over my lack of ability, I will not mention my humble profession or my profession of humility, and I will not plead my commonplace, not to say mediocre, position and name. Whenever I mention anything like this you do not regard it as a reasonable excuse, but as a mere pretext for not answering your letters promptly. According to your mood you call my quite legitimate modesty sometimes indiscretion and at other times false humility, and now you tell me it is pride. So I will not make any more of what you regard as dubious excuses, I will merely point out to you as a friend what you must believe to be a fact, namely that because of the short summer nights and the full days I have not had one moment of leisure in which I could attend to your business since your messenger left me . . . not the present one but the former. As it is, your letter has found me so occupied that even to recount all I have to do would take too long. I scarcely had time to read it when it came during my dinner. And now by getting up early I am just able to scribble, on the quiet, this brief reply. Whether or not you will be satisfied with its brevity is your affair.

2. To tell the truth, dear Oger, although my conscience bears witness that I am only trying to serve charity yet, for your sake, I cannot but be exasperated with all my cares. I bear them only for the sake of charity, because I am debtor to the wise and unwise; only for her sake am I prevented from complying with your requests. Does charity prevent me from doing what you ask in the name of charity? You have asked, you have implored, you have knocked, but charity has closed the door to you. Why be angry with me? If you wish, if you dare, you should be angry with charity. In the name of charity you have been bold to demand, and charity herself has refused you. Already she complains of this long screed and is vexed with

you for imposing it. Not that she is displeased with your zeal, for she gave you that, but she would have you rule zeal with knowledge and not try to hinder greater matters with things of lesser consequence. See, even now I have become vexatious to lady charity, who urges me to make an end, but drawn on by my delight in conversing with you and by my desire to please you I am loath to be torn from a long letter and still have not finished. There is so much to answer in your letter. If only it were right for me to do as I please, I could probably satisfy both you and myself. But she who commands otherwise is mistress or, I should say, lord for 'God is charity'. Such is her authority that I must obey her rather than you or myself. So although I do not refuse what you ask, I must unwillingly and sadly defer it for the time, because I must obey charity, which is God, rather than men. Otherwise I, a mere worm of the earth, in my desire humbly to please you, would be setting myself, under the cloak of humility, but with a real pride, against that stronghold of authority which, as you well say, can command even the angels in heaven.

3. As for that booklet of mine, even before your messenger arrived I had asked for it back from the man to whom I had lent it. But I have not got it yet. I will do what I can to have it here when you come (if you ever do come), so that you may see it and read it, but not copy it.[1] That other one I lent you I had meant you only to read, but you tell me you have had it copied. What use that can serve or whom it can possibly benefit is your responsibility. I did not intend that you should send it to the Abbot of St. Thierry, but I do not mind. Why should I mind him seeing it when I would gladly lay bare my whole soul for him to see if I could. Alas that the mention of such a man should arise in so short a letter which even now clamours to be finished, when I would gladly dwell on his welcome memory! Do

1. It is said that St. Columba was sued in the court of the king at Tara by St. Finnan in the 6th century for having secretly copied a manuscript which belonged to him, and that St. Finnan won his case, and St. Columba was ordered to give up the copy he had made.

not hesitate, I beg you, to find an opportunity of going to see him, and do not on any account allow anyone to see or copy the aforesaid booklet until you have been through it with him, discussed it with him, and have both made such corrections as may be necessary, so that every word of it may be supported by two witnesses.[1] I leave to the judgement of you both whether it shall be published, or shown to only a few, or to no one at all. I also leave to you both to decide whether the preface you have put together out of my other letters will stand or whether it would not be better to compose another.[2]

4. I had almost forgotten the complaint at the beginning of your letter that I had accused you of falsehood. I do not remember saying any such thing about you. But if I did (I would sooner believe I had forgotten than that your messenger had lied), it could only have been in fun that I said it and not seriously. How could I possibly believe that you were a trifler or one of those to whom Yes and No are the same. May such a suspicion of you be very far from me who know full well that you are happy to carry the yoke of truth from your youth and restrain the years of indiscretion[3] with the gravity of your conduct. I am not so simple as to believe that a simple statement from the lips without duplicity of heart can ever be a formal lie, nor am I so indifferent to you as to have forgotten what you have had at heart for so long and the obstacle that impedes its accomplishment.

    1. *ut in ore duorum testium stet omne verbum.* Literally: 'That in the mouth of two or three witnesses every word shall stand' (*Deut.* 19.15 and *Matt.* 18.16).

    2. The booklet referred to here is plainly the *Apologia* of St. Bernard. It was inscribed to Abbot William of St. Thierry, which accounts for why Oger sent it to him without instructions. There is a reference to the preface here mentioned in Letter 87.4.

    3. *lascivos annos morum superas gravitate.*

To the same

This letter is of interest for Saint Bernard's vivid description of the labour of literary composition.

I FEEL you may be annoyed or at least surprised that I answered your long letter with only a short note. But I beg you to remember those words of the Wise Man, 'All things have their season: there is a time for speaking and a time for keeping silence'. And what time would there be for silence if conversation claimed even these holy days of Lent, and a sort of conversation all the more laborious for being so engrossing? When we are together it is possible quickly to say what we want, but being absent from each other we must laboriously compose what we want to ask or reply. And where, I ask you, is the leisure, where the quiet of silence when one is thinking, composing, and writing? You say that all this can be done in silence. I am surprised that you can seriously mean this. How can the mind be quiet when composing a letter and a turmoil of expressions are clamouring and every sort of phrase and diversity of senses are jostling one another? When words spring into the mind, but just the word one wants escapes one; when literary effect, sense, and how to convey a meaning clearly, and what should be said, and in what order it should be said, has to be carefully considered; all the things which those who understand these matters scrutinize carefully? And do you tell me there is any quiet in all this? Can you call this silence, even if the lips are not moving?

2. It is not only that I have not the time, it is also that the sort of work you want me to do is not suited either to my profession or ability. Not teaching, but lamenting is the duty of the monk I am supposed to be and of the sinner that I am. There could not be anything more silly than for an untaught

man such as I confess I am, to presume to teach what he knows nothing about. An untaught man is not competent to teach, a monk does not dare to do so, and a penitent does not want to do so. It is in order to avoid this that I have flown far away and dwelt in solitude, and like the Prophet have determined to 'take heed of my ways that I sin not with my tongue', because, according to the same Prophet, 'a glib tongue shall not have its way upon earth'; and according to another, 'the tongue holds the keys of life and death'. Isaias calls silence 'the work of justice' and Jeremias says that 'it is good to await the salvation of the Lord in silence'. Therefore so that I shall not seem entirely to ignore your request I invite and incite you, who by speaking press me to teach what I do not know, and, if not by my teaching, at any rate by the example of my silence, all those who like you wish to grow in virtue, to foster this 'work of justice', the mother, the support, the guardian of all the virtues.

3. But what am I doing? I wonder you do not laugh. For, while appearing to condemn strongly much speaking, I still continue to pour out words, and in recommending silence to thwart silence by my verbosity. Our dear Guerric,[1] concerning whose life of penance you wish to be assured, to judge by his fruit is walking worthily, you may be sure, before God, and bringing forth worthy fruit of penance. But the little book you ask for I have not by me, for another friend, who was just as anxious to read it as you are, has had it for a long time and not yet returned it. However, so as not to ignore your request completely, I am sending you another booklet which I have lately published, in praise of the Virgin Mother. As I have not got the original I beg you to return it as soon as you can or, if you are coming here in the near future, to bring it with you.

1. Guerric was made Abbot of Igny in 1138.

To the same

I HAVE answered your short letters with short letters, glad to have an excuse in your brevity for being brief myself. For true and, as you rightly say, eternal friendships are not helped by exchanging vain and empty words. However much you try to show your friendship by verses, phrases, and quotations, I feel sure you express less than you feel; and you would not be wrong if you believed the same thing of me. When your letter was delivered into my hands, you were already in my heart. While I write this letter you are present to me, as I am sure I shall be present to you when you read it. We wear ourselves out in scribbling to each other, and we exhaust our messengers in sending them backwards and forwards between us. But is the spirit ever weary with loving? Let us stop this tiring business of exchanging letters and turn ourselves to what the more we do the easier it becomes. Let us give our heads a respite from dictating, our tongues from chattering, our hands from writing, our messengers from running to and fro, and apply ourselves to meditating day and night on the law of the Lord, which is the law of charity. The more we rest from doing this, the less rested we become; the more we apply ourselves to it, the more repose we derive from it. Let us love and be loved: benefiting ourselves by loving, and others by being loved.[1] We find rest in those we love, and we provide a resting place in ourselves for those who love us. To love anyone in God is charity, to try and make ourselves loved for God's sake is the service of charity.

2. But what am I doing? I promise brevity but cling to prolixity. If you wish to know about Brother Guerric, or rather

---

1. *Amemus, et amemur; in altero nobis, in altero nostris consulentes.* Eales translates: 'Let us love and be loved, striving to benefit ourselves in the other, and the other in ourselves'.

because you do, I can assure you that he so runs not as one uncertain of the course, and so fights not as one beating the air. But he knows that the effect comes from God's mercy, not from man's will, or man's alacrity, so he begs you to pray God for him that he who gives the power to fight and run may also give the power to conquer and achieve the goal. I greet your abbot through you, for he is dear to me not only on your account, but also because of what I have heard of him. It will give me great pleasure to meet him at the time and place you have arranged. I must tell you that for some time now the hand of the Lord has been heavy upon me. I reeled under it and had well nigh fallen, the axe was laid to the barren tree of my body, and I feared it was already being cut down, but on account of your prayers and those of my other friends the Lord has spared me this time, yet only in the hope that I shall show some fruit in future.

[95]

To Henry I, King of England

This letter refers to the foundation of Rievaulx, which took place on March 5th, 1132. Rievaulx was the first daughter of Clairvaux in these islands but not the first Cistercian house, for Waverly dates from the year 1129. The first abbot was William, the scribe of St. Bernard's letter to Robert of Châtillon and an Englishman, but the chief glory of Rievaulx is St. Ailred, the third abbot. The founder was Walter Espec, who in 1138 rallied the barons and yeomen of Yorkshire and drove back David, King of Scotland, at the battle of the Standard. Note how Saint Bernard uses military phraseology to describe the making of a monastic foundation. Saint Benedict speaks of his monks as soldiers fighting with the bright arms of obedience.

To Henry, the illustrious King of England, that in his earthly kingdom he may faithfully serve and humbly obey the King of heaven, from Bernard, styled Abbot of Clairvaux.

IN your land there is an outpost of my Lord and your Lord, an outpost which he has preferred to die for than to lose. I have proposed to occupy it and I am sending men from my army who will, if it is not displeasing to you, claim it, recover it, and restore it with a strong hand. For this purpose I have sent ahead these men who now stand before you to reconnoitre. They will investigate the situation carefully and report back to me faithfully. Help them as messengers of your Lord and in their persons fulfil your duties as a vassal of their Lord. And may he for his honour, the salvation of your soul, and the health and peace of your kingdom, bring you safe and happy to a good and peaceful end.

[97]

To Duke Conrad

This was Conrad, Duke of Zeringen. Mabillon dates this letter 1132 and quotes Samuel Guichen to the effect that Conrad was at this time contemplating hostilities against Amadeus I, Count of Geneva. This letter is just one example of St. Bernard's beneficent influence in curbing the sultry passions of the mediæval barons.

ALL power comes from him to whom the Prophet says: 'Thine, Lord, the power, of all princes art thou the overlord'. So it seems to me fitting, illustrious Prince, that I should write and admonish your Excellency to bow down before the terrible One who strikes with terror the hearts of princes. The Prince of Geneva, as I have heard from his own mouth, has of-

fered himself to justice and is ready to make satisfaction to you
in all that you have against him. So if, on the top of this, you set
out to invade his territory, destroy churches, burn down home-
steads, and shed human blood, there can be no doubt at all that
you will seriously anger him, who is 'father to the orphan and
gives the widow redress'. If he is angry it would advantage you
nothing to fight no matter how great your military strength.
It makes no difference to the omnipotent Lord whether armies
are great or small, he gives victory where he pleases. When he
wished he gave one man power to put thousands to flight, and
two men ten thousand.

2. A poor man myself I am stirred by the cries of poor men
to write to you knowing that it would be more honourable for
you to yield to the humble than to submit to the enemy. Not
that I believe your enemy to be stronger than you are, but I
know the omnipotent God to be more powerful than either of
you, and that he resists the proud and gives his grace to the
humble. I would have had an audience with you on this matter, if it had been possible, but now I send in my place these
brethren of mine in the hope that by their entreaties united with
mine they may obtain from your Highness a complete treaty
if possible, or at any rate an armistice until we can explore the
ground for a firm peace to your honour, the good of your country and in accordance with the will of God. Otherwise, if you
will neither receive the satisfaction offered you nor listen to
my entreaties, or rather, if you will not heed the voice of God
warning you through me for the good of your soul, then may
he be your judge. I know full well that two armies can hardly
close in combat without terrible slaughter on both sides, which
is what I fear so much.

To a certain Religious

I AM returning Brother Lambert to you. When he arrived here he was rather unsettled in certain respects, but your
prayers have restored calm to him and he is no longer troubled
by his former scruples. I have carefully enquired into the
cause of his coming here and also the reason and nature of his
leaving you. His intentions seem to have been above reproach,
but there is certainly no excuse for his leaving you in the way
he did, namely without permission. And so having scolded him
for this as he deserved, I am returning him to you suitably
chastened and now quite composed. When he comes back I beg
you, dearest brothers, to be lenient in the matter of his presumption, for he is quite simple about it and without any malice whatsoever. He came straight here without turning to right
or left, because he knew that all of us here are your loyal friends
and faithful followers. As spiritual men, I beg you to receive
him in the spirit of gentleness, confirming the charity which is
in him and forgiving, on account of his good intentions, his mistaken departure. I am sure that, by the mercy of him who is
all-powerful, any annoyance you may have felt at his irregular
exit will soon vanish when you see the change in him for the
better.

[103]

To a certain Abbot

*This letter is an excellent commentary on the 28th chapter of
St. Benedict's Holy Rule.*

ABOUT that troubled and troublesome brother who
has no respect for his superiors, my advice to you is brief but
trustworthy. It is the devil's endeavour to go around the house
of God seeking whom he may devour, and it is your duty to
keep a sharp look-out so that he does not find a way in. The
more he tries to separate a weak lamb from the rest of the
flock, so that he can carry him off all the easier for there being
no one to rescue him, the more it behoves you to withstand
him with all your might, so that he can never snatch a lamb
from your hands and boast: 'I have prevailed against him'. Do
all that charity requires of you to save the brother, spare neither
kindness, wholesome advice, rebukes in private, exhortations
in public, and if necessary sharp words and sharp floggings,
but above all, what is usually more efficacious than anything
in these cases, do you and the brethren pray for him.

2. If you have tried all this and availed nothing, then you
must have recourse to the advice of the Apostle and 'put away
the evil one'. The evil one must be put away lest he lead others
into evil. A bad tree can only give bad fruit. So I say 'put him
away', but not in the way he would want. That is to say do not
let him go with your licence, for if you do he will deceive himself into thinking that he can legitimately live contrary to his
vows outside his monastery, beyond all reach of discipline, as
his own master and according to his own sweet will. But turn
him out as a diseased sheep is turned out of the flock, as a gan-
grenous limb is cut off from the body. Let him understand
clearly that from henceforth you will regard him as 'a heathen
and a publican'. Do not have any fear that by thus preserving

the peace of all at the cost of one,[1] you will be acting contrary to charity. The malice of one brother can easily disturb the unity of the whole. Let those words of Solomon comfort you: 'No man can set him straight at whom God looks askance', and those of our Saviour: 'Every plant which my heavenly Father hath not planted, shall be rooted up', and what the blessed John has said about schismatics: 'They went out from us because they were not of us', and again the words of the Apostle: 'If the unbeliever depart, let him depart'. The godless ought not to be left in the domain of the just, else the just will stretch out their hands to wickedness. Better that one should perish than the unity of all.

[105]

To Master Walter of Chaumont

Saint Bernard did not, of course, think that no one could be saved except he became a Cistercian, but neither did he think that the Cistercian way of life was only for a chosen few, a tiny body of select souls. This is a modern conception of more modern orders such as the Trappists. In the Saint's view the Cistercian way of life was a microcosm of the Church, a net let into the sea, a way of life open to all men of average physical strength, and perhaps rather more than average good will.

I AM filled with sadness for you, my dear Walter, when I think of the flower of your youth, the brightness of your intelligence, the ornaments of your knowledge and scholarship and, what more becomes a Christian than all these, your noble bearing, all being wasted in futile studies and the pursuit of what is merely passing, when they would be so much better

1. *Ne timeas esse contra caritatem si unius scandalum multorum recompensaveris pace.*

used in the service of Christ. God forbid that a sudden death should snatch them from you, that all should suddenly wither like grass in the fury of a burning wind, fall from you like leaves from autumn trees. What fruit will you have then of all your labours upon earth? What return will you be able to make to God for all he has given you? What will you have to show for all the talents he has entrusted to you? What will happen to you, if with empty hands you stand before him who, although he willingly gave you all your gifts, will nevertheless exact a strict account of how you have used them? He will come, he will soon come, who will demand back with increase what was his own. He will take away all those gifts which have earned you such spectacular, but such treacherous, applause in your own country. Noble birth, a lithe body, a comely appearance, a distinguished bearing, are great acquisitions, but the credit of them belongs to him who gave them. You may use them for your own advantage, but there is one who will enquire into it and judge if you do.

2. Let us suppose that you may, for the time being, claim all the credit for yourself, that you may glory in your renown and the title you have of master, and win for yourself a great name on earth. What will happen to all this when you are dead? What will be left of it but the memory, and even this only upon earth, for it is written: 'There they sleep on, empty handed, the warriors in their pride'? And if this is to be the end of all your labours, will you pardon me for asking, what more have you than the beasts of the field? When your charger is dead, what more can be said of it than that it was a good beast? Ask yourself how you will answer at that terrible judgement for having received your soul, and such a soul, in vain, if you have paid no more attention to your immortal and rational spirit than any brute beast whose soul ceases to exist the moment it ceases to animate its body. Wherein, think you, lies your worth, you who are made in the image of your creator, if you care not for this, your sole title to the great dignity you

enjoy as a man? Because you do not understand this, because you concern yourself with nothing spiritual or eternal but, like the brute beasts whose soul dies with their body, are content only with passing and material things, because you are blind to the counsel of the Gospel: 'Labour not for the bread that per-isheth but that which endureth for life everlasting', you are become 'like the brute beasts and not better than they'. It is written that only he shall go up the mountain of God who 'has not received his soul in vain', and not even he shall do so unless he be also 'guiltless in act and clean of heart'. It is for you to decide whether you can dare say this of yourself. If you cannot, then consider what reward will be meted out to wickedness, if mere unfruitfulness incurs damnation. Certainly thorns and briars will not be spared when the axe is laid to the unfruitful tree, stinging plants will not escape when the unfruitful tree is threatened. Woe therefore, and woe again to him of whom it can be said: 'He should have borne grapes, but he bore wild grapes instead'.

3. I know that you can think all this out clearly and fully without my prompting you, but that the love you have for your mother prevents you from following your convictions by completely abandoning what in your heart you despise. What can I say about this? You live with your mother and were I to tell you to leave her it would seem inhuman. But on the other hand it is not for her good that she should be the cause of your perdition. Perhaps you can serve both the world and Christ? But no man can serve two masters. Your mother wishes what will impede your salvation and so impede hers as well. Choose which you prefer: you can either serve her wishes or both her salvation and yours. If you truly love her, it is for her good that you should leave her. If you leave Christ in order to be with your mother, on your account she too will perish. She who gave you birth would be ill paid if she were to perish on your account. But how could she not perish who has destroyed the son to whom she gave birth? I have spoken in this way in

consideration to the flesh and in deference to natural affection. But it is a true saying, worthy of all acceptance, that although it is wicked to disregard one's mother, yet to do so for Christ's sake is most righteous, for he who said, 'Honour thy father and mother,' also said, 'He who loves father or mother more than me, is not worthy of me'.[1]

[106]

To Romanus, a Subdeacon of the Curia
at Rome

To his dear friend Romanus, all that he could wish for a friend, from Bernard Abbot of Clairvaux.

YOU did well, my dear friend, to renew by your letter the pleasant memory I have of you and excuse the tiresome delay. Forgetfulness of you can never steal you from the hearts of those that miss you but, I must confess, I had begun to think you had almost forgotten about yourself. Have done with delay and do at once what you say in your letter you intend to do! Prove by what you do the sincerity of what you write. Why delay to give birth to the spirit of salvation which you have conceived already? Nothing is more certain for mortals than death, nothing more uncertain than the hour of death: like a thief in the night it will come. Woe to them that are with child in that hour! If it should come upon and forestall that life-giving birth, alas, it will undermine the house and destroy the holy seed: 'For when they shall say peace and security; then shall sudden destruction come upon them, as the pains upon her that is with child'. I do not wish you to escape death, but I do wish that at any rate you should have no cause

1. St. Jerome, *Ep.* 14.

to fear it. The righteous man, although he does not guard against death, yet he does not fear it.[1] 'Though he should die before his time, rest shall be his.' He dies certainly, but his death is safe, for as he departs this life he enters a better one. It is a good death which dies to sin that it may live to righteousness. And this death to sin must come first if that final death is to be safe. While you are still in this life, lay up treasure which will last for ever in the next. Die to the world while you are in the body that after the death of the body you may live for ever in God. What matter if death does rend your bodily raiment if it straightway clothes you in joy? How 'blessed are the dead, who die in the Lord', they shall hear the Spirit say 'from henceforth now you may rest from your labours'! And not only shall they rest from their labours, they shall also experience a great joy from the newness of life which will be theirs, and the safety that will last for ever. The death of the righteous is good because of its rest, better because of its new life, and best of all because of its safety. On the other hand, 'the death of the wicked is very evil'. It is very evil because for them loss of the world is grievous, separation from the body worse, and the twofold suffering of worm and fire worst of all. Come then, make haste, go forth and depart, die the death of the righteous that your end may be the same as theirs. How precious in the sight of the Lord is the death of his saints! Fly, I implore you, and linger no more where sinners walk. How can you live where you would be afraid to die? And, you can be sure, I shall be ready, according to the words of the Prophet, 'to bring out bread' to you in flight.

1. *Justus quippe mortem, etsi non cavet, tamen non pavet.*

[107]

To Henry Murdac

Henry Murdac was a Yorkshireman who became a monk of Clairvaux and returned to Yorkshire to be Abbot of Fountains and finally Archbishop of York. He seems to have been a rather dour character.

To his dear friend Henry Murdac, health, and not only in this life, from Bernard, styled Abbot of Clairvaux.

WHAT wonder if you are tossed about between prosperity and adversity since you have not yet gained a foothold on the rock. But if you have sworn and are determined to keep the just commandments of the Lord, neither prosperity nor adversity can sever you from the love of Christ. Oh if you only knew, if only I could explain to you! 'Such things as were never known from the beginning, as ear never heard, eye never saw, save at thy command, thou, O God, hast made ready for all that await thy aid.' I hear, brother, that you are reading the Prophets; think you that you understand what you read? If you do, you will perceive that it is to Christ which they refer. And if you would grasp him, you will do so sooner by following him than by reading of him. Why seek the Word amidst written words, when in the flesh he stands before your eyes? He has long since left his hiding place in the Prophets and appeared unto the Fishermen. Like a bridegroom from his bridal bed he has leapt from the shady coverts of the mountain sides and run into the open pastures of the Gospels. Let him who has ears to hear, hear him crying out in the Temple: 'Whosoever thirsts, let him come to me and drink', and: 'Come unto me, all ye who labour and are burdened, and I will refresh you'. Are you afraid that you will break down where Truth himself has promised to refresh you? Certainly if the 'dark waters from the clouds of the air' please you so much, you will be more than delighted with the clear water that springs from the fountains of the Saviour.

2. If you could but once taste for a moment the 'full ears of corn on which Jerusalem feasts' how gladly would you leave the dry husks for Jewish hacks to gnaw! If I could but have you as my fellow in the school of piety of which Jesus is the master! If only I might submit the vessel of your heart when it has been purified to the unction which teaches all things! How gladly would I share with you the warm loaves which, still piping hot, fresh, as it were, from the oven, Christ of his heavenly bounty so often breaks with his poor! Would that when God sweetly deigns to shed on his poor servant a drop of that heavenly dew which he keeps for his chosen, I might presently pour it forth upon you and in turn receive from you what you feel! Believe me who have experience, you will find much more labouring amongst the woods than you ever will amongst books. Woods and stones will teach you what you can never hear from any master. Do you imagine you cannot suck honey from the rocks and oil from the hardest stone; that the mountains do not drop sweetness and the hills flow with milk and honey; that the valleys are not filled with corn? So many things occur to me which I could say to you that I can hardly restrain myself. But as it is for prayers and not a sermon that you have asked me, I will pray God that with his laws and his commandments he may open your heart. Farewell.

P.S. Ivo and William join me in saying the same.[1] What more can I add to what I have said? You know very well that I wish to see you and the reason why; but how much I wish to see you, that you could never guess, nor I tell you. I pray God that he will give you the grace to follow me where you should

---

1. *Idipsum epsi Willelmus et Ivo.* Eales translates: 'Let William and Ivo too have share in this my prayer'. Mabillon believes that Ivo is the brother of William to whom Letter 104 is addressed.

have led the way. I believe you to be so great a master in humility that you would not object, although a master, to following your disciples.

[108]

To Thomas, Provost of Beverley

To Thomas, Provost of Beverley, and a youth of great promise, that he may learn by the example of his namesake, the Apostle, from Bernard, the servant of the Poor of Christ at Clairvaux.

IVO who knows you has suggested to me, whom you do not know, that I should write to you; and charity prompts me to do so. He has told me all he wished of what he knew about you, and charity, which believes all things, could not hear and remain idle. Not idle, I say, as regards myself, because as soon as I had heard what Ivo had to say of you, I was compelled by charity to write to you, to exhort you, to pray for you. Whether with any effect or not rests with you. I confess that what I have heard of you from those who know you, pleases me. I do not mean your noble lineage, your courtly bearing, your handsome figure, your riches, or your exalted rank. All these and the like are mortal things and will fade like the flowers of the field. I refer to your strong character, your noble demeanour, and especially to that love of holy poverty which, I am told, you have lately conceived amidst your riches. And so while warmly congratulating you, I have conceived great hopes for you, which I trust will not be disappointed. May this my joy speedily reach even to the angels in heaven who are prepared to make great joy over you, as they are over the conversion and repentance of all sinners. If only it were to fall to my lot to husband the flower of your youth, to gather such an example of good dispositions; if only I were permitted to save it intact for God, to offer it unblemished, a sweet fragrance acceptable to the Lord.

2. Perhaps your conscience will answer to this that I have spoken too late, that your youth has already been soiled with too many sins for it to be possible to preserve it unblemished. This does not dismay me. A sinner myself, I feel no repugnance towards a sinner. I do not spurn the diseased, since I am aware that I too am diseased. Even if you believe me to be whole, I do not refuse 'to become weak to a weak man, that I may gain the weak'; I gladly listen to Paul in this matter, when he says: 'You who are spiritual, instruct such an one in the spirit of meekness, considering thyself lest thou also be tempted'. The gravity of the sickness is nothing to me when I consider the skill of the Physician, and also his pity which is so well known to me in my own grievous ills. No matter how great your sins may be, how foul may be your conscience, even though you may be conscious that your youth is polluted with dreadful atrocities, even though grown old in years ill spent 'you have become rotten like a beast on a dung heap', yet you shall be cleansed and become whiter than snow, and your youth shall be restored as the eagle's plumage. I know who it is that says: 'Where sin abounded grace did more abound'. The good Physician heals all mortal ills, and contents all our desires for good.

3. A good conscience is a mine of wealth. And in truth what greater riches can there be, what thing more sweet than a good conscience? What is there on earth to give such peace and such serenity? A good conscience fears no material loss, no invective can touch it, and no physical pain can hurt it; death itself cannot bring it low, but only lift it up. What, I ask, amongst the goods of the earth is there to compare with such happiness as this? What thing like this can the world, for all its blandishments, offer to its lovers? What thing like this can the world, for all its lies, hold out to fools? Vast estates, a prelate's robes,

the sceptre of a king; all this, yes. But not to mention all the hazards without which such things cannot be won or held, is it not true to say that at the first touch of death all is lost? It is written: 'There they sleep on, empty handed, the rich men in their pride'. But the wealth of a good conscience lives again, it does not wither away in travail, it does not pass away in death, it flowers again. It gives joy to the living, it consoles the dying, it refreshes the dead. But why dwell in words upon the truth of what I am ready to prove by deeds. It is for you to prove me a liar or yourself a rich man. Only come and see. With what joyous steps will I not run out 'with bread to meet the fleeing man,' with what glad embraces shall I not receive my youngest son. 'Quickly shall the first robe be brought forth for you and a ring put on your finger, and I shall say: This my son was dead but he lives again, was lost and is found.'

[109]

To the same

This Thomas had promised himself to Clairvaux.[1] *But as he showed great reluctance to fulfill his promise, St. Bernard wrote the following letter to encourage him. But the warning and encouragement of the saint fell on deaf ears, for Thomas died suddenly, his promise still unfulfilled.*

To Thomas, his dear son, from Bernard as to a son.

WHAT need of words? A fervent spirit and eager heart cannot be expressed by the tongue alone. I need your presence also to tell me of your good will. If you were present

---

1. *Thomas iste Ordini Cisterciensi in Claravalle sese devoverat* . . . , so Mabillon. But surely not as Eales translates: 'Thomas had taken the vows of the Cistercian Order at Clairvaux'.

you could both explain yourself and know me better. Even now we are tied to each other by a mutual debt, I by a debt of faithful care for you and you by the debt of humble obedience to me. I wish you to apply to yourself and to prove in me that saying of the Only-Begotten: 'The works which the Father has given me to perfect, they give testimony of me'. So in truth, even so the Spirit of the Son bears testimony to our spirit that we too are sons of God when he lifts us from the works of death and bestows upon us the works of life. It is not from the leaves or the blossom but from the fruit that we can tell a good tree from a bad, for it is 'by their fruits that ye shall know them'. It is therefore by their works that the sons of God are distinguished from the 'sons of unbelief', and it is by works that you too will prove the sincerity of your own desire and put mine to the test.

2. I long for and, indeed, require your promised and expected presence here. Do you ask why? It is not because I look for any natural satisfaction in your presence, but simply because I wish both to profit you and profit by you. The nobility of your birth, the strength of your body, the comeliness of your appearance, the grace of your youth, your estates, mansion, and gorgeous furniture, the marks of your high station, and on the top of all this your worldly wisdom; all these are of the world, and the world loves its own. But for how long? Certainly not for ever, since the world will not last for ever, but not even for a long time. The world will not acknowledge all these things in you for long because you will not have them for long: the days of man are short. The world and its glory pass; and it will part with you before it passes. Why does this love, which you will so soon lose, please you so unboundedly? I love you for your own sake and not for the sake of your possessions, let these go to where they belong. Remember your promise and do not deny me any longer the satisfaction of your presence, I who love you so truly and will love you for ever. United by a pure love in life, we will not be separated

in death. Those things which I desire in you, or rather for you, do not belong to the body, they are not subject to time, so they do not fail with the body or pass with time, rather when the body has been laid aside the joy of them increases and they last for ever. They have nothing in common with the things I have enumerated above, things with which the world, but not the Father, has endowed you. These all vanish at the hour of death, if they have not vanished before.

3. It is the best part which will never be taken away. And what is this best part? 'Eye has not seen, ear has not heard, nor has it entered into the heart of man to conceive it.' A man who lives as a man or, to speak more clearly, a man who complies with flesh and blood, knows nothing of it, because flesh and blood do not disclose it, but only God by his Spirit. The merely animal man is never admitted to this secret, he does not perceive the things that are of God. Blessed are those who hear, 'I have called you friends, because all things, whatsoever I have heard from the Father, I have made known to you'. How wicked is the world, which only favours its friends so as to make them the enemies of God and accordingly unworthy of the counsel of the blessed. Clearly the world which wishes to be your friend is the enemy of God.[1] And if the servant knows not what his lord does, how much less does the enemy! Moreover the friend of the Bridegroom stands and is so overjoyed at the voice of the Bridegroom that he says: 'How my heart melted at the sound of his voice!' And so the friend of the world is excluded from the counsels of the friends of God, who have not received the spirit of this world but the Spirit of God that they may know what God has given them. I praise thee, my Father, because thou hast hidden these things from the wise and prudent and revealed them to children. Even so, Father, because it seemed good in thy sight, not because they have deserved it of themselves. For all have sinned and are destitute of thy glory, so that thou sendeth thy Spirit, without their deserving it,

1. *Plane enim qui amicus vult esse tuus, inimicus Dei constituitur.*

crying in the hearts of these, thy adopted sons, 'Abba, Father'. Those who are led by thy Spirit are thy sons, and will not be left out of the counsels of their Father. Within them they have dwelling the Spirit which searches even the hidden things of God. Of what could they be ignorant who are taught all things by the unction of God?

4. Woe to you, children of this world, foolish in your prudence, knowing nothing of the life-giving spirit, nor sharing in the counsels which well up only between the Father and the Son and him to whom the Son will reveal them. For 'who has known the mind of the Lord or who has been his counsellor?' Not indeed no one ever, but only someone sometimes, only those who can truthfully say: 'The only-begotten Son who is in the bosom of the Father, he hath declared to us'. Woe to the world for its clamour! The Only-Begotten cries among the people like an angel of great counsel: 'Who hath ears to hear let him hear'. And since he can find no ears worthy to hear the secret which the Father has imparted to him, he disguises it under parables for the crowd, that hearing they may not hear and seeing they may not understand. But to his friends he whispers apart: 'To you it has been given to know the mysteries of the Kingdom of God', and he also says to them: 'Fear not, little flock, for it has pleased your Father to give you a kingdom'. And who are these friends of his? Without doubt those 'whom he foreknew and predestined to be made conformable to the image of his Son, so that he might be the firstborn among many brethren'. This is his great and secret counsel. The Lord knows who are his own, but what was hitherto only known to God has now been revealed to men. He does not deign to allow others to share in this great mystery, unless they are those whom he has known and foreordained to be his own. Those whom he has foreordained, he has also called. Who else indeed would be admitted to the counsels of God but those who are called? And 'those whom he has called, them he has also justified'. Over them the Sun rises, not the sun which is seen to shine every day

on the good and bad alike, since only to those who are called is the prophetic promise made: 'Unto you that fear my name the Sun of Justice shall rise'. While the sons of unbelief stay out in the darkness, the sons of light go out from the power of darkness into this new light, providing they can truthfully say to God: 'We partake with all them that fear thee'. Do you see how fear must go first so that justification may follow? Perhaps it can be said that we are called by fear and justified by love. Finally: 'The just man lives by faith', the faith surely 'that worketh by charity'.

5. And so let the sinner hear and be afraid and approach the Sun of Justice to be enlightened and see what he has to love. What is that? 'Those who fear the Lord know no beginning or end of his mercy'. They know no beginning on account of their being preordained, and they know no end because their blessedness shall never end. The first has no beginning and the latter has no end. Those whom he has foreordained from the beginning, he makes blessed without end, their calling and justification, at least in the case of adults, coming between. Thus from the rising up of the Sun of Justice, the great mystery concerning predestination and beatification, hidden from before the beginning of time, begins at last to come forth from the depths of eternity, while each one who is called by fear and justified by love dares to believe that he also may be among the blessed, knowing that 'whom he has justified, them also he has glorified'. What then? The soul hears her call and is struck by fear. She then feels herself to be justified and is swamped with love. Does she doubt that she is also to be glorified? Initiated and then lifted up, can she despair of the consummation? If fear of the Lord, in which I have said the call consists, is the beginning of wisdom, what else is the love of God but progress in wisdom, the love, that is, which for the time being comes from faith and is the source of our justification? If this is so, what else but consummation in wisdom is that glorification from the divine and deifying vision which we hope for in the end? 'So one depth

makes answer to another amid the roar of the floods', when in terror of his judgements, that immense eternity and eternal immensity, of whose wisdom none can make a reckoning, leads in terror of his judgments but with wonderful goodness and power the corrupt and inscrutable heart of man into his eternal light.

6. For example, let us suppose a man in the world still held by love of the world and the flesh; a man carrying the image of an earthly man, still resting in earthly things. Who, but one himself sitting in the same shadow of death, could not see that such a man is wrapped about with horrible darkness? No sun of salvation has yet shone on him, no interior inspiration bears testimony to him of his eternal salvation. But if at some time the mercy of heaven should graciously regard him and send down on him the spirit of compunction, so that he comes to his senses with a groan, changes his life, calls upon God, and decides in future to live for God and not the world, would not such a one, in this undeserved visitation of heavenly light, in this sudden change of the right hand of the Most High, see himself to be no longer a son of wrath but of grace? Would not such a one, having experienced in himself the effect of divine goodness which had hitherto been so hidden from him that he could not know whether he was worthy of hatred or love, but seemed by the witness of his life to be worthy of hatred, for darkness was over the face of the abyss, would not such a one appear to have been rescued from a most deep and dark pit of horrible ignorance, and plunged into a pleasant region bright with eternal light?

7. Then at last the darkness is, as it were, divided from the light when the sinner is enlightened by the Sun of Justice, casts aside the works of darkness and puts on the arms of light; when he who by his former life and conscience was doomed as a true son of perdition to the eternal flames, draws breath in such a great visitation of the day star from on high and begins, beyond all expectation, to glory in the hopes of the children of God. As

he is ravished by the near prospect of this vision, gazing upon it in the light which has newly come to him, he cries: 'The sun of thy favour shines out clear above us; thou hast made me glad at heart'. 'O Lord, what is man that thou shouldst notice him, or the son of man that thou shouldst give heed to him?' Already, O loving Father, that most vile worm, worthy of everlasting hatred, is confident that it is loved because it feels that it loves: or rather because it divines that it is loved, it is ashamed not to love in return. Now in thy light, O Light Inaccessible, it becomes clear what good things thou hast had in store for that miserable thing man even when he was evil. He loves indeed, but not without reason, for he knows that he is loved without desert; he loves without end because he knows that he was loved before the beginning of time. A great secret which from all eternity has remained hidden in the bosom of eternity has now been revealed in the light of day for the consolation of the wretched: God does not want the death of a sinner but that he should be converted and live. As a witness, O man, to this secret you have the Spirit which justifies testifying to your own spirit, that you, even you, are a son of God. See the design of God in the justification of yourself and declare and say: 'Thy decrees are my counsellors!' Your present justification is both a revelation of the divine plan and a preparation for future glory. Or rather predestination itself is the preparation for it and justification the approach to it. It is said: 'Do penance, for the kingdom of heaven is at hand'. Now hear how predestination is the prepa- ration for it: 'Possess you the kingdom prepared for you from the foundation of the world'.

8. Let no one who loves God have any doubt that God loves him. The love of God for us precedes our love for him and it also follows it. How could he be reluctant to love us in return for our love when he loved us even when we did not love him? I say he loved us. As a pledge of his love you have the Spirit, and you have a faithful witness to it in Jesus, Jesus crucified. A double and irrefutable argument of God's love for us. Christ

died and so deserved our love. The holy Spirit works upon us and makes us love him.[1] Christ has given us a reason for loving himself, the Spirit the power to love him. The one commends his great love to us, the other gives it. In the one we see the object of our love, by the other we have the power to love. The former provides the occasion for our love, the latter provides the love itself. How shameful it would be to look with ungrateful eyes upon the Son of God dying for us! But this could easily be were the Spirit lacking. 'The charity of God is poured forth in our hearts by the Holy Ghost who is given to us'. Loved we love in return, and loving we deserve to be still more loved. If while we were still his enemies we were reconciled to God by the death of his Son, how much more being reconciled shall we be saved through his life. Why so? 'He that spared not even his own son, but delivered him up for us all, how hath he not also, with him, given us all things?'

9. Since then we hold a twofold token of our salvation, the double pouring forth of Blood and Spirit; neither avails without the other. The Spirit is not given to any but those who believe in Christ crucified, and faith avails not unless it is actuated by love. But love is the gift of the Holy Spirit. And if the second Adam (I mean Christ) became not only a living soul, but also a quickening spirit, by one dying and by the other raising the dead, how can that which died in him avail me without that which gives life? 'The flesh profiteth nothing, it is the spirit that quickeneth'. And what else does quickeneth mean but justifieth? Since sin is the death of the soul (for the 'soul that sinneth, the same shall die') the life of it is undoubtedly righteousness, for 'the just man lives by faith'. And who is just, but he who pays his debt of love to God who loves him? And this can never be except the Spirit reveal by faith the eternal designs of God for his future salvation. And this revelation is nothing else but an infusion of spiritual grace through which, while mortifying the works of the flesh, a man is made ready for the king-

1. *Spiritus afficit et facit amari.*

dom which flesh and blood cannot possess. He receives at the
same time and in the same Spirit both the audacity to believe
himself loved and the power to love in return, so that he should
not be loved without return.

10. This is that holy and secret counsel which the Son receives in the Holy Spirit from the Father, and communicates
to his own whom he knows, by the same Spirit, justifying them
by communicating it, and communicating it by justifying them.
Thus a man is justified so that he begins to know himself even
as he is known; that is, he begins to experience something of
his future blessedness, as it has lain hidden from all eternity in
God who foreordained it, to appear all the more plainly in him
when he confers it. And for this great blessing which he has
received let him rejoice for the time being in hope, but not yet
in security. How pitiful on the other hand are those who as yet
hold no token of their call to such a joyful council of the just!
'What credence, O Lord, to such news as ours!' Oh that they
may be wise and understand. But except they believe they shall
not understand.

11. O unhappy and foolhardy lovers of this world, you too
have your counsels, but they are far apart from the counsels of
the just! Scale adheres to scale, there is no vent between you.[1]
You too, I say, even you, O impious ones, share a counsel together, but one against God and against Christ. For if, according
to Scripture, 'piety is the worship of God', it follows that whoever loves the world more than God is guilty of idolatry and
impiety in that he worships and serves creatures rather than
the Creator. But between the counsels of the impious and those
of the righteous there is fixed a great gulf. For as the righteous
keep far aloof from the counsel and council of evildoers, so the
wicked shall not rise to plead their cause, nor sinners have any
part in the reunion of the just. For there is a counsel of the just,
a grateful shower, which God has kept for his chosen, a truly
secret counsel, coming down nevertheless like dew onto fleece.

1. *Squama squamæ conjungiture, et non est spiraculum in vobis.*

It is a sealed fountain of living waters of which no stranger may partake. It is the glory of the Sun of Justice which rises only on those who fear God.

12. When the Prophet adverts to the impious who remain in their aridity and blindness and are not privy to the rains and light of the just, he mocks at them and points them out as persons wrapt in gloom, confused and overcast, saying: 'Here is the people who will not listen to the voice of God'. O wretched people, you will not say with David: 'Let me listen to the voice of the Lord God within me'. You pour yourselves out on the vanities and follies, and will not listen to the intimate and most excellent words of truth. 'Great ones of the world, will your hearts be always hardened? Will you never cease setting your hearts on shadows, following a lie?' Will you always remain deaf to the voice of truth, ignoring the counsel of God who bears peace in his mind and speaks words of peace to his people, his holy ones, those whose hearts are turned unto him? 'Now you are clean', he said, 'by reason of what I have spoken to you.' And accordingly those who do not hear what he has said to them are not clean.

13. But do you, dearest son, if you would prepare the ear of your heart to hear the voice of God, sweeter than honey and the honeycomb, fly exterior cares, so that, with your spiritual sense free and unimpeded, you can say with Samuel: 'Speak, Lord, for thy servant heareth'. This voice is not heard in the market place nor does it sound in public. A secret counsel demands a secret hearing. Without doubt it will give you great joy and delight if you lend a prudent ear to it. Abraham was commanded to go forth from his country and from his kinsfolk that he might see and possess the land of the living. Jacob when he left his brother and home crossed the Jordan and was received by the embraces of Rachel. Joseph, after he had been sold in secret and taken from his father and home, ruled in Egypt. The Church is commanded to forget her nation and the house of her fathers, so that her beauty may delight the king.

The child Jesus was sought by his parents among their friends and relations, but he was not found there. So do you also fly your brethren if you would find your salvation. Fly from the midst of Babylon, fly from the sword of the North wind. In the words of the Prophet, I am ready 'to meet you with bread' when you are in flight. You call me your abbot: for the time being I will not refuse that title for the sake of complaisance. Complaisance, I say, not that I may demand it from you but that I may show it to you, just as 'the Son of man came not to be ministered unto, but to minister and to give his life a redemption for many'. If you deem me worthy, accept me as your fellow disciple whom you have chosen as your abbot. One master in Christ we will both have, and so let this letter end with his name, for 'the end of the law is Christ unto the justice of everyone that believeth'.

[110]

To Thomas of Saint Omer, after he had broken his promise to become a Monk

To his dearest son, Thomas, that he may walk in the spirit of fear, from Brother Bernard, styled Abbot of Clairvaux.

YOU do well to admit the debt you have incurred by your promise and to admit your guilt in delaying the payment of it. You must consider not only what you have promised but also to whom you have promised it. I too remember well your making the promise, but although you made it in my presence you did not make it to me and I claim no share in it. So you need not fear that I, who was only the witness and not the Lord of it, shall upbraid you for your futile delay in the fulfilment of it. I saw and was glad; and now it only remains for me to pray that my joy may be complete, but this will only be when you have honoured it. You set yourself a limit which you ought not to have passed. You have passed it, but that is not my responsibility: 'To your own Lord you stand or fall'. But because the danger of your position is so menacing I have decided, not indeed to threaten or reprove you, but to advise you, and this only in so far as you can take it in good part. If you hear me, well and good; if you do not, it will not be for me to judge you; there is one who will see and judge, even the Lord who judges us all. What is especially a matter for fear and remorse is that you have lied, not to man, but to God. You have asked me to spare your blushes before men and I will do so, but is your shamelessness to be left unashamed before God? Why are you afraid of what men might think of your conduct and yet not afraid of God's frown? 'Perilous is his frown for wrongdoers.' Are you more afraid of the reproaches of men than the torments of hell? Do you fear the tongue of flesh and scorn the sword that smites all flesh? Are these the fine principles which you tell me you are acquiring in your pursuit of knowledge, the knowledge you follow with so much love and zeal that you do not care if the fulfilment of your promise is impeded?

2. I ask you, what sort of tribute to virtue is this, what sort of advance in knowledge, what sort of result is this of your erudition, to fear where there is no cause to fear and yet to have no fear of the Lord? How much better for you to learn Jesus, Jesus crucified. This, of course, is not an easy knowledge to acquire, save for one who is crucified to the world. You deceive yourself, my son, if you think you can learn from the masters of this world what is a gift of God and can be obtained only by those who follow Christ and scorn the world. This is a knowledge imparted, not by books, but by grace; not by the letter but by the Spirit; not by mere book learning but by the practice of the commandments of God. 'Sow for yourself in right doing and reap in mercy and be enlightened with the light of knowledge.' You see the light of knowledge cannot

properly be acquired unless there first enter the soul the seed of righteousness from which may come the grain of life and not the straw of vainglory. Do you who have not yet sown for yourself in right doing nor yet gathered your sheaves of mercy, fancy that you are following true knowledge? Perhaps you fancy that the knowledge which puffs up is true knowledge? If so you err stupidly 'by always spending and having no bread to eat, always toiling and never a full belly'. Come to your senses, I implore you, and consider that this extra year which you have permitted yourself at the cost of offending God, is not at all a year acceptable to him, but a seed-bed of disunion, an incentive to wrath, a feeding ground for apostasy, a year which will extinguish the spirit, impede grace, and induce the tepidity which God vomits from his mouth.

3. Alas, it seems to me that you are led by the same spirit as your namesake Thomas, one time Provost of Beverley. He, like you, promised himself with all his heart to our Order and this house; then, like you, he began to make delays, and little by little to grow cold until a sudden and terrible death snatched him away while he was still a complete secular and in bad faith, a double child of hell. May the all-merciful God save him, if possible from the terrible consequences! The letter which I wrote to him in vain still exists. By doing what I could to warn him of what must soon befall him, I only succeeded in saving myself from any responsibility for him. If he had only listened to me, how happy he would have been! But he equivocated and I am innocent of his blood. Yet I am not satisfied by this. Although I am not to blame in the matter, yet I am impelled by the charity which seeketh not its own to lament for the parlous state in which he died by his own fault. How mysterious are the judgements of God! How fearful his counsels for the sons of men! Here is one to whom he gave his Spirit, but only to take it away again, so that thereby he sinned a sin beyond all measure. Grace was given to him and for this his transgression was all the greater. Yet this was not the fault of the giver, but of

him who rejected the gifts and so added sin to sin. Using ill the freedom which was his he saddened the free Spirit by his own free choice, he scorned the grace which was given him, and failed to put into effect the inspiration of God, so as to be able to say: 'The grace of God has not been rendered void in me'.

4. If you are wise you will wash your hands in the blood of the sinner by learning from his folly and taking pains quickly to escape from the pit of perdition and release me from the terrible fear I have for you. I confess that I feel your turning away just as if my heart were being torn from my body, for you are very dear to me and I regard you with all the affection of a father. For this reason every time I think of you I feel a sword of anxiety pierce my soul, and I feel it all the more bitterly when I consider that you yourself have no fear at all in the matter. Of such as you it was written: 'For when they shall say peace and security, then shall sudden destruction come upon them'. I see many fearful things threatening you while you delay to come to your senses, for I have had much experience and only wish that you could profit by it too. Believe me who have had experience, believe me who am fond of you, and understand that because of my experience I am not deceived, and because of my affection for you I would not deceive you.

[111]

To the distinguished youth, Geoffrey of Péronne
and his companions

Geoffrey of Péronne was one of a band of noble youths whom St. Bernard converted when he was in Flanders. They are said to have numbered thirty in all.

To his dear son Geoffrey and all his companions, the spirit of counsel and strength, from Bernard, styled Abbot of Clairvaux.

THE news of your conversion has resounded abroad edifying many and rejoicing the whole Church. 'The heavens rejoice, the earth is glad' and every tongue praises God. 'How the earth shook, how the sky broke at the coming of God', pouring down more copiously than usual the gracious shower that God keeps for his chosen. Never more will the Passion of Christ appear of no effect in you, as in the many 'children of unbelief'. While they put off their conversion from day to day they are snatched away by an unexpected death and in the twinkling of an eye they are plunged into the pit. Like a tree in spring the cross has burst into flower, the cross on which the Lord of glory hung not only for the Gentiles, but also for the scattered sons of God that he might gather them together in one. It is he and no other who has gathered you together, he who loves you so well has gathered you as the precious fruit of his cross, as the worthy reward of the blood he shed. If the angels of heaven rejoice over the conversion of one sinner, what will they do over the conversion of so many who were sinners too, who for their very renown in the world, for their birth and youth, were such a bad example to so many? I read that God did not choose 'many noble, many wise, or many mighty' but now contrary to the usual rule he has converted by his wonderful power a whole band of such. They have deemed the glory of this world worthless; they have trampled on the flower of their youth; they have held their noble lineage of no account; they have considered worldly wisdom foolishness; they have defied flesh and blood; their natural affection for relations and friends they have renounced; all the privileges, honours, and dignities of their position they have treated as things no better than dung that they might gain Christ. If I thought you had done all this of yourselves, I would praise you; but it is the finger of God, the power of his right hand that has done it. It is that best of gifts, that most perfect of gifts, which has come without doubt from the Father of lights. Therefore it is right that we should sing our praises to him who alone does marvellous things, who has seen that the copious redemption which he has to offer has not been wasted in you.

2. What remains for you to do, my dear sons, but to endeavour to put your praiseworthy intention into effect. See that you persevere, for perseverance is the only virtue which is crowned. Do not be of those who say 'yes' one minute and 'no' the next, but true sons of your heavenly Father 'in whom there is no change nor shadow of alteration'. May you be 'transformed into the same image, going from glory to glory as by the spirit of the Lord', being ever watchful that you do not become fickle, unstable, wavering. It is written: 'A doubleminded man is inconstant in all his ways', and again: 'Woe to the man who will go two ways about it to enter the land of his desires'. I congratulate you, my dear sons, and myself also, for I have heard that I am deemed worthy to help you in your good purpose. I will do what I can to advise you and I promise to help you as I am able. If I seem necessary to you or at least if you deem me worthy, I shall not grudge the trouble and I shall try not to fail you. If it should be the will of heaven, I will earnestly take this burden on my shoulders, although they are already bowed with care. Joyfully and, as the saying is, with open arms I will receive you as fellow citizens of the saints,

servants of God's household. How gladly will I not, in the
words of the Prophet, 'bring out bread' to those who fly from
the sword; water to those who thirst. I leave the rest for my or
rather your Geoffrey to say. Whatever he tells you in my name
you can regard as coming from me.

[112]

To the parents of the afore-mentioned Geoffrey, to console them

*This fine letter expresses well Saint Bernard's attitude towards
the monastic life.*

IF God is making your son his own, as well as yours, so
that he may become even richer, even more noble, even more
distinguished and, what is better than all this, so that from being a sinner he may become a saint, what do either you or he
lose? But he must prepare himself for the kingdom which has
been prepared for him from the beginning of the world. He
must spend the short time which remains of his life on earth
with us in order to scrape off the filth of secular life and shake
off the dust of the world, so as to be fit to enter the heavenly
mansion. If you love him you will surely rejoice because he is
going to the Father, and such a Father! It is true that he is going
to God, but you are not losing him, on the contrary, through
him you are gaining many sons. All of us at Clairvaux or of
Clairvaux will receive him as a brother and you as our parents.
    2. Knowing that he is tender and delicate perhaps you are
afraid for his health under the harshness of our life. But this is
the sort of fear of which the Psalm speaks when it says: 'Fear
unmans them where they have no cause to fear'. Have comfort,
do not worry, I shall look after him like a father and he will be

to me a son until the Father of mercies, the God of all consolation, shall receive him from my hands. Do not be sad about
your Geoffrey or shed any tears on his account, for he is going
quickly to joy and not to sorrow. I will be for him both a
mother and a father, both a brother and a sister. I will make
the crooked path straight for him and the rough places smooth.
I will temper and arrange all things that his soul may advance
and his body not suffer.[1] He will serve the Lord with joy and
gladness, 'his song will be of the Lord's, for great is the glory
of the Lord'.[2]

[118]

To a Nun of the Convent of St. Mary
of Troyes

I HAVE been told you are thinking of leaving your
convent under the pretext of seeking a harder way of life, and
that although you will not listen to your Reverend Mother and
sisters trying every argument to dissuade you and every means
to prevent you from doing this, you are yet prepared to take
my advice in the belief that whatever I suggest would be for
the best. You had done better to have chosen someone more
experienced to counsel you on this matter, but as you have

1. . . . *ut spiritus proficiat*—a reminiscence undoubtedly of the *Holy Rule*
of St. Benedict, where he says of the monk who has been ordained priest
that he should not make his priesthood an occasion for pride but *magis ac
magis in Deum proficiat*: 'advance ever more and more in God'.

2. Cf. *Holy Rule*, Prologue. 'We have, therefore, to establish a school of
the Lord's service, in the institution of which we hope to order nothing that
is hard or rigorous. But if anything be somewhat strictly laid down, according to the dictates of equity, for the amendment of vices and preservation of
charity, do not therefore fly in dismay from the way of salvation, whose
beginning cannot but be strait. But as we go forward in our life and faith,
we shall with hearts enlarged and unspeakable sweetness of love run in the
way of God's commandments.'

preferred myself I will not hide from you what I think best. I have been turning this plan of yours over in my mind ever since I heard of it and I am still puzzled as to your motives. It might be that you are inspired by zeal for God, in which case your plan would be excusable. But all the same I do not see how it can be wise for you to follow it. Do you ask why? 'Is it not wise', you say, 'to fly riches, crowded towns, and delicate meats? Would not my modesty be safer in a desert where I could live in peace with a few others or even quite alone, so as to please him alone to whom I have pledged myself?' By no means. For anyone wishing to lead a bad life the desert supplies ample opportunity. The woods afford cover, and solitude assures silence. No one can censure the evil no one sees. Where there is no fear of blame the tempter approaches more boldly, and evil is committed with greater freedom. In a convent, if you would do good there is no one to stop you; if you would do evil, you are not able. Soon everyone would know about it, it would soon be blamed and corrected, just as on the other hand all would admire, respect, and imitate the good they saw. Therefore you see, my daughter, that in a convent greater glory awards your deserts, and a more prompt correction your faults, for amongst others you set an example by a good life and give offence by a bad one.

2. But I will take away from you all excuse for error by the distinction made in the Gospel. Either you are one of the foolish virgins (if indeed you are a virgin) or you are one of the wise. If you are one of the foolish, the convent is necessary for you; if you are one of the wise, you are necessary for the convent. If you are one of the wise and well tried virgins, the reform which has been lately introduced into your convent and praised on all sides would be much discredited and weakened were you to leave, which is what I fear. It would be said that had the convent been good you would never have left. But if you are known to be one of the foolish virgins and depart, we will say that you left because being evil you could not live up

to the high standards of the convent and had gone off to seek somewhere where you could live as you pleased. And there would be some reason for this inasmuch as before the reform of your house you never, so I am told, mentioned this plan of yours, but only when Religion began to flourish there did you suddenly become holy and, fired by an unexpected fervour, begin to think of the desert. I recognize, my daughter, I recognize in this, and only wish you could do so too, the poison of the serpent, the guile of the deceiver, the imposture of the trickster.[1] The wolf lurks in the wood. If you, a little sheep, penetrate the shadows of the wood alone, you are offering yourself as a prey to the wolf. But listen to me, daughter, listen to a faithful counsel. Whether you are a saint or a sinner do not cut yourself off from the flock or you will fall a prey to the wolf and there will be none to rescue you. If you are a saint, try to edify your sisters by your example. If you are a sinner, do not pile one sin on the top of another but do penance where you are, for if you leave your convent you will incur great danger, as I have tried to show, give scandal to your sisters, and set the tongues of many wagging against you.

[121]

To Beatrice, a Noble and Religious Lady

I MARVEL at the zeal of your devotion and the strength of your affection. My good lady, what can I mean to you? Why are you so anxious for me? If I were related to you by any tie of blood, if I were your son or nephew, I could regard your many kindnesses, your frequent messages, and the

1. *versipellis astutiam.* When an adjective, as we assume it is here, *versipellis* means 'that changes its form or shape', as the devil is apt to pose as an angel of light. On the other hand, the word may be used as a substantive in which case it can mean 'were-wolf' or one that can change himself into a wolf.

innumerable and daily marks of your esteem, as the fulfilment of a duty and no matter for surprise. But since I know you only as a great lady by birth[1] and not as my mother, it is no wonder that I wonder, it would only be wonderful if I were able to wonder enough. Who of my relations and friends show the same care for me? Who ever even enquires after my health? To my friends, relations, and neighbours, 'I am discarded like a broken pitcher'. Only you never forget me. You ask after the state of my health, about the journey from which I have just returned, and the monks whom I have moved to another place. To all of which I briefly reply that 'from a wilderness, from fearful desert spaces' the brethren have come unto an abundance of everything, of buildings and friends; into a fertile land and a dwelling place of great beauty. I left them very contented and peaceful and came home myself also contented and at peace, except that for a few days, but in no small way, my fever returned and I become so ill that I thought I should die. But God had mercy on me and I soon got over it so that now I feel stronger and better than I did before the journey.

[133]

To Louis 'Le Gros', King of France

On November 8th, 1134, *Pope Innocent promulgated a bull, convoking a Council at Pisa for May* 26th *of the following year. For some reason, Louis 'le Gros' was not at all favourably disposed towards the project. It is not easy to understand why this was so. He may have been jealous of the Emperor Lothair, or his* amour propre *may have been injured in some way by the Pope. In any case he forbade the French bishops to attend*

---

1. *Nunc autem cum genere tantum dominam, non matrem te cognoscamus.* Eales has: 'But as, in common with the rest of mankind, we recognize in you only a great lady, and not a mother'.

the Council on grounds that the heat would be too great. This
called forth the following letter from St. Bernard, and Louis
was sufficiently mollified to withdraw his ban on the Council.

To the most excellent Louis, King of France, and to his beloved
wife and children, Bernard, styled Abbot of Clairvaux, sends
health from the King of kings and Lord of lords.

THE kingdoms of this world and their prerogatives
will certainly only remain sound and unimpaired for their
lords so long as they do not contravene the divine ordinances
and dispositions. Why, my lord, does your wrath rage against
the elect of God, whom your Highness has also received and
chosen as a father for yourself, as well as a Samuel for your
son?[1] Your royal fury is arming itself, not against a stranger,
but against yourself and your family. How well do the Scriptures say: 'The anger of man worketh not the righteousness of
God', for it not only renders you insensible to the damage you
are doing to your own interests and honour, but it also often
blinds you to what everyone else can see is dangerous to yourself. A Council has been convoked. What is there in this to detract from your royal honour or menace your royal interests?
There it will be commemorated and remembered how you,
with a ready and special devotion to the universal Church,
were the first of all the kings, or among the first, to set forth as
a Christian in strong defence of your mother against the rabid
fury of her persecutors. There the thanks which are due to you
will be rendered by the assembled multitude. There prayers
will be offered up for you and yours by a thousand holy men.
2. No one is ignorant that a council of all the bishops is
most necessary at this time, unless it be some hard-hearted
individual who pays no attention to the straightened circumstances of the Church. You say the heat will be too great. We
are not made of ice! Or is it that our hearts are frozen within

1. A reference to the consecration of Louis *le Jeune* at Rheims in 1131.

us, so that, in the words of the Prophet, 'there is none who care for the ruin of Joseph'. But of this another time. Now I, who of your subjects am the least in dignity, though not in fidelity, tell you that it is not desirable for you to try and hinder such a great and necessary good as this Council will be. I have very good reasons for saying this which would make the matter quite clear to you, and I would state them more fully were I not convinced that I have already said enough for a wise man such as you are. But if the Apostolic See has, in its severity, issued decrees which have deservedly troubled your royal serenity, then all your loyal subjects who are present at the Council will endeavor with all their power to have them changed or revoked in accordance with your honour. Amongst these I too will not hesitate to do anything I can.

[137]

To Pope Innocent

This letter and the five that follow were written during the papal schism when Gregory, Cardinal Deacon of S. Angelo, and Peter Leonis, Cardinal Priest of St. Calixtus, divided Christendom between them in their struggle for the See of Peter. Saint Bernard threw himself into the scales on the side of Gregory who was undoubtedly the better man of the two and his claim was unquestionably the stronger. But it was Bernard who saved him and won the world to his side.

To his most loving father and lord, the Supreme Pontiff Innocent, the humble devotion of Brother Bernard.

THE opposition of Cremona has hardened, their prosperity is their undoing; the Milanese have become arrogant, their over-weening self-confidence deceives them. I am un-

done and my efforts are frustrated by those who put their trust
in horses and chariots. I was sadly leaving when I received some
consolation from you. Although the trials I endure for the sake
of Christ are many, so also are the consolations I receive through
him. When I received your welcome letter my heart was gladdened by the assurance it gave of your safety, of the misfortunes of the enemy, and of the successes of our allies. But when
I came to the sad conclusion, my joy was a little dampened.
Who would not fear your anger? I admit that it is reasonable,
and therefore all the more to be feared. My opinion is that
what has not yet been accomplished, should be done; but in
God's good time. Then you can just as readily do what you intend, and perhaps with less risk. By intemperate action, how
soon could all you have accomplished with these people by the
mercy of God, and at the cost of so much labour on the part of
yourself and your servants, be reduced to nothing! And it
would be surprising if such an action were to please him who
exalts mercy over justice. Unhappy the lot of that bishop who
has been transferred to Ur of the Chaldees from a sort of paradise, 'to have dragons for his brothers, and ostriches for his company'. What can he do? He would like to obey you, but the
beasts of Ephesus bare their teeth at him. Very prudently he is
trying to disguise his sentiments for the time being, but only to
incur thereby the very much more fearful wrath of yourself.
On all sides he is beset by difficulties; unless he should find it
more satisfactory to be without a people than without a lord,
since he very properly prefers the favour of his Pope to his See
of Milan. Can you doubt his loyalty? If any evil-minded person
has tried to suggest to you the contrary, he only proves himself disloyal by spitefully persecuting with venomous tongue
a man of excellent character. I implore you, most loving father,
to have consideration for this most loyal servant of yours, for
the work that has only just been started, for this newly planted
tree; I beg you to spare the people who have only lately at-
tached themselves to you and to remember the benefits which,

as you rightly say, you have only recently conferred upon them. Remember, dear lord, those words of your Lord: 'I have been coming to look for fruit on this fig tree for three years, and cannot find any'. You have waited scarcely three months, and yet you are already preparing the axe! If you had waited already three years, we would still be entitled to expect a faithful servant of the Lord to wait yet a fourth. Therefore I say: Let it be for this year and permit him to whom you have entrusted the sterile ground of Milan, to dig it about with the spade of penance, to dung it with his tears, so that he can induce it to bring forth fruit.

[140]

To the People of Milan

The Milanese, after having been reconciled to Pope Innocent, began again to waver in their allegiance. In this letter the Abbot of Clairvaux exhorts them to loyalty and reminds them of the unfortunate results of their last rebellion. The letter is of note for the Saint's clear exposition of the claims of the Holy See. However much Bernard might criticise the actions and person of any Pope he never wavered in his support of the office. Flattery was impossible to him, unorthodoxy unthinkable.

GOD has favoured you and the Roman Church has favoured you; he as a father, and she as a mother. What more could have been done for you, that has not been done already? You asked that eminent persons might be sent to you from the Curia for the honour of God and yourself, and it was done.[1] You asked that the unanimous election of your venerable Father should be confirmed, and it was done. You asked that

---

1. They had stirred up a schism after the deposition of their Archbishop Anselm. Guy of Pisa, Matthew of Alba, and Geoffrey, Bishop of Chartres, were the 'eminent persons' sent to reconcile her to the Holy See.

your See might be raised to metropolitan rank,[1] a thing which the canons deem unlawful, except in cases of great necessity, yet it was permitted. You asked that your citizens might be released from their bondage to the people of Piacenza, a thing which I am neither willing nor able to pass over, and it was done. In fact what petition which a daughter could reasonably have asked from a mother has there been even any delay in granting you? And to crown all, you will soon have the pallium. Now listen to me, renowned people, noble race, glorious city. Listen to me, I say, who love you and am anxious for your good. I speak the truth and do not lie to you. The Roman Church is very forbearing, but nevertheless she is powerful. I offer you good advice, worthy of attention: do not try too far her forbearance or you will feel her power.

2. But someone may say: I will show her due reverence, but nothing more. So be it, do as you say. If you show the reverence that is due to her, it will be a reverence without reserve, for the Apostolic See, by a unique privilege, is endowed with a full authority over all the Churches of the world. Anyone who withstands this authority sets his face against the decrees of God. She can, if she judge it expedient, set up new bishops where, hitherto, there have been none. Of those which already exist she can put down some and raise up others just as she thinks best; so that, if she deem it necessary, she can raise bishops to be archbishops or the reverse. She can summon churchmen, no matter how high and mighty they may be, from the ends of the earth and bring them to her presence, not just once or twice, but as often as she sees fit. Furthermore she is quick to punish disobedience if anyone should try to oppose her wishes. This you have discovered at your cost. What advantage did you derive from your last rebellion and opposition to which you were unfortunately incited by your false prophets?[2] The only re-

1. Milan had always been a Metropolitan See. But in punishment for schism it was reduced to a suffragan status for a time.
2. A reference to the schism and the consequent penalty.

sult was that, under your suffragans, you were deprived of all your power, honour, and glory. Who was able to stand up for you against the most just severity of the Apostolic See when, provoked by your excesses, it determined to deprive you of your ancient privileges and cut off your members? And even to-day you would be lying shamed and stripped had not the Apostolic See been merciful rather than firm with you. But now, were you to provoke her again, none could save you from far greater penalties. So be careful that you do not suffer a relapse, because, unless I am very mistaken, you would not find a remedy for the consequences so easily. If anyone should advise you, to obey in some things but not in others, you should know, since you have experienced once the severity of the Apostolic See, that he is either deceived or a deceiver. Do what I say, for I do not deceive you. Be humble and patient because God gives his grace to the humble and the patient inherit the land. Be careful to keep in the good graces of your mistress and mother now that you have returned to them, and try in future to please her, so that she may be pleased, not only to keep safe for you what she has given back, but even to add what she has not yet given.

[143]

To the Emperor Lothair

Another example of the Saint's fearless attitude toward those in high places.

I WONDER at whose instigation or advice you have allowed yourself to be so hoodwinked that a people who have, beyond any doubt, deserved of you a double honour, should have been treated quite to the contrary. I refer to the Pisans who were the first and, at one time, the only people to stand out in defence of the Empire. How much better it would have been if the royal wrath had flamed up against those who dared to take any occasion they could for attacking a bold and devoted people, at a moment too when they had set out in their thousands to encounter the tyrant, avenge the injury inflicted on their territory, and defend the interests of the imperial crown. I may very aptly apply to this people what was said of David, and ask you, 'What city of thine was ever so loyal as Pisa; one who ever does thy errands, obedient to thy commands?' These were the men who raised the siege of Naples and put to flight your only powerful enemy. These were the men who, wonderful to say, at one attack overcame Amalfi, Ravello, Scala, and Atrani, all rich and well protected cities, hitherto reputed impregnable by all who had tried to take them. How much more right and fitting, how much more reasonable and just it would have been had the territory of these loyal men been protected from hostile invasion, at any rate while they were engaged on these campaigns, both out of respect for the presence of the Supreme Pontiff whom they sheltered and served with great honour, and still do, when he was exiled from Rome, and in the interests of the Emperor in whose service they themselves were suffering banishment at that time? But the contrary has happened. Those who were hostile to you have met with favour from you, and those who were loyal have incurred your wrath. Perhaps you did not know. But now that you do know, it is vital and, what is more, only right and proper that you should change your attitude both in word and in deed towards these people. Let them receive from you in future the royal favour and liberality to which they are entitled. How well have the Pisans deserved of you, and how much they could still do for your interests! But a word is enough for a wise man.

[144]

To the Monks of Clairvaux

To his dear brethren at Clairvaux, monks, lay-brothers, and novices, a lasting joy in the Lord, from Brother Bernard.

YOUR own experience can tell you how much I am suffering. If my absence is irksome to you, you can be sure it is much more so to me. You are suffering from the absence of one person, but I am suffering from the absence of each and all of you, and this is something quite different and much more hard to bear. I cannot but have as many anxieties as I have sons at Clairvaux; I cannot but fear for the safety, and grieve for the absence of each one of you. This twofold grief will never leave me until I am restored to you, for you are part of my life. I have no doubt of what you are feeling for me, but I am only one person. You have only one reason for your grief, but I have many because I grieve for each of you. It is not only that I am obliged, for the time being, to live away from you, when even to be king would be but a sorry servitude without you; but also because I am forced to move in affairs that trouble the peace of my soul, and are not perhaps very compatible with my vocation.

2. As you know all this you ought to sympathize with me and not be angry at my delay which the needs of the Church render necessary. Indeed I hope that my presence here may not be necessary for very much longer, but you must pray that it may bring forth fruit. We must reckon as gain the loss we suffer, for it is all in the cause of God. He can easily make good, and more than make good, what we lose, for he loves us and is all-powerful. So we must be of good cheer for God is with us and, no matter how great the distance which seems to separate us, we can always be united to each other in him. Any of you who are well disposed, humble, reverent, zealous in read-

ing, attentive in prayer, fervent in fraternal charity, can be quite sure I am not far away from them. How could I not be present in spirit to those with whom I am thus united in heart and soul? But if there should be any one amongst you scheming, double-faced, grumbling, rebellious, insubordinate, restless and flighty, or unblushingly eating the bread of idleness, then even though I were present to such a one in body, yet my spirit would be far from him, in manner of life if not in material space, because he would be alienating himself from God.

3. In the meantime, dear brothers, serve God with fear until I return, so that the time may come at last when, delivered from the hand of the enemy, you may serve him without fear. Serve him with hope, because he is faithful in his promises. Serve him thankfully, because he has claims on our gratitude. He has every right to claim that we should devote our lives to him, if for no other reason than that he gave his own life for us. Who is better entitled to my life than he who gave his that I might live, than he who has purchased for me eternal life at the cost of his own? And whom can it be more necessary for me to serve, than him who threatens me with everlasting fires? But I serve him willingly because charity sets me free. To this willing service I exhort you, dearest brethren. Serve him with the 'charity which has no room for fear', for which nothing is too much, which looks for no reward, and which yet impels as nothing else can. No fear has the same power to spur us on, no reward can so attract us, no sense of obligation can demand so much of us. Let this be the bond between us, by this let me be ever present to you, especially at the hours of prayer, dearest brothers.

[145]

To the Cistercian Abbots in
Chapter at Cîteaux

As the following letter shows Bernard was all this while suf-
fering from his terrible gastric complaint that made it difficult
for him to retain his food and which was at last to bring him
to the grave.

WEAK in body and (God knows) anxious of heart I
write to you—a wretched man, born to labour, but yet your
brother. Would that I might merit to have the Holy Spirit, in
whose name you are come together, as my advocate to impress
upon your hearts the misfortunes from which I suffer, to por-
tray to your loving eyes the picture of myself sad and on my
knees before you. It is not my prayer that he should create in
you a new spirit of pity, for I know how habitual to you is that
virtue. But I do pray that you may understand from the bottom of your hearts how badly I need your pity. Then I am
sure tears would well up from the fount of your love, and that
with sighs and groans you would storm the gates of heaven so
that God should hear you and have pity on me and say: 'Go
back to your brothers, you shall die amidst your own and not
amidst strangers'. I am afflicted by so many labours and worries
that life itself often becomes a burden to me. To speak in a human way because of my great weakness, I desire to be spared
until I can return, so that I shall not die until I am with you.[1]
For the rest, dear brothers, 'amend your lives and your likings'
and determine and observe what is good, what is honest, and
what is wholesome; but above all endeavour to preserve unity
in the bonds of peace, and so the God of peace will be with you.

1. How ill the Abbot of Clairvaux was when he wrote these letters, we
have no means of ascertaining precisely; but we do know he lived an active
life for many years after writing them.

To the Monks of Clairvaux

MY soul is sorrowful and will not be comforted until I return to you. What consolation can there be for me in this evil hour, in this land of my exile? There is only yourselves. Wherever I am your dear memory never leaves me. But for this very reason your absence is all the more hard to endure. Unhappy am I to be doomed to an exile ever prolonged! In the words of the Prophet, 'Hard was my hurt to bear and these have added to it', who separate me from you. The exile from God, which we all endure while we are in the body, is hard enough to bear; but added to this I have to endure an exile from you which almost renders me impatient with my lot. To be involved for so long in the vanity of everything here, to be shut in by the rotten feculence of the body, to remain still bound by the bonds of death and still subject to sin, to be for so long without Christ, this is a continual affliction, a wearisome suspense. I had but one remedy for all this, a truly heaven-sent gift, and it was the sight, instead of God's glorious countenance which is as yet hidden from us, of you who are his holy sanctuary. From this it seemed an easy passage to that glorious sanctuary for which the Prophet sighs when he says: 'One request I have ever had of the Lord, let me claim it still, to dwell in the Lord's house my whole life long, gazing at the beauty of the Lord, haunting his sanctuary'.

2. What more can I say? How many times has not that one comfort of mine been frustrated! Unless I am mistaken this is the third time that my sons have been torn from me, weaned before their time. I am prevented from rearing the sons I have 'begotten in the Gospel'. I am obliged to leave my own to undertake the cares of others. I do not know which is the more painful: to be taken away from the former or to be saddled with the latter. O good Jesu, 'for very misery my strength ebbs

away, my frame is wasted, and my years are but sighs'. For me 'death is more welcome than life', only let it be amongst my own brethren, my own family, my own dear sons! As everyone knows, it is sweeter, safer, and more natural to die thus. It were a loving act 'to give me some respite, some cooling breath of comfort, before I go away and am known no more'. If it please my Lord, let my sons be allowed to close the eyes of their father, albeit I am not worthy to be their father; let them be present at my last end and console my passing away; if it should seem good to thee, let my soul be lifted up on the wings of their prayers to the company of the blessed; let my poor body be buried by their hands amongst the bodies of the poor. If I have found favour in thy eyes, grant this my one great desire for the sake of the prayers and merits of my brethren. Yet not my will, but thine be done. 'I do not wish to live as my own master or die as my own master.'

3. As I have told you of my sorrows, it is right that I should also mention my consolations. First, it is for God's sake that I am suffering all this grief and misfortune; it is in the cause of him for whom all things live. Whether I wish it or not, I cannot but live for him who has purchased my life by laying down his own; for the merciful judge who is able and willing to reward on that last day the sacrifices we have made for him. If I should fight his cause unwillingly, it will only be by his dispensation that I am doing so, and I shall be a wicked servant; but if willingly, then I shall have glory. It is this thought that gives me some respite amidst my troubles. And it is true to say that, for no merits of my own, he has given my labours a happy issue; I can tell from many things that 'the grace he has given me has not been without fruit', something of which you will probably know. I should like to tell you, for your consolation, how necessary my presence here is or was at this juncture, were it not that it would savour of boasting. It is better that you should learn this from others.

4. Sorrowfully and reluctantly, weak and sickly, and (I

must admit) ever haunted by the wan spectre of pale death, I have bowed before the urgent request of the Emperor, the command of the Apostolic See, the prayers of the Church and of secular princes, and suffered myself to be dragged to Apulia.[1] Pray for the peace of the Church, pray for my health, pray that I may see you again, live with you, and die with you. So live that your prayers may avail. Pressed for time and with ebbing strength, my words are broken by tears and sobs, as our dear brother Baldwin,[2] who has taken this letter down for me, can testify. He has been called to serve the Church in another sphere and in another post. Pray for him, because he is my only comfort now and my spirit finds great refreshment in his company. Pray for our lord the Pope who cherishes myself and all of you with fatherly affection. Pray for the lord Chancellor who is like a mother to me, and for all those who are with him . . . my lord Luke, my lord Chrysogonus, and Master Ivo, who are as brothers to me. Brothers Bruno and Gerard[3] are with me and they too beg you to pray for them.

[147]

To Peter the Venerable

To his most reverend lord and father, Peter, Abbot of Cluny, the entire devotion of his Bernard.

MAY the day star on high visit you, O most excellent man, for you have visited me in a foreign land, and consoled

1. The Emperor Lothair, having come to Italy in order to help the Pope, was preparing to return home without having finally defeated the redoubtable Roger of Sicily. As soon as Lothair's back was turned he fell upon Campagna. It was left to St. Bernard to face him. He warned Roger that if he showed battle he would be defeated. Roger scorned his words and attacked the forces of Pope Innocent. But the saint's prophecy was fulfilled, and Roger was forced to leave the field in disorder.

2. Baldwin, the first Cistercian Cardinal, was raised to the sacred purple by Innocent at Clermont in 1130.

3. Gerard, Bernard's brother.

me in the place of my exile! You have done well thus to 'take thought for the poor and needy'. You are a great man concerned with great affairs, and yet you do not forget me when I am absent, even when I have been absent for a long time. Blessed be your holy angel for putting the kind thought into your mind, and blessed be our God for prompting you to follow it! In your letter, that letter wherein you have poured forth your soul to me, I have something to be proud of amongst strangers. I am proud to think you keep me, not only in memory, but also in favour. I am proud to enjoy the privilege of your affection, and I am refreshed by the great goodness of your heart. I am also proud of my troubles, if I may be counted worthy to suffer them for the sake of the Church. But most of all it is the triumph of the Church of which I am proud and which keeps my head erect. If we have shared in her labours, so also shall we share in her consolation. But we must work and suffer with our Mother, or else she will complain of us, saying, 'Old companions shun me. I am assailed by enemies that grudge me life itself.'

2. I give thanks to God who has given her victory, who has 'cherished her and brought her safely through all her strivings'. Our sorrow has been turned to joy, and our tears to the praises of the harp. 'Winter is over now, the rain has passed by, the flowers have begun to blossom, the pruning time has come', the fruitless growth, the rotten branch has been lopped off. That impious one, who made Israel to sin, has been swallowed up in death and gone down into the pit. In the words of the Prophet he 'made terms with death and a compact with hell' and therefore, according to Ezechiel, 'only ruin was left of him, for ever vanished and gone'. That other one too, the greatest as he was the worst enemy of all, he also has been cut off.[1] He had been a friend of the Church, but one of those of whom she complained, saying: 'Friends and neighbours keep their distance now'. If any remain, we can only hope that they may soon meet with a like fate. The time is approaching for me to return

1. This was probably Gerard of Angoulême.

to my brethren and, if I should live to do so, I hope to visit you on my way back. In the meantime I commend myself to your holy prayers, and beg you to remember me to brother Hugh the Cellarer[1] and to the others who are with you, as well as to all your holy brethren.

[150]

To Humbert, Abbot of Igny

Humbert had been a Benedictine at La-Chaise-Dieu for twenty years before entering Clairvaux. After nine years as a monk of Clairvaux he became Abbot of Igny in the diocese of Rheims. In the year 1138 he called forth the following strong letter from St. Bernard by attempting to lay down his heavy burden for one that was lighter. However it appears that fuller information as to the circumstances modified the saint's attitude, for Humbert retired to Clairvaux and when he died in 1148 the Abbot preached the funeral sermon and referred to him in it as a man after his own heart.

GOD forgive you, what have you done! Who could believe that one so highly endowed as you, should break out into such evil! How is it that such a good tree has been able to bring forth fruit so very bad? 'How terrible is God in his dealings with men!' I do not wonder that the devil has been able to do it, but I do wonder that God should have permitted it after all your years of what I believe to have been humble and sincere service. What will he do with me who am but a slothful and careless servant if, even for a time, he can deliver up you, his faithful servant, to the will of his enemies? What sense is

1. *salutamus fratrem Hugonem Camerarium.* Eales translates *Camerarium* as 'chamberlain'. This may be correct, but Du Cange quotes Peter the Venerable describing the office as that of a procurator or cellarer: . . . *hoc est fratrum procuratorio officio functus.*

there, or rather what is not impious in your flight from duty, over which your sons lament and your adversaries make merry? I wonder that you were not scared by the example to Abbot Arnold.[1] His audacity was not unlike yours, and it met with a speedy but fearful retribution. Yet he, as I know well, had some excuse, while you have none at all. You have no disobedient monks, none of your lay-brothers are slothful in their work, you have no neighbours laying violent hands on your property, you do not suffer from scanty or insufficient means of support, so that you might feel obliged to leave those whom you can neither feed nor rule.

2. Have a care lest those words of God 'They have hated me without cause' be applied to you. What ought he to have done for you that he has not done? He has planted for you a chosen and beautiful vineyard, and hedged it about with the vows of continence. He has dug therein a winepress of the strictest discipline and built a tower of poverty reaching almost to the heavens. He has put you in as husbandman and set you over it as the guardian. 'He has cherished you and will bring you safely out of all your striving' if you but permit him. 'But you are shamefully levelling his wall for every passer-by to rob his vineyard of its fruit. Ah! who will now prevent the wild boar from ravaging it, and the lone dweller in the woods from finding his pasture therein?' I am surprised that you think this is a proper way to prepare for death, as you say in your letter; that you have no fear at all of death finding you in a state of such great scandal and under the anathema of the Pope. If it were really necessary for you to do this, could you not have found some other time for it, but just now when I am kept by the needs of the whole Church so that I cannot come to the help of the poor community you have left exposed to danger. I implore you by him who was crucified for you, spare to torture those who are already sufficiently afflicted; and cease, I beg you, from adding to my already accumulated sorrows. To tell the

1. Cf. Letter 4.

truth I am so upset by this general and grave schism of the Church that life has become a burden to me, even if you and yours are able to live in peace.

[157]

To Philip, the Intruded Archbishop of Tours

When the see of Tours fell vacant in 1133, Geoffrey, the Count of Tours, for some inexplicable reason expelled the Chapter from the city. When the Chapter met, elsewhere than in their own city, one party of them elected, quite uncanonically, a young monk of Fontaines-les-Blanches, by the name of Philip. Philip went off to the anti-Pope, Anacletus, to have his election confirmed. Then he returned to Tours and took possession of his See. The other party had in the meantime elected a certain Hugh, who was consecrated at Le Mans. Philip fled from Tours and carried off with him the treasure of the Cathedral. Pope Innocent entrusted the matter to Saint Bernard giving him full authority to enquire into it and act as he thought best. The result of this was that the Saint annulled Philip's election. The supporters of Philip appealed to the Pope over the head of Saint Bernard. The Pope supported the decision of the Saint and Philip sought refuge with the anti-Pope. He later repented, became a monk of Clairvaux, and was Prior there when the Saint died. In this very 'Bernardine' letter, the saint addresses himself to Philip. Almost certainly it was written after Philip had gone to Rome to have his election ratified by Anacletus, but before he had returned to Tours, and been forced to retire again.

YOU are causing me great sorrow, my dear Philip. I beg you not to mock at my grief, because, if you do not see why I should grieve for you, then there is all the more reason why I should do so. Whatever you think of yourself, I think that your condition calls for a whole fount of tears. My grief is no matter for mockery, but for sympathy. My sorrow has no mere human cause, it is not occasioned by the loss of any fleeting chattels, but of you, Philip. I cannot better describe how great is the cause of my sorrow than by saying that Philip is the cause of it. When I have said this, I have declared what is a great source of distress for the Church, who once cherished you in her bosom when you were growing like a lily, and blossoming with every heavenly gift. Who would not have said then that you were a youth of fair hopes, a young man with great gifts. But alas! how your blossom has faded. From what great hopes has France fallen who gave you birth and nourished you![1] Oh, if you did but know, even you! If you set yourself to learn, you soon will know grounds for grief; and then in your grief, my grief will bear fruit. I would say more were I to follow my inclination, but I do not wish to say much while I am still uncertain, lest I be like one beating the air. I have written this, so that you should know how greatly I care for you, and that I am always at hand if God should inspire you with the wish to talk to me and afford me the pleasure of your company. I am at Viterbo and you, I hear, are in Rome. Be so good, I beg you, to answer this letter and tell me how it strikes you, so that I may know what to do, whether I should grieve more or less for you. And if you scorn everything I have said and refuse to hear me, I will not lose the fruit of this letter, for it proceeds from charity, but you will have to answer for your contempt before that fearful tribunal.

1. *A quanta spe decidit Francia.* Watkin Williams *(op. cit.)* sees here a reminiscence of the *Quanta de spe decidi* from the *Heautontimor* of Terence (II.iii.9).

To Geoffrey, the Abbot of
St. Mary's Abbey, York

The fat slumbers of the great Benedictine abbeys were stirred with uncomfortable dreams when the Cistercians arrived in Yorkshire. St. Mary's Abbey, York, was the first to suffer a dramatic awakening. The abbey had become rich and had adopted all and, if one may believe the hints of early chronicles, rather more than all the traditional modifications of the Holy Rule. Yet there remained an élite who were not satisfied with the comfortable life of the abbey. At length, Richard, the prior, and Gervase, the sub-prior, presented on behalf of their followers a scheme of necessary reforms to Geoffrey, the abbot. The abbot, who appears to have been a weak character and was certainly old, instead of giving a clear answer tried to temporize. The reforming party were not satisfied and asked for permission to break away and live a life strictly in accordance with the Rule. The abbot refused and bitterly reproached them with levity, disobedience, and causing dissension in the community. Richard appealed to Thurstan, Archbishop of York. The archbishop summoned the abbot, the prior, and the sub-prior to conference before witnesses at his house. During the conference the abbot said he could do nothing without the consent of his chapter. Whereupon the archbishop offered to meet the chapter and hear the matter discussed. On the appointed day he arrived at the abbey and was forbidden entrance by the abbot. When he expostulated, the monks raised a clamour and attempted violence. He thereupon laid the abbey under an interdict, at which one of the monks cried out that a century of interdict would be preferable to episcopal interference. An attempt was made to seize Richard and his party and thrust them into prison. They took refuge in the entourage of the archbishop who returned to his home taking them with him. That was October 17th, 1132. There were thirteen monks altogether and they remained with the archbishop for three months. During this time two of them, Gervase and Ralph, returned to their mother house; but Gervase rejoined the reformers later on. It was at this moment that the Abbot of St. Mary's appealed to St. Bernard and received the following letters.[1]

On Christmas day of the same year Archbishop Thurstan installed Richard and his companions on land of his own in Skeldale, a solitary and uncultivated wilderness. And then, having presided at the election, he blessed Richard as the first abbot of the new community. Such were the turbulent beginnings of the great Cistercian abbey of Fountains.[2]

YOU write from across the sea to ask my advice, and I could wish you had gone to someone else. You have put me into a dilemma, for if I do not answer you my silence will appear rude; if on the other hand I do answer you it is difficult to know what I can say without offending anyone or without seeming to favour anyone unduly or to countenance anything unwisely. I can say that it was not with the knowledge, advice, or encouragement of myself or of any of the brethren here that your monks have left you. But I believe it to have been by the inspiration of God because, in spite of all your efforts, they remain firm in their purpose. And I believe that those very brothers feel the same who implore me for my advice about themselves, I suppose because their conscience gnaws at them for going back, otherwise, according to the words of the Apostle, if they are not troubled in their conscience for what they

1. Vacandard dates this letter and the following two letters at the May or June of 1133.

2. For the story of Fountains see *Monastic Order in England,* Knowles, Vol. I, pp. 231-239.

have done, 'they are fortunate'.[1] And now what shall I do so as not to give offence either by not answering your letter or by what I answer? Perhaps it would be best for me to send you to one more learned than myself, one whose prestige and holiness entitle him to speak with greater authority than I. In his book on Pastoral Care[2] St. Gregory says: 'The second best is unlawful for one who has chosen the best'. And to confirm this he quotes the words of the Evangelist: 'No man who puts his hand to the plough and then looks back is fit for the kingdom of heaven'. From this he concludes that anyone is guilty of looking back who, having once undertaken great things, leaves them for something less perfect. And likewise in his third homily on Ezechiel he says: 'There are some who while leading as good a life as they know, decide, while leading it, on something more perfect, but afterwards change their minds and retract the good intentions they had. They continue in the good way they had begun, but fall away from the better one they had intended. Such persons appear to do well before the eyes of men, but before God they have fallen away.'

2. Behold a mirror! May they consider in it not only their

---

1. *Credimus autem ex Deo fuisse, quod nec tantis potuit dissolvi conatibus. Credimus hoc idem et ipsos sentire fratres, qui nostrum tantopere de seipsis consilium flagitant, credo remordente eos conscientia quod retro abierint. Alioquin beati sunt secundum Apostolum, si se non judicant in eo quod probant.*

The whole tone of the letter, as well as the background of it, and the words and syntax, seems to make it clear that this passage refers to the two monks who left the reformers and returned to St. Mary's. They were Gervase and Ralph. Evidently they must have been uneasy about themselves and given Abbot Geoffrey no peace until he had written to St. Bernard. Gervase, we know, rejoined the reformers. Likewise at the end of the letter, it seems quite clear that the saint is referring to the two monks who returned to St. Mary's when he says, *Quidnam vero majus aut minus, superius aut inferius, arctius sive remissius sit, quod videlicet reliquerunt, an ad quod redierunt.*

However, Dr. Eales has thought differently and translated accordingly. The words *remordente eos conscientia quod retro abierint* he translates, 'their conscience troubling *them because they quitted you*', i.e., the Abbot of St. Mary's. And the words . . . *quod videlicet reliquerunt, an ad quod redierunt* he translates, 'the state which they have left or that which *they have embraced*'.

2. Chap. 28.

bodily features, but the facts of their turning back. Herein let them examine and judge themselves, their thoughts answering for and against them, according to what that spiritual man has said who judges all things, but is himself judged by no man. It is not for me rashly to decide, but for them to make up their minds whether what they have left or what they have returned to is greater or less, higher or lower, harder or easier. St. Gregory has spoken to them. But to you, reverend father, I can say with the assurance of complete certainty and the naked truth that it would not be well for you to try to extinguish the spirit: 'Suffer him to do good who may, and thou thyself, when thou mayest, do good'. Rather should you take a pride in the progress of your sons, because it is written that a wise son is the pride of his father. For the rest let no one be offended with me because I have not hidden the righteousness of God in my heart,[1] unless it should seem to anyone that in order to avoid giving offence I have said less than I should.

[169]

To the same

To the venerable Dom Geoffrey, Abbot of the Church of St. Mary at York, greetings in the Lord from Bernard, styled Abbot of Clairvaux.

IT has pleased your Reverence to consult me by letter on some doubtful matters. But I am fearful of delivering a decided opinion on these and like matters in proportion as, regarding as clearly as a man may the designs of Divine Providence, I hesitate to shock others by saying what they do not

1. Cf. *Rule of St. Benedict*, Chap. 2.

wish to hear.[1] And this is especially the case with those whose conscience is troubled by the worries of a too subtle mind and bemused in a fog of difficult and tortuous reasoning. But it is the avenger of its own voluntary blindness because, while it tries to justify to itself what it has done it suffers pricks and twinges from the truth which it remembers. The psalmist bewails the bitterness of such a frame of mind and prays: 'Bring my soul out of prison, O Lord, that I may praise thy name'. Do not therefore, I beg your Reverence, attribute it to any craftiness on my part if I am not able to answer your enquiries in the way you want, or if I do not venture to say what I want quite openly. Your letter takes its complexion from the complaints with which it begins. You bemoan the fact that in your old age some of your monks should have dared to desert you in order to pass to a more straight and safe way of life. Take care that your grief is not the grief of this world which 'worketh death'.

2. Surely if reason counts for anything in the opinions of men it should not be a matter for grief that someone should sometimes try to observe the laws of his Creator more strictly. And indeed we superiors are not watching over the souls of our sons with sufficient holiness and fatherly care if we resent their spiritual progress. If you want sound counsel, as I have no doubt you do, then I advise you not only to make it your business to see that those who remain with you in a mitigated observance of the Rule do not fall away, but also, according to the words of the Prophet, to 'bring out bread' to meet those

---

1. The text here is not quite obvious. *Verum de his et similibus tanto quid certum respondere pertimescimus, quanto minus divinæ voluntatis beneplacitum, sicut homines, ad purum intuentes, proximorum animos, si quicquam aliud quam volunt edicimus, offendere dubitamus.* Eales, who claims to have translated the text of the letters literally, has: 'But I am afraid to give any decisive answer; and hesitate the more to do so, inasmuch as if men with the purest intentions are unable to discern the minds of their nearest companions, they are still less able to discern the secret designs of the Divine Will. Again, I am afraid in so speaking to wound those who do not share my own opinion . . .'

whose conscience did not suffer them to continue living in a manner out of keeping with the full purity of their vows and who have passed from the good way in which they began to a higher state of life. It should be your especial care to see that the former do not become reckless to their own ruin, and to encourage the latter that they may progress to their own glory. Surely those who have 'set their heart on the upward journey', who go from virtue to virtue, will deserve all the more joyously to see the God of gods in Sion for having tried to follow more exactly a purer way of life.

3. And now about those two monks, Gervase and Ralph, who set out in the company of the others with the paternal and episcopal sanction of the Lord Archbishop Thurstan, having been released (as you admit) by yourself. I am sure that had they persevered in the pure state of life to which they had risen, they would have done, not wrongly, but well. But I am also sure that if they wished to resume again that pure state from which they heedlessly fell away, they would be all the more praiseworthy on account of their courage, as soldiers are all the more glorious for their victory when they have returned willingly to the field of battle after having once shamefully deserted. It is my opinion that although the release you gave can be revoked, yet it cannot be rendered void before the judgement-seat of God. You admit their way of life is more holy yet you say that on account of the frailty of the flesh and the ties of personal relationship they cannot sustain for long the hardship of it. But you go on to say that their presence is necessary to you and to express grave doubt as to whether they can remain without fault in a position in which they did not place themselves without scandal.

4. One must distinguish between different sorts of scandal, and carnal affections must be completely cut off for the love of Christ. The Gospels thunder exceedingly, the whole of Scripture cries out on every page, that worldly advantage must be abandoned for the good of the soul, and to ignore this is not

only wrong, it is almost heretical. I am not at all sure that such a return as you hope for ought not to be regarded as a grave sin. It is a most dangerous thing, not far short of a catastrophe, to presume on the mercy of God at the expense of his justice and, as it were, to play one off against the other, or in the words of Scripture 'to add sin to sin, and say: The mercy of God is great'. It is a mistaken sort of discretion to put small things before great, and to place the worse on the same footing as the better.

5. After this you go on to demand vigorously why those who return should be called apostates seeing that they are only trying to fulfil their vows according to the recognized customs of their house. It is not for me to condemn them. The Lord knows who are his own and everyone shall bear his own burden. He whom the darkness does not comprehend shall be known as the Lord on the day of judgement, and 'the wicked shall contrive their own undoing'. Let everyone judge of himself as leniently as he likes, but I shall say what I think of myself. I, Bernard, if I had in will and deed passed freely from something good to something better, from something dangerous to something safer, and then afterwards wilfully returned again to what I had changed for the better, I would very much fear that I had rendered myself not only an apostate, but also unfit for the Kingdom of God. And this is what blessed Gregory says: 'Whoever', he says, 'attempts the best renders the second best unlawful for himself, since it is written: "No one who puts his hand to the plough and then looks back is fit for the Kingdom of God". And whoever once he has undertaken great things falls back on something less excellent is guilty of looking back'. With regard to a certain excommunication you wish to discuss, to my mind it would not profit you to consider it, nor me to give an opinion on it. The law judges no man without a hearing and it is rash to launch an excommunication against an absent person.

[170]

To Thurstan, Archbishop of York

To his most dear father and reverend lord Thurstan, by the grace of God Archbishop of York, greetings from Bernard, Abbot of Clairvaux.

THE splendour of your work and your reputation amongst men have combined greatly, as I know, to your credit. Your deeds prove that yours is no undeserved or empty reputation for facts themselves bear out what hitherto has everywhere been reported of you. How, especially of late, has your zeal for righteousness shone forth, your priestly activity stood out and been strong in the defence of poor monks who had no helper! All the Church has told of your deeds of mercy and alms-giving, but this you have in common with many others for it is the duty of all who possess the substance of this world. But this episcopal work, this eminent example of fatherly piety, this truly divine fervour and zeal wherewith he without doubt has inspired and girded you for the protection of his poor, who 'has made his angels like the winds, the servants that wait upon him like a flame of fire', all this is wholly yours, the ornament of your dignity, the mark of your office, a glorious jewel in your crown. It is one thing to fill the belly of the hungry, and another to have a zeal for poverty. The one is the service of nature, the other the service of grace. 'Thou shalt visit thy kind and not sin', the Scriptures say, therefore we care for others that we may not sin, but when we honour the holiness of another we benefit ourselves. Hence it is also said: Let your alms grow warm in your hand until you find a just man to whom you may give them. For whose advantage? 'He that receives a just man in the name of a just man, shall receive the reward of a just man.' It is because you do both these things, fulfilling both the service of nature and the service of grace, that I admire you and recognize that it is given to you from above to do this, so that the praise of all you have done to relieve our temporal necessities may mingle for ever with the divine praises, O most truly reverend and most deservedly lovable father!

[171]

To Richard, Abbot of Fountains, and to his Brethren

Vacandard dates this letter at 1133-34.[1] *The Geoffrey mentioned at the end of the letter is Geoffrey of Ainai, an experienced and elderly monk, whom St. Bernard sent to Fountains in order to instruct the religious in Cistercian observance. The formal affiliation to Clairvaux took place about 1134-35.*

WHAT great things have I heard and known, and our brothers, the two Geoffreys, have told me of you! How you have been inflamed anew by the fire of God, how from weakness you have risen to strength, how you have blossomed afresh into a holy newness of life! This is the hidden work of the finger of God, sweetly renewing and wholesomely changing the spirit within you, not, indeed, from evil to good, but from good to better. Who will grant that I may come over and see this great sight? Your progress from good to better is no less wonderful, no less gratifying, than a conversion from evil to good. It is much more easy to find many men of the world who have been converted from evil to good than it is to find one religious who has progressed from good to better. Anyone who has risen even a little above the state he has once attained in religion is a

1. Vacandard, *Vie de S. Bernard*, 1927 edn., Vol. I, p. 413 u.

very rare bird indeed.¹ But your most salutary and remarkable action has not only given great joy to myself who wish so much to serve your holiness, but also to the whole Church, since it is all the more celebrated for being so rare. The merest prudence demanded that you should rise above the mediocrity which is so near to apostasy and leave behind you that tepidity which God vomits from his mouth; but it was also a matter of conscience. You yourselves discovered whether or not it were safe for those who have vowed to observe the Holy Rule to remain in a stage below what is required by it. I regret deeply that the pressure of my daily cares and the impatience of the messenger oblige me to limit the expression of my full heart and to compress my affection for you within the compass of a short note. But Brother Geoffrey will supply for my brevity by word of mouth.

[172]

To David, King of Scotland

This letter was written about 1134 *in favour of the new foundation at Fountains.*

To the Lord David, the most excellent King of Scotland, worthy of all love in Christ, greetings and eternal life, from Bernard, styled Abbot of Clairvaux.

     I HAVE long since learned to love you, most illustrious king, your fair renown has for long stirred in me the desire to meet you in person. This is my desire and relying on the words, 'The Lord has heard the desire of the poor', I am confident in the Lord that one day I shall see you in the body whom even now I delight to gaze upon in spirit and imagination, and

    1. Horace, *Satire*, 2.26.

whom I constantly think of with such pleasure and joy. Our brothers at Rievaulx were the first to experience the effects of your mercy. You opened to them the treasury of your good will and anointed them with the oil of your compassion and kindness, so that the house of the King of heaven was filled with the odour of your ointments. I am not ungrateful for this, I am as grateful as if you had shown your favours to me personally. And now there are other brothers in the same neighbourhood who have lately joined us. I do not think that your Highness can be ignorant of how these brothers, inspired from on high, came forth into a desert place from the Church of the blessed Mary at York where the observance was perfunctory. They have had to endure many persecutions and injuries inflicted on them sometimes with force and sometimes with guile. They were rich and they abounded in the goods of this world, but they have chosen to become poor for the love of Christ, true followers of the apostolic life and sanctity. If they had been of the world, the world would have loved them, according to the words of the Lord. But now that they are not of the world, the world persecutes them. With the help of God they bear patiently whatever the world does to them but we, who fear God, should help his servants in their troubles. To you therefore, most merciful king, I commend these aforesaid servants of Christ that you may comfort them in their poverty, looking to Christ, the King of kings, for the meed which he will distribute to the just in his eternal kingdom.

[175]

To Thurstan, Archbishop of York

Thurstan remained at his post as archbishop until he felt the approach of death, and then he went to the Abbey of Pontefract, where he died a monk of Cluny in the year 1141. In the

concluding remarks of the Saint on the consideration given to
weakness and age, we see once more how far the early Cister-
cians were from any narrowness and over rigidity.

To his reverend father and lord, Thurstan, by the grace of
God Archbishop of York, health more of the soul than of the
body,[1] from Bernard, styled Abbot of Clairvaux.

     I PRAISE your desire for quiet and your wish to rest
peacefully in the Lord. But the reasons you give do not seem
to me in themselves sufficient for abandoning your pastoral
care, unless perhaps (which I am sure is not the case) you have
committed some grave sin or have obtained the permission of
the Holy See,[2] for I am sure you are not ignorant of those
words of the Apostle: 'Are you married to a wife? Then do
not go about to free yourself'. No promise such as you say you
have made[3] can be binding on a bishop so as to impede the
ministry to which he is called.

    2. It seems best to me, if I can say so without prejudice to the
wiser opinions of wise men, that you should stay where you are
and exhibit in a bishop the dress and holy life of a monk. But if
there is some secret reason for your resignation or if the Lord
Pope has gratified your wish for quiet, my advice, such as it is,
is that you should not be put off from joining some house
where you see great purity of observance by fear of any degree
of poverty or rough clothes and victuals. Bear in mind that in
such houses, although the soul is the first concern, yet due regard is always given to physical weakness and age. I am your
servant so as always to pray God fervently for you that he may

---

    1. . . . *salutem non tam in via, quam in patria.* Eales translates: ' . . .
wishes health in the present life and in the future life eternal'.
    2. St. Bernard recognizes two reasons which would justify a bishop relin-
quishing his office, *viz.* some grave crime or the permission of the Holy See.
    3. Thurstan made a promise in his early youth to become a monk of
Cluny.

inspire you to do what is best and grant that you may bear the burden and heat of the day, so as to receive in the evening of your life the meed of your labours in coin that bears his image.

[177]

To St. Ailred, Abbot of Rievaulx[1]

In this letter St. Bernard urges St. Ailred to write something on charity. This letter always appears as an introduction to St. Ailred's Speculum Charitatis *as from Gervase, Abbot of Louth Park, but Dom André Wilmart has proved conclusively that the writer of it is St. Bernard of Clairvaux.[2] And indeed, as Prof. David Knowles observes,[3] the style* clamat dominum.

THE great virtue of the saints is humility, but a sincere and discreet humility. True humility does not consort with untruthfulness and it is in no way helped by the sacrilege of disobedience. I have besought you, I have commanded you, I have even charged you in the sacred name of the Most High, to

1. The 'Bernard of the North'. One of the most attractive figures in English monasticism. Not only a true Cistercian and a true disciple of St. Bernard, but also an able administrator. His works are printed in *P.L.*, t. cxcv, col. 209-796, with the exception of the *Sermon on the Saints of Hexham*, edited by J. Raine and published by the Surtees Society; the *Regula Inclusorum*, printed by the Maurists as an appendix to St. Augustine; and *De Jesu Puero Duodenni*, printed by the Maurists in St. Bernard's works. He was by birth completely English and connected with landed families between Hexham and Durham. He became associated with the Scottish Court and held the post there of steward or seneschal. *Vide The Monastic Order in England*, by David Knowles, Vol. I; also *Vita Ailredi*, by his disciple Walter Daniel, and an appreciation of his character by his friend, Gilbert, Abbot of Swineshead, written on hearing of his death: *Gilberti Hoilandensis, Serm.* 41 *in Canticum*, printed in the appendix of St. Bernard's works by Mabillon.

2. Andre Wilmart, *L'Instigateur du Speculum Charitatis d' Aelred Abbé de Rievaulx* in *Revue d' Ascétique et de Mystique*, Oct., 1933.

3. David Knowles, *op. cit.*

write some little thing for me whereby the grievances might be answered of those who are trying to follow the narrow way after a life of self-indulgence. I do not condemn, I do not blame your excuses, but I do reproach your obstinacy. It was an act of humility to make excuses, but it is not humble to disobey. Where is the humility in refusing to consent to my wishes? Indeed to defend oneself in this way smacks of the sin of the soothsayers, such stubbornness is like the sin of idolatry. You complain that it would be too heavy a burden for weak shoulders and that it would be more prudent to refuse to undertake it than to break down under it. I grant that I am placing on you a heavy burden, that it is hard, even impossible. But even so you have no excuse. I persist in my opinion and I repeat my command. What will you do? Surely what he, to whose Rule you have vowed obedience, has said that a monk should do in such circumstances: 'If a superior still persist in his command, let the young monk know that it is expedient for him; and let him obey out of love, trusting in God'.[1] You have done what you ought to have done to excuse yourself, if not more than you ought to have done. You have gone as far as is allowed. You have pointed out all the reasons why you cannot obey. You have said that you are ignorant of grammar, that you are almost illiterate; that you have come to the desert, not from the schools, but from the kitchen; that you have since lived a rustic and rough life amidst rocks and mountains, earning in the sweat of your brow your daily bread with axe and maul; and that flights of oratory ill become your poor fishermen's clothes.[2] I

1. For the understanding of this passage it is necessary to read the whole reference in the Rule of St. Benedict, Chap. 68: 'If on any brother there be laid commands that are hard and impossible, let him receive the order of his superior with all meekness and obedience. But if he sees that the burden altogether exceeds his strength, let him lay before his superior the reasons of his incapacity patiently and in due season, without showing pride, or resistance, or contradictoriness.'

2. The 'kitchen' is a reference to the post St. Ailred held as steward in the Scottish Court. But in speaking of himself as 'ignorant of grammar' and 'almost illiterate' (*minus grammaticum et pene illiteratum*) he was using a

most gratefully accept your excuses, they serve rather to inflame than extinguish the spark of my desire, because knowledge that comes from the school of the Holy Spirit rather than
the schools of rhetoric will savour all the sweeter to me and
because you 'have this treasure in an earthen vessel, that the
excellency may be of the power of God'. What a joyous thing
it is, what a presage of the future, that you should have come
to the desert from the kitchen, so that as one who has been entrusted for a time with providing food for the body in a royal
kitchen, you may now provide spiritual food for spiritual men
and feed the hungry with the food of God's word in the house
of the King of kings. What you say about your mountains and
rugged rocks does not disconcert me at all, nor am I horrified at
the thought of your great valleys, for now 'the mountains drop
down sweetness, the hills flow with milk and honey, and the
valleys are filled with corn', now 'honey is sucked out of rocks
and oil out of the hardest stone', and rocks and mountains are
the pasture of the Lord's sheep. And so I think that with that
maul of yours you will be able to strike something out of those
rocks that you have not got by your own wits from the bookshelves of the schoolmen, and that you will have experienced
sometimes under the shade of a tree during the heats of midday
what you would never have learned in the schools. Not unto
yourself, not unto yourself give the glory, but render it unto
him who has not only rescued you from 'the pit of misery and
mire of dregs', from the house of death and the unclean place,
but 'hath made a remembrance of his wonderful works, being a
merciful and gracious Lord', and so as to raise more generously
the hopes of sinners he has given sight to the blind, knowledge
to the ignorant, instruction to the unskilled. And so why do
you blush and hesitate to give what I ask, when everyone who

---

very strong hyperbole. St. Ailred would have been better educated than
most so-called educated people of to-day. Though he was not trained in the
schools he had clearly been well taught by one who was familiar with the
new humanism. *Vide* David Knowles, *op. cit.*

knows you will know it is not yours that you give? Why do
you dissemble? Why do you refuse to give even at the command of him who gave you all you have to give? Do you fear
the envy of some or to be thought presumptuous? As if anyone has ever written anything useful without incurring envy!
Or as if anyone could accuse you of presumption who are only
obeying your abbot! I therefore order you in the name of Jesus
Christ, and in the Spirit of our God, that you do not delay to
write down those thoughts that have occurred to you, in your
long meditations, concerning the excellence of charity, its fruit,
and its proper order, so that we may see in what you write, as
if in a mirror, what charity is, how great sweetness there is in the
possession of it, how much heaviness and sorrow there is in
cupidity which is the contrary of it, and that exterior troubles,
so far from diminishing it, as many believe, only serve to increase it, and finally what discretion there should be in the
exercise of it. But, for the sake of your modesty, let this letter
be put at the beginning of the work, so that whatever in the
Mirror of Charity (for that is the name I give it) should displease the reader shall be imputed to me who have commanded
it and not to you who have obeyed by writing it.

[210]

To the King of France

It is very probable that the following letter was written by the
saint on his election to the see of Rheims.

I AM very glad you are so sincere in all that appertains
to the glory of God. For, not to mention other things, you
would surely not be so very anxious to promote such a wretched
person as myself except for the glory of God; what other reason
could you have since I am poor and destitute? You were not

satisfied with simply consenting to my election, you also added your request that I should accept it. You show me favour, you open wide to me your kind heart and, so that I should not be scared of the burden, you promise to help me with your royal protection. Whence such condescension in a king, such maturity in one so young? But, O king, I am a timorous character, broken in body, and there only remains for me the grave, I cannot on any account 'stretch forth my hands to great works'; unfitted and unequal to such a holy office, I cannot possibly venture to accept it. Those responsible for my election should have considered this. If they are able to overlook my insufficiency, I cannot because I have read 'thy own self befriend, doing God's will'. Or if they believe me suitable because of the religious habit I wear, they must understand that in the habit there is the appearance of holiness, but not the virtue. No one is better known to me than myself, no one knows me so well as I know myself. I cannot believe against my conscience those who only see me from without and judge me only by appearances. I and the sons God has given me are here and, although sinners, we pray for your kingdom and your person. To part us would be difficult and cruel, and would induce sorrow rather than prayers. So much for myself. Now, I beg you, deign to listen to what is in my mind about the church.[1] The queen amongst the churches sits in sorrow, 'her cheeks are wet with tears', all dim now and discoloured the beauty that once shone so fair, faded her ancient glory, her splendid apparel is trodden under foot, her nobility has been brought into contempt, her liberty turned to servitude. I am tortured in this flame, and can find no thought to comfort me, until he shall come who will console her. May reverence for her spouse touch your heart, the spouse by whose blood she was redeemed, in the likeness of whom she was adorned, and with whose heritage she was endowed. And may you remain firm in your purpose lest this well loved bride of our Lord be overwhelmed even now with such a mass of

1. The church of Rheims?

evil, that she is no longer pleasing to his eyes. I tell you, I tell you as your true friend, that such a thing would certainly not advantage you. So may you administer your kingdom of France, great and mighty king, as to obtain the Kingdom of heaven.

[215]

To the Canons of the Church of Lyons

The Canons of Lyons had instituted a feast of the Conception of the Blessed Virgin and by doing so called forth the following well-known remonstrance from the Abbot of Clairvaux. St. Bernard maintains that it is impossible on purely rational grounds for her conception to have been holy; that there is no evidence at all for it in Scripture, the Fathers, or the tradition of the Church, and that if her conception were not holy there could be no justification for a feast in its honour. It remains to say that he uses the term 'conception' in a different sense to the Church in her dogma of the Immaculate Conception. In this doctrine the Church teaches that the Blessed Virgin was, by a unique privilege and solely by virtue and in anticipation of the redeeming death of our Blessed Lord, preserved from all taint of original sin from the first moment of her existence, that is to say from the moment she was quickened in her mother's womb. There is no real evidence that the use of the term 'conception' in this sense ever occurred to St. Bernard. He believes that the Blessed Virgin was cleansed from original sin, or sanctified in the womb, after her conception but before her birth, in the same way as St. John the Baptist, but more abundantly, so as to preserve her from all actual sin throughout her life.

The authenticity of this letter has occasionally been questioned in the past, ostensibly on the grounds that in it St. Bernard speaks of himself as 'the especial son of the church of

Lyons'. But he was born and lived his whole life in the province of the metropolitan church of Lyons, and was therefore perfectly justified in regarding himself as a son of that church. Furthermore, the style of the letter is unmistakably the saint's: ... clamat dominum.

AMONG all the churches of France the church of Lyons is well known to be pre-eminent for its dignity, sound learning, and praiseworthy customs. Where was there ever so flourishing strict discipline, grave conduct, ripe counsels, and such an imposing weight of authority and tradition? Especially in the offices of the Church, has this church, so full of judgement, appeared cautious in adopting novelties, and careful never to permit its reputation to be sullied by any childish levity. Because of this I marvel exceedingly that some of you should wish to tarnish the lustre of your good name by introducing at this time a new festival, a rite of which the Church knows nothing, of which reason cannot approve, and for which there is no authority in tradition. Are we more learned or more devout than the Fathers? To introduce something which they, with all their prudence in such matters, passed over in silence, is a most dangerous presumption. It is not as if they would have passed it over without good reasons, for it is a thing that could not have escaped their attention.

2. You say that the Mother of the Lord should be highly honoured. You are right, but 'the honour of the queen loves justice'. The Virgin has many true titles to honour, many real marks of dignity, and does not need any that are false. Let us honour her for the purity of her body, the holiness of her life. Let us marvel at her fruitful virginity, and venerate her divine Son. Let us extol her freedom from concupiscence in conceiving, and from all pain in bearing. Let us proclaim her to be reverenced by the angels, desired by the nations, foretold by the patriarchs and prophets, chosen out of all and preferred before all. Let us magnify her as the channel of grace, the mediatrix

of salvation, the restorer of the ages, and as exalted above the choirs of angels to the very heights of heaven. All this the Church sings in her praise and teaches me too to sing. What I have received from the Church I firmly cling to and confidently pass on to others; but, I confess, I am chary of admitting anything that I have not received from her.

3. Certainly the Church has taught me to keep that day with the greatest veneration on which, when she was taken up from this evil world, she brought a festival of great joy to heaven.[1] But I have also learned in the Church to celebrate the birth of the Virgin, and from the Church to hold it as a festival and holy, believing most firmly with the Church that she entered the world already holy because she had been sanctified in the womb.[2] And I read of Jeremias that he too was sanctified before he left the womb, and I believe the same of John the Baptist who from the womb felt the presence of the Lord in the womb. It is a matter for consideration by you whether it would be permitted to think the same of David, in that he said to God, 'By thee I have been confirmed from the womb, from my mother's womb thou art my protector'; and likewise, 'From my mother's womb thou art my guardian, depart not from me'.[3] And to Jeremias it was said: 'I claimed thee for my own before ever I fashioned thee in thy mother's womb; before ever thou camest to birth, I set thee apart for myself'. How beautifully the divine Word distinguishes between formation in the womb and birth from the womb. It shows that the former was only foreknown, but that the latter was blessed beforehand with the gift of sanctity, so that no one should consider the privilege of the

1. *Accepi sane ab Ecclesia illum diem cum summa veneratione recolendum, quo assumpta de sæculo nequam, cælis quoque intulit celeberrimorum festa guadiorum.* Eales translates this sentence: '. . . when I have received from the Church that day to be reverenced with the highest veneration, when being taken up from this sinful earth, she made entry into heaven; a festival of most honoured joy.'

2. . . . *firmissime cum Ecclesia sentiens, in utero eam accepisse ut sancta prodiret.*

3. See par. 8 *ad fin.*

prophet to have been only a matter of foreknowledge or pre-destination.

4. Let us grant this in the case of Jeremias. What shall we say of John the Baptist whom the angel pronounced would be filled with the Holy Spirit while yet in his mother's womb?[1] Certainly I do not think that this can refer only to predestination or foreknowledge. Without any doubt the words of the angel were fulfilled in their own time, as he said they would be; and it is not permissible to doubt that he was filled with the Holy Spirit as the angel had foretold, and in the time and place that he had foretold. And certainly the Holy Spirit sanctified him when he filled him. But I would not venture to say how far this sanctification availed over original sin either for John the Baptist, or for the prophet, or for anyone else who was thus prevented by grace. Yet I have no hestiation in saying that they were sanctified whom God sanctified, and that they came forth from the womb with the sanctity they received in the womb, and that the original sin they contracted in conception had no power at all to hinder or rob them in their birth of the blessing they had already received before their birth. And who would venture to say that a child filled with the Holy Spirit still remained a child of wrath, and that he would suffer the penalty of damnation if he should happen to die in the womb, having received the fulness of the Spirit? This is very severe. But I would not at all venture to define anything about it on the strength of my own opinion. However this may be, the Church, which judges and declares the death but not the birth of the saints precious, makes a unique exception in favour of him concerning whom the angel said, 'Many shall rejoice in his birth', and honours his nativity with festal joy. And why should not the birth of him be holy and so a festival and joyous, who was able to rejoice even whilst in the womb?

5. We cannot for a moment suppose that a privilege which

1. The Vulgate: *Adhuc ex utero matris suæ*. St. Bernard quotes *adhuc in utero matris suæ*. Eales translates according to the Vulgate.

has been accorded to some, though very few, mortals, was denied to that Virgin through whom all mortals have entered life. Beyond all doubt the Mother of the Lord was holy before she was born. Holy Church is certainly not mistaken in keeping the day of her birth holy and celebrating it every year throughout the world with a glad and joyous festival. I, for my part, believe that she received a more ample blessing which not only sanctified her in the womb, but also preserved her thereafter free from sin throughout her life. This is something which we do not believe to have been accorded to any other born of woman. This unique privilege of sanctity whereby she was enabled to live her whole life without sin surely well becomes the Queen of Virgins who, in giving birth to him who destroyed sin and death, obtained for all of us the reward of life and righteousness. Therefore her birth was holy because great sanctity from the womb made it so.

6. Is it possible to think of any other honours that we can add to these? That her conception which preceded her honoured birth should also be honoured because there would have been no birth to honour if there had been no conception? What if another should maintain for the same reason that festal honours should be accorded to both her parents? And the same thing could also be claimed with the same reason for her grandparents and her great-grandparents, and so on without end, so that there would be festivals beyond count. Such a repetition of joys would be more fitting for heaven than for here below, for citizens than for exiles.[1] But they show records of, so they say, heavenly revelations; as if anyone could not equally well show records of how the Virgin had been seen commanding the same honours for her parents, according to the commandment, 'Honour thy father and mother'. I find it hard to be moved by records of visions which are unsupported by sound

---

1. In fact an ordinary Calendar of the Church now has a good 280 feasts, not counting Sundays, out of the 365 days of the year. But whether everyone regards this as a foretaste of heaven is a matter open to enquiry.

reason or good authority. How does it follow that her conception would be holy because her birth was holy? Was it because
it preceded a holy birth? It preceded so that there should be a
birth, but not so that the birth should be holy. Whence that
holiness which could be passed on to what was to follow?
Would it not be more true to say that, because her conception
was not holy, she was sanctified after she had been conceived
so that her birth was holy? Or shall we say that perhaps the
conception shared in the holiness of the birth which followed
it? It would certainly be true to say that the sanctification of
what had already been conceived could be transmitted to the
birth that followed, but it is quite impossible that the holiness of
the birth could be retrospective and sanctify the conception
which preceded it.

7. Whence therefore the sanctity of the conception? Can it
be said that she was conceived holy because she was already
holy before her conception, so that, on account of this, her
conception would be rendered holy, just as her birth was rendered holy because of the sanctification she received while in
the womb before her birth? But she could not have been holy
before she existed, and before her conception she did not exist.
Or was sanctity present in the act of her conception, so that
she would be holy at the same time as she was conceived? But
reason cannot accept this, for how can anything be holy without the presence of the Sanctifying Spirit, and how can the
Holy Spirit have any part in sin, and how can there not be sin
where there is carnal lust? Perhaps someone might say that she
was conceived of the Holy Spirit and not of man, but this is a
thing hitherto quite unheard of. I read that the Holy Spirit
came upon her, but not that it came with her, when the angel
said: 'The Holy Spirit shall come upon thee'. If it is permitted
to say what the Church thinks, and the Church thinks what is
true, I say that she conceived of the Holy Spirit, not that she
herself was conceived of the Holy Spirit; that she gave birth as
a virgin, but not that she was born of a virgin. Otherwise

where would the unique privilege of the Mother of the Lord be, whereby she alone is believed to be able to glory in both the birth of a child and in the virginity of her body, if we concede as much to her mother? This is not to honour the Virgin, but to detract from her honour. If therefore it was quite impossible for her to have been sanctified before her conception, because she did not then exist; or in the act of her conception, because of the presence of sin; it remains that she was sanctified after her conception, when she was already in the womb, and that this sanctification excluded sin and rendered her birth, but not her conception, holy.

8. And so, although it has been given to very few of the sons of men to be born holy, it has not been given to any to be conceived holy, so that the prerogative of a holy conception might be reserved for him alone who sanctified all of us; the only person who, being conceived without sin, cleansed all sinners. It is true for all the sons of men what one of them humbly and truly admitted of himself: 'I was born in sin; guilt was with me already when my mother conceived me'.[1]

9. This being so, what reason can there be for a feast of the Conception? How, I ask, can a conception be holy which was not of the Holy Spirit, not to say that it was of sin; and how can a feast be kept in honour of what was not holy? Gladly will the mother of God forgo an honour by which either sin is honoured or by which a false holiness seems to be implied. A novelty, the mother of rashness, the sister of superstition, the daughter of levity, presumed against the practice of the Church, can in no wise at all be pleasing to her. If you thought such a feast advisable, you should have first consulted the Holy See, and not have followed so hastily and so unadvisedly the simplicity of the uneducated. In fact I have before now observed this very error amongst some persons, but in order to spare the devotion of simple hearts for the Virgin, I have overlooked it. But when I find this superstition amongst learned men in the

1. See par. 3 *ad fin.*

noble church of which I am specially the son, I doubt whether I could overlook it without grave offence to you all. I have said all this in submission to the judgement of anyone wiser than myself, and especially in submission to the authority of the Roman Church, to whose decision I refer all that I have said on this or any other such subject, prepared to modify anything I may have said, if it should be contrary to what she thinks.

[224]

To Henry, Archbishop of Sens

This is the same Archbishop of Sens to whom St. Bernard addressed the long and important letter, included among his regular treatises, on the life and duties of a bishop. He seems to have been a strong-willed prelate, not to say imperious. He was surnamed 'The Wild Boar'. In the year 1136 he seems to have got himself into serious trouble and been suspended for a time.

I CONFESS that I have often intended to write to you for your own sake on behalf of other people, and then have decided not to do so on account of your hateful hardness: but charity shall prevail. I want to keep your friends for you, but you will not condescend to it. I wish to reconcile your enemies to you, but you will not suffer it. You will not have peace, you are set on rushing to your own shame, confusion, and deposition. You are multiplying your accusers and driving away your supporters. In everything your own sweet will is law, you think only of power and not at all of the fear of God. All your enemies are laughing about you, all your friends complaining. How could you have unfrocked that man when he had not been, I do not say convicted in court, but even summonsed.

Everyone will be shocked by this, everyone will be whispering about it, everyone will jeer at it, everyone will be indignant. Do you really think that the whole world is as void of all sense of justice as you seem to be, so that you can deprive a man of his archdeaconry in this way without causing remark? Or perhaps it pleases you more to give it and then take it away, than to retain his gratitude for the gift of it?[1] Do not, I pray, do not do this thing, which will shock everyone and please no one. Perhaps I have written more boldly and more bitingly than you could wish, but if you will correct your ways you will see it has been for your good.

[239]

To Pope Innocent

To his most loving father and lord, Innocent, by the grace of God Supreme Pontiff, the entire devotion, for what it is worth, of Brother Bernard, styled Abbot of Clairvaux.

THERE must be scandals; they are an unpleasant necessity. Therefore the Prophet says, 'Had I but wings as the dove has wings, to fly away and be at rest', and the Apostle desires to be dissolved and be with Christ, and Elias declares, 'I can bear no more, Lord; put an end to my life; I have no better right to live than my fathers'. This I have in common with the saints, although it is a matter only of the will and not of merit, that I too wish to be taken out of it all, overcome, I admit, by 'the fears that daunt me and the storm around me'. But I fear that I should not be found so well prepared as I am well disposed. I am weary of life; and I know not whether it would be

---

1. *Sed vos forsitan plus amatis reddere et perdere, quam gratiam de beneficio retinere.* Eales: 'But you perhaps are better pleased to give it back after seizing it, rather than to deserve his gratitude by suffering him to retain it'.

well for me to die. Perhaps for this reason I am removed even in my wish from the saints who were spurred on by their desire for better things, whereas I am constrained to go forth only to escape scandals and troubles. In fine he says, 'It were better to be dissolved and be with Christ'. Therefore in the saint the desire was uppermost, in me feeling. But in this most miserable life he was not able to have the good he desired, nor I to be free of the anxieties which I suffer. And so while we are both alike in our wish to go forth, we differ in our motives for wishing it.

2. Fool that I am, I was but now promising myself rest, when the madness of the lion had been quelled and peace restored to the Church.[1] And now the Church is at peace, but not I. I did not realize I was in the vale of tears, I was forgetting that I was still in 'a land where all is forgotten', I did not stop to consider that the earth on which I dwell brings forth thorns and troubles for me, and that, when they have been cut back, new ones will grow again, and other new ones after these, and so on without end. I had heard this to be sure, but experience, I have now discovered, gives a better comprehension to the hearing. Grief transcends and never ends for me,[2] my sorrows have increased because evils have gained strength; first the frost, then came the snow. Who can endure this cold? In it charity grows cold so that iniquity abounds. We have escaped the lion only to fall victims to the dragon who is, perhaps, more dangerous lurking in his lair than the lion raging in the open. Although he is no longer lurking in his lair: would that his poisonous writings were still lurking in their shelves, and not being discussed at the crossroads! His books have wings: and they who hate the light because their lives are evil, have dashed into the light thinking it was darkness. Darkness is being brought into towns and castles in the place of light; and for honey poison or, I should say, poison in honey is being offered on all sides to everyone. His writings 'have passed from country to country, and from one king-

1. A reference to Peter Leonis, the anti-Pope.
2. *Innovatus est dolor, non exterminatus.*

dom to another'. A new gospel is being forged for peoples and for nations, a new faith is being propounded, and a new foundation is being laid besides that which has been laid. Virtues and vices are being discussed immorally, the sacraments of the Church falsely, the mystery of the Holy Trinity neither simply nor soberly. Everything is put perversely, everything quite differently, and beyond what we have been accustomed to hear.

3. Goliath advances tall of body, girt in the noble accoutrements of war, and preceded by his armour-bearer, Arnold of Brescia.[1] Scale is joined to scale, and there is no breathing space between.[2] The bee that is in France[3] has murmured to the bee in Italy, and they have joined forces against the Lord and against his anointed, 'they have strung their bows, have arrows ready in the quiver, to shoot from their hiding places at unoffending hearts'. In food and clothing they have all the appearances of piety, but they reject its virtue, and they deceive all the more people by transforming themselves into angels of light, whereas they are Satan. Therefore Goliath, standing between the two armies with his armour-bearer, cries out with a loud voice to the ranks of Israel, and taunts the forces of the saints, all the more audaciously for there being no David to defy him. He insults the Doctors of the Church by holding up the philosophers for exaggerated praises. He prefers their ideas and his own novelties to the doctrines and faith of the Catholic Fathers; and, when all have fled before him, he calls me out, the least of all, to single combat.

4. At his request the Archbishop of Sens wrote to me fixing the day of the meeting, on which Abelard, in his presence and in the presence of his brother bishops, should establish, if he could, his perverse doctrines, against which I have dared to croak. I refused because I am but a child in this sort of warfare and he

1. A pupil of Abelard, heretic, and demagogue.
2. *Squama squamæ conjungitur, nec spiraculum incedit per eas.* Eales translates: 'Scale overlaps scale, and there is no point left unguarded'.
3. The French bee is Abelard; the Italian, Arnold of Brescia. Perhaps an allusion to *Isaias* 7.18.

is a man habituated to it from his youth, and because I deemed it an unworthy action to bring the faith into the arena of controversy, resting as it does on sure and immutable truth. I said that his writings were evidence enough against him, and that it was the business of the bishops to adjudicate on the doctrines of which they were the ministers, not mine. But he lifted up his voice all the more for this, called upon many, and assembled all his accomplices. I would rather not say what he wrote about me to his disciples. He spread it about on all sides that he was going to answer me at Sens on the day appointed. The word of it went forth to everyone, and I was not able to hide myself. At first I did nothing, not greatly caring for what people were saying. Yet, unwillingly and sorrowfully, I bowed to the advice of my friends, who saw how everyone was preparing as if for a show, and feared that my absence would serve only to increase the influence of the man and the scandal of the people, also it seemed that his errors might appear to be confirmed if there were no one to answer and refute them. And so I went to Sens at the time appointed, unprepared, unprotected, except by those words which I had in my mind at the time: 'Take no thought how or what to speak: for it will be given you in that hour what to speak', and 'With the Lord to aid me, I have no fear of the worst that man can do'. Besides the bishops and abbots, there were many religious men present, and also masters of the schools from the cities, and many educated clerics, the king too was there. And so, in the presence of all, face to face with my adversary, I took certain headings from his books. And when I began to read these, he refused to listen and walked out, and appealed from the judges he had chosen, which I do not think was permissible. When these aforesaid headings from his books had been examined, they were found by the judgements of all to be contrary to the faith, to the truth. I have written all this on my own behalf in case I should be thought to have shown levity or at least rashness in so grave a matter.

5. But you, successor of St. Peter, will judge whether this

man who has attacked the faith of Peter should find a refuge in
the see of Peter. You, I say, the friend of the Bridegroom, will
find a way of freeing the bride 'from treacherous lips, the per-
jured tongue'. But, to speak a trifle more boldly to my lord,
look also to yourself, most loving father, and the grace of God
that is within you. Did not God set you up over nations and
kingdoms when you were yet small in your own eyes? And for
what other purpose than that you should pull up and destroy,
build and plant? Consider, I beg you, how much he has done
for you who took you from your father's house, and anointed
you with the oil of his mercy; how much for his Church, by
means of you; how many things in the field of the Lord, heaven
and earth being witnesses, have been powerfully and wholesomely pulled up and destroyed; how many things have been
well and truly built, planted, and propagated. God has raised
up crazy heretics in your time that by your hand they may be
crushed. I have seen a fool well rooted, and straightway his
beauty was cursed. I have seen, I say, an impious man lifted up
and exalted like the cedars of Lebanon; and I passed by, and
lo! he was not. There must be heresies and schisms, that they
also, who are approved, may be made manifest among you.[1]
God has proved you and found you true. But so that nothing
should be lacking to your crown, heresies have now arisen. For
the perfection of your virtue, it now only remains for you not
to be found to have done less than the great bishops, your
predecessors. Catch for us, most loving father, the foxes that
are destroying the vine of the Lord, while they are yet young;
lest, if they should grow and multiply, what was not done for
their extermination by yourself, may be the despair of those
that come after you. Although now they are no longer so small
or so few, but well grown and numerous, and only to be exter-
minated by your strong hand. Jacinctus has borne us much ill-
will, but he has not hurt us because he could not. I thought I
ought to bear patiently in my own person, what he has not

1. See Vincent of Lérins, *Commonitorium*, x.15.

spared either yourself or the Curia. All this my Nicholas, who is yours too, can tell you better by word of mouth.

THE ERRORS OF ABELARD

St. Bernard wrote a long letter (Benedictine Edition, 190) on the errors of Abelard but, on account of its doctrinal importance and great length, it is included among the treatises of St. Bernard.

The Archbishop of Rheims, in a letter to Pope Innocent (Benedictine Edition, 191), begged the Holy Father to suppress the evil teaching of Abelard. In much the same phraseology as St. Bernard he describes how many are being led astray by Abelard's false doctrines and hints at the fear that there may be some in the Curia itself who favour his errors. He describes what happened at Sens, and ends by saying that the remedy now rests with the Pope.

[253]

To Peter, Dean of Besançon

Apparently Guy, Abbot of Cherlieu, was being persecuted by Peter, Dean of Besançon, and had gone to Rome in order to put his case before the Pope. News of this fracas called forth the following letter from the Abbot of Clairvaux. Cherlieu was a daughter house of Clairvaux, founded 1131.

I hear such an account of the journey of the Abbot of Cherlieu that I regard him as if he were already dead. I am sorry to say that you especially are to blame for any danger that threatens him,[1] any trouble that he has to undergo. I did not expect this of you because I have not deserved it. I thought you were a different sort of person from what I find you to be. Those who were present at the affair testify that you did not conduct yourself either sincerely or honourably. I partly believe them, for neither is the Abbot of Beauvais very pleased

---

1. The journey to Rome in those days could never have been easy and not always safe. A chronicle records how once an envoy to Rome fell into the hands of an anti-Pope and had his nose cut off.

with you. Do not, I beg of you, persecute the servants of God, of whom you read what he himself says: 'He that touches you, touches the apple of my eye'. Do not utterly uproot from my heart whatever good opinion I may have had of you. I have written in this way to you, not because I am not fond of you, but because I wish to remove any obstacle there may be to my affection for you. Speaking as a friend, I tell you that it would not do either you or your church any good if the Pope were to hear of how you have acted.

[254]

To Pope Innocent, concerning the matter of the above letter

I THINK that the injury done by the aggressor, the innocence of the sufferer, and callousness of the judge are sufficiently evident in the case which my dear friend Guy, Abbot of Cherlieu, is bringing before you. The poor man has been compelled by the violence of his opponents as well as by the impossibility of obtaining justice, to have recourse to you, despite the trouble and expense of the journey, and the danger of the times. This lover of quiet has been obliged to shake hands with death in order to preserve his peace. Look kindly, I beg you, upon this poor and needy man, and lend a fatherly ear to his complaints, lest such a great expenditure of slender resources be all in vain. I have twice written to you in the past of that man who is assailing the abbot, to testify that he was violating his profession and squandering the goods of his monastery. And now I grieve to tell you that he is an enemy of the cross of Christ, an oppressor of the holy men in his neighbourhood, and a deceiver of the poor. As he now has almost nothing of his own to waste, he descends upon his neighbours with force and makes free of their possessions. His monastic habit is a lie for, in fact, he is a robber, completely unmindful of regular observance, anl utterly regardless of the canons. He is brazen faced, quite unscrupulous, impervious to piety, prone to anger, bold in crime, ready to inflict injury. I am most surprised that the abbot of Chaise-Dieu, a religious man, can overlook or be ignorant of so many great vices in one of his monks.

2. But what has all this to do with me? Let him look to it: he stands or falls to his own Lord. For me it is enough to be liberated from his hands, and this is what I earnestly implore of you. I have attempted to achieve it in other ways, but without success. 'I have looked around, and there was none to help me.' It has come to the common refuge to which we all fly, there we are sure to be set free. Only let there be pity in the heart, for power is not lacking to the hand. It is clearly one of the privileges of the Apostolic See that, in the last resource, men should have recourse to your supreme authority and power. Indeed it is the rescue of the poor man from the clutches of the strong which, among all the other notable marks of your primacy, has rendered yours a glorious apostolate. To my mind there is no more precious jewel in your crown than that zeal with which you are wont to strive for the down-trodden and prevent 'the rule of the godless in the domain of the just', doubtless because of what follows, 'else the just too might soil their hands with guilt', or because of what is written elsewhere, 'The heart of the oppressed burns within them, when the schemer that has entrapped them is triumphant', and the bodily torture of the one, is the spiritual loss of the other.

3. There is a monastery not far from here,[1] which is similarly harassed by the grievous assaults of evil men, and 'there is none to rescue it, none to bring it aid'. And for this also your child does not hesitate to besiege your heart with his sorrowful prayers. The abbot who bears this letter will explain truthfully by word of mouth who these men are and what is the occasion of

1. Clairfontaine?

their machinations. May the Omnipotent God preserve you for
many years to be the protector of all of us who live a poor life
in the garb of poverty and under the vows of repentance, that
'delivered from the hand of our enemies, we may serve him
without fear'.

[255]

To the same, on the same subject

FOR how long will the schemer triumph, and the heart
of the oppressed burn within them? For how long will such
great innocence be harassed by such arrant impudence? It must
be due to our sins that my lord is so late to discover those who
lie to him, so slow to hear those who call upon him in this matter. In other cases I know it is the custom of my lord quickly
to apprize the situation and readily to render help. For the sake
of him who has chosen you, and made you a refuge for the
down-trodden, now at last put an end to the wickedness of the
oppressor, and the troubles of the afflicted: both have been sufficiently shown up and exposed. At the command of my lord
the affair has been discussed and settled; it only remains that
the results should receive the confirmation of your authority.
Shall that man of lies be heard if he comes to you against the
witness of such great men as the bishops of Valence and Grenoble? Again I supplicate you and cast myself down before you
with the greatest anxiety possible lest you should suffer that
religious monastery to be wrecked by a treacherous and cruel
foe. For he who has nearly destroyed his own is not likely to
spare ours. Therefore with my usual presumption I add: if you
believe me, your child, send this man who abuses your kindness
back into his cloister, and command the Lord Abbot of Chaise-
Dieu that he promote a religious man to the position which he
uselessly holds, and that he set the monastery in order accord-

ing to the Rule. Clearly this would be a thing worthy of your apostolate, a thing pleasing to God; this would be for the honour of the Lord Abbot of Chaise-Dieu and his monastery. So also you would free the soul of that aforesaid man and the monastery which he burdens.

[271]

To the Bishop of Rochester

This letter was apparently written about the year 1142 after Ascelin had been consecrated Bishop of Rochester. It concerns one Robert Pullen, an Englishman of great learning and the first English cardinal. He reconstituted the schools of Oxford.

I HAVE not deserved your severe letter. What have I done wrong? I advised Robert Pullen to spend some time in Paris for the sake of the sound doctrine which is known to be taught there, because I thought it necessary and I still do so. I asked your Highness to permit this and would ask the same thing again, were I not sensible of your anger at my first petition. I said that he was supported by many friends whose influence in the Curia was not small, because I feared for you and I still do so. I did not think your action in seizing the goods of a man after he had appealed was a matter for praise, and I am still of the same opinion. But I never advised him to go against your will, and I do not do so now. I am your servant and am always ready to uphold and honour your authority with due and fitting reverence. On the strength of my good conscience in this affair I venture once more to advise and pray you to allow Master Robert to depart for a short time to Paris with your full favour. May God reward you for your kindness to my children, I mean my sons whom I have sent to Ireland.

[272]

To the Queen of Jerusalem

This letter is addressed to Melisande, daughter of Baldwin II, King of Jerusalem, and wife of Fulk V of Anjou. In the year 1143 Fulk of Anjou died, leaving the kingdom to his widow Melisande during the minority of her son Baldwin III, a boy of twelve years of age.

MEN say that I have some influence with you, and many who are to set out for Jerusalem beg me to commend them to Your Excellency. Amongst whom there is this young man, a kinsman of mine; a youth strong, they say, in arms and polished in manners. And I am delighted that for the time being[1] he has chosen to fight for God rather than for the world. Act according to your custom and, for my sake, see that all is well with him, as it has been for all my other kinsmen who were able to introduce themselves to you by means of myself. For the rest, take care that the pleasures of the flesh and the glory of the world do not hinder your journey to the heavenly kingdom. What profit is it to reign for a few days on earth, if the eternal kingdom is lost? But I am confident in the Lord that you will do better than this. And if it is true what my dear uncle Andrew says of you, and he is a man in whom I have every confidence, you will reign by the mercy of God both here and in eternity. Take care of the pilgrims, the needy, and especially the prisoners,[2] for God is gained by such sacrifices. Write to me often because it will not hurt you and it will benefit me to know fully and for certain of your state and dispositions.

1. . . . *ad tempus.* Eales: '. . . . at his age'.
2. *inclusis.*

To the same

A letter written to Melisande on the death of Fulk, her husband.

To the most illustrious Queen of Jerusalem, Melisande, that she may find favour with the Lord, from Bernard, styled Abbot of Clairvaux.

WERE I only to regard the glory of your kingdom, your power, and your noble lineage, my writing to you amidst all the many cares and occupations of your royal court might seem rather inappropriate. All these things are seen by the eyes of men, and those who have not got them envy those who have and call them happy. But what happiness is there in possessing what will 'soon fade like the grass and wither away like the green leaf'? These things are good, but they are transient and changeable, passing and perishable, because they are the goods only of the body. And of the body and its goods it has been said: 'Mortal things are but grass, the glory of them is but grass in flower'. So, when writing to you, I must not hold in too much awe those things of which we know 'the comeliness to be vain, and the beauty a snare'. Receive, therefore, what I have to say in a few words, for although I have many things to say to you, I will do so briefly because of your many affairs and mine. Receive a brief but useful word of advice from a distant land, as a small seed which will bear a great harvest in time. Receive advice from a friend who is seeking your honour and not his own ends. No one can give you more loyal advice than one who loves you and not your possessions. The king, your husband, being dead, and the young king still unfit to discharge the affairs of a kingdom and fulfil the duty of a king, the eyes of all will be upon you, and on you alone the whole burden of the kingdom will rest. You must set your hand to great things and, although a woman, you must act as a man by doing all you have to do 'in a spirit prudent and strong'. You must arrange all things prudently and discreetly, so that all may judge you from your actions to be a king rather than a queen and so that the Gentiles may have no occasion for saying: Where is the king of Jerusalem? But you will say: Such things are beyond my power; they are great matters which far exceed my strength and my knowledge; they are the duties of a man and I am only a woman, weak in body, changeable of heart, not far-seeing in counsel nor accustomed to business. I know, my daughter, I know that these are great matters, but I also know that although the raging of the sea is great, the Lord is great in heaven. These are great affairs, but great too is our Lord, and great his power.

[274]

To the same

To his beloved daughter Melisande, Queen of Jerusalem, the mercy of God our saviour, from Bernard, styled Abbot of Clairvaux.

I AM surprised that I have not had any letter from you or received any of your accustomed greetings for such a long time. I cannot forget your old affection for me which I have put to the proof in so many ways. I have heard certain evil reports of you, and although I do not completely believe them I am nevertheless sorry that your good name should be tarnished either by truth or falsehood. But my dear uncle Andrew has intervened with a letter signifying better things of you, and I cannot disbelieve anything he says. He tells me that you are behaving peacefully and kindly; that you are ruling yourself and your kingdom wisely with the advice of wise men; that you love the Brothers of the Temple and are on friendly terms

with them; and that, according to the wisdom given you by
God, you are providently and wisely meeting the dangers
which threaten the Holy Land with sound counsels and help.[1]
These are actions which become a strong woman, a humble
widow, a great queen. It is not beneath your dignity as a queen
to be a widow, and you need not be one if you do not wish it.
I believe that it is much to your honour, especially among
Christians, to live as a widow no less than a queen. You are a
queen by succession, but a widow by virtue. You are the former by reason of your lineage, the latter by the grace of God.
You have the former by the good fortune of your birth.
the latter you have obtained by courage. A double honour is
yours, the one according to world, the other according to God:
but both are from God. Do not think the honour of widow-
hood is a small thing, for the Apostle says: 'Honour widows that
are widows indeed'.

  2. You are familiar with the wholesome and sound advice of
the Apostle by which you are taught to 'watch your behaviour
not only before God, but also before men': Before God as a
widow, before men as a queen. Remember that you are a queen
whose worthy and unworthy actions cannot be hidden under
a bushel, but are set up on high for all men to see. Bear in mind
that you are a widow whose concern it is to please not man but
God. Blessed are you if you make the Saviour a wall for the
protection of your conscience, a breastwork to ward off dis-
grace. Blessed are you if, alone and a widow, you give yourself
wholly to God to be ruled by him. Unless you are well ruled,
you will not rule well. The Queen of the South came to hear
the wisdom of Solomon, that she might learn how to be ruled
and so how to rule. Now there is one greater than Solomon
here: I speak of Jesus and him crucified. Give yourself unto him
to be ruled, and to be taught how you ought to rule. Learn of

  1. The fact is that Melisande exposed the whole Latin Kingdom to the
attacks of Zengi, the Emir of Mosul, by breaking the alliance made by Fulk
with the Emir of Damascus. In 1144 Edessa, the bulwark of Jerusalem, was
captured by Zengi.

him as a widow, for he is meek and humble of heart; learn of him as a queen, because he gives the poor redress and rights the wrongs of the defenceless. When you think of your dignity, bear in mind that you are a widow because, to speak plainly, you cannot be a good queen unless you are also a good widow. You ask how you can tell a good widow? From what the Apostle says: 'If she have brought up children, if she have given shelter, if she have washed the saints' feet, if she have ministered to them that suffer tribulation, if she have diligently followed every good work'. If you do these things 'blessed thou art and all good shall be thine'. May the Lord that dwells in Sion bless thee, renowned daughter in the Lord, worthy of all respect. I send my admonition first, now I shall expect an answer. I have given you an opportunity and shall take no excuse if our friendship is not renewed in future by frequent and friendly letters and messages from you.

[282]

To Pope Innocent, on behalf of the
Bishop of Salamanca

The bishop referred to is Peter who, when his diocese was rent by a threefold schism, was summoned to Rome, and, together with the other leaders, degraded from his office. In this letter we have one of many examples of how ready Saint Bernard was to forgive and forget even the most serious misdemeanours and sins at the first sign of repentance.

THAT distinguished man, the former Bishop of Salamanca, did not consider it was too much trouble for him to turn aside on his way back from Rome to visit me, your child; nor did he consider it beneath his dignity to implore the help of myself, good-for-nothing though I be. When I heard what he had to say, I thought of those words of the Prophet: 'Every mountain and every hill shall be levelled'. This is your amusement, to level down the high-minded, to repress those who are swollen with pride, and to reduce the overbearing to their measure. When the man told me the whole story of his tragedy as it had happened, I had nothing but praise for the judge and approval for the judgement; but, I must tell you, I was moved by pity for the judged. The whole theme of his story was those words of the Prophet: 'I have been lifted up only to be cast down and left bewildered', and 'so low hast thou brought me who didst once lift me up on high'. When I thought of your justice and your strong character, which I used to know so well, I thought at the same time of your great mercy which I have experienced on so many occasions, and I said: 'Who can tell whether he will not relent and forgive, and leave behind him a blessing?' Certainly, I say, he is ready everywhere and always to be jealous and yet to forgive; 'to subdue the proud, and yet to spare the vanquished', except that, after the example of his master, he is also wont to prefer mercy to justice. I consented with my usual presumption to speak to my lord, even I who am but dust and ashes. And I found grounds for hope, confidence for my petition, a reason for my pity, in that I saw the man did not, as is usual in such cases, turn away in fury, and return to his native land, there to stir up scandals and foment schisms; but that he gave place to wrath, adopted an attitude of meekness, and turned his steps towards your monks of Cluny there to throw himself at the knees of the humble monks and fortify himself with their intercession, as with powerful arms from God. With these weapons he is determined to strive with you, and with these engines of devotion he will try, as he declares, to undermine that wall of your severity by which he is confronted. He is sure that you will hear the prayers of the humble, and not spurn their intercession, and that you, before whom the princes of the world tremble, will be overcome by piety. I too

with confidence stretch out my hands in company with such
men, bow my knees before you, and supplicate for the suppli-
cant. I boldly pronounce that this poor man who has already
been hindered enough by his haughtiness, ought now to be
helped by his humility; that it is not right for only vice and not
virtue to receive its due.[1]

[283]

To the same, on behalf of Peter of Pisa

The reconciliation of the Cardinal Priest Peter of Pisa to Inno-
cent II at the height of the schism was one of the great personal
triumphs of St. Bernard. He met him at Salerno and after ad-
dressing him a moving appeal in the presence of Roger of Sicily,
he took him by the hand and led him off to Pope Innocent.
There can be no doubt at all that Innocent pardoned him and
confirmed him in his office. But Innocent in difficulties was a
very different person from Innocent victorious as, much to his
disappointment, St. Bernard was to discover. Hardly was the
schism ended than Innocent, who before had been so reasonable
and long-suffering, began reprisals, much to the very openly
expressed indignation of the saint. At a council held at the
Lateran during the April of 1139, *all the supporters of the anti-*
Pope were ignominiously deprived of office without any dis-
tinction being made between those who had remained in schism
right to the very end, so that it was not so much they who left
the schism as the schism which left them, and those who, like
Peter of Pisa, were reconciled with Innocent while the schism
was still at its height. This letter must have been written soon
after 1139, *but unfortunately it appears that its only effect was*

1. Peter might have been reinstated in his office had not envoys from King
Alfonso arrived in Rome in haste to obtain the see for a friend of the king.

to lose St. Bernard the friendship of the Pope. It was not until four years later, during the pontificate of Celestine II, that Peter was reinstated in his honours.

WHO shall judge between us? If I had a judge before whom I could bring you, I would soon show you (I speak as one in travail) what you deserve. There is the tribunal of Christ, but God forbid that I should summon you before that, far sooner would I stand up and defend you there, should such a thing be necessary for you or possible for me. And so I hasten to him whose duty it is in the present time to judge all things, and that is yourself. I arraign you against yourself, to judge between yourself and myself. What, I ask you, have I, your son, done to deserve so ill of you that you must brand and blazon me with the name and stigma of a traitor? Were you not pleased to appoint me as your representative for the reconciliation of Peter of Pisa, should God deign through me to call him from the foul condition of schism? If you deny this, I can prove it by as many witnesses as there were men in the Curia at the time. And after this was not the man received back to his position and honours according to your plighted word? Who is it then who has advised you, or rather beguiled you to revoke what you had once granted, and to go back on the word your lips had uttered? I say this not to blame your severity, or the zeal with which you were fired by God against the schismatics, the zeal and severity with which you 'wrecked the ships of Tharsis' and, after the example of Phinees, slew the fornicators, according to those words of the Prophet: 'Lord, do I not hate the men who hate thee, am I not sick at heart over their rebellion?' But it is clear that the punishment ought to fit the crime, it ought not to be the same for a small sin as a great one, nor is it right that he who forsook the schism should fall under the same sentence as those whom the schism forsook. For the sake of him who, that he might spare sinners, did not spare himself, remove this reproach against me and, by re-installing him whom you have once installed, honour your first wise and un-biased decision. I have written to you on this matter before, but because I never received an answer, I suppose my letter did not reach you.

[305]

To Peter the Venerable, Abbot of Cluny

It would certainly not be surprising if relations between the Abbot of Clairvaux and the Abbot of Cluny had become rather strained as a result of the rivalry between the two Orders, the dispute over the election at Langres, and the exemption of the Cistercians from paying tithe; and the following letter seems to indicate that this had indeed been the case. But the Benedictine editor of the letters refuses to admit that there had been any estrangement between the two men, and maintains that St. Bernard was writing only facetiously and rhetorically.

To the reverend father and lord Peter, by the grace of God Abbot of Cluny, the humble devotion of Bernard, styled Abbot of Clairvaux.

SO YOU are pleased to jest? Courteously and kindly I would admit, if I could be sure you were not ridiculing me. Do not be surprised at my saying this, for your sudden and unexpected urbanity makes me a little uneasy. It is not so long ago that I greeted you in a letter with all the respect that is your due, yet you never answered one word. And it is not long since I wrote to you again from Rome, but even then I did not get a reply. Are you therefore surprised that I did not presume to trouble you with my trifles when you got back from Spain? If it is blameworthy not to have written for some reason or other, how can you be free of blame for having neglected, not to say disdained, to write in answer to my letters? So you see what I might urge in justice on my behalf (for that is what you implored me to do), if I did not prefer to welcome your renewal of favour towards me rather than to delay it by futile excuses or accusations. I have only said this so as to be quite open with you and not to keep anything back from you, for this true friendship demands. Because charity believeth all things, I have put away all my misgivings and am glad that you have warmed to the memory of an old friendship, and recalled a wounded friend. Being recalled I am happy to return, happy to be recalled. I have now put out of mind all grievances. Here I am, now as ever, your devoted servant, and full of gratitude for being once more your intimate friend, as you were kind enough to write. If I had perhaps grown cold towards you, as you reproach me for having done, there is no doubt that cherished by your love I shall soon grow warm again.

2. I welcomed your letter with open hands. I have read it and re-read it greedily and gladly, and the more often I read it the better pleased I am. I must say I enjoy your fun. It is both pleasantly gay and seriously grave. I do not know how it is you are able to be both gay and grave, so that your fun has nothing about it of frivolity, and your dignity loses nothing by your gaiety. You are able to keep your dignity so well in the midst of your fun that those words of the holy man might be applied to you: 'I smiled on them though they were never so ill at ease, and the encouragement of my glance never failed them'. So you see I have answered you, and now I think I am entitled to demand more than you promised! It is only right that you should know how things are going with me. I have decided to stay in my monastery and not go out, except once a year for the general chapter of Abbots at Cîteaux. Here, supported by your prayers and consoled by your good will, I shall remain for the few days that are left to me in which to fight, 'until the time comes for me to be relieved at my post'. May God be merciful and never alienate his mercy or your prayers from me. I am

broken in body and have a legitimate excuse for not going about as I used to do. I shall sit still and hold my peace, so that perhaps I may experience something of that inner sweetness of which the Prophet sings: 'If deliverance thou wouldst have from the Lord, in silence await it'. And, so as not to appear the only one to make fun of me, I suppose you will not now dare to reproach me with my silence and, in the way you have, to call it sloth! As a matter of fact I think Isaias has more suitably and properly called it 'the service of righteousness'; and, inspired by God, he also says, 'In quietness and in confidence lies your strength'. Commend me to the prayers of your holy brethren at Cluny having first, if you think fit, greeted them from me as the servant of them all.[1]

PETER THE VENERABLE TO ST. BERNARD

In a very long reply to the Abbot of Clairvaux (Benedictine Edition, 229), Peter, in a most affectionate greeting expresses his delight with Bernard's last letter and describes how he could not refrain from kissing it before he read it out to his brethren. He excuses himself from the charge of not answering Bernard's letters on the grounds that the letter from Rome was in reply to one of his, and that he has no recollection of the previous letter. He then goes on to express his regrets for the mutual distrust and rancour which was dividing the monks of their two Orders. He attributes this first to the difference between their customs, and declares that it is childish and stupid, because quite unreasonable, to allow such things to cause any ill-feeling. If such differences in customs and observances were a valid reason for quarrelling there would be no charity left anywhere. The Church herself has a hundred different customs and usages in various parts of the world. 'What', he asks, 'does it matter if monks, united by one profession, should observe different customs, so long as all alike attain to eternal life?' As for their different interpretations of the Rule, the Rule itself allows the greatest liberty to the abbot in the ordering and arranging of

1. *Commendate me orationibus sancti conventus Cluniacensis, salutato prius ex me servo omnium, si dignum judicatis.* Eales more literally: 'Commend me to the prayers of your sacred convent of Cluny; salute it first from me, the servant of all, if you think fit'.

all things for the salvation of souls. In fact this is all that matters, the salvation of souls; and for this we should cultivate that single eye which renders the whole body full of light. He then urges his own monks who have adopted certain mitigations in the letter of the Rule, but not against the mind of the legislator, to cultivate this single eye which regards solely, not the mote in another's eye, but the glory of God and the salvation of souls. He prays that his Cistercian brethren may do the same and not scorn their Cluniac brothers, who, like them, are seeking only God's glory and the salvation of souls. As for the different colour of their habits, it were sheer folly to quarrel about such a trivial thing. Yet he had seen black monks looking askance at their white-robed brethren of Cîteaux, and vice versa! As if both white and black were not sheep of the same heavenly shepherd! What human shepherd, not to say God, would ever quarrel about the different colour of his sheep's wool? It is not the colour of the habit that matters, but the colour of the soul. The Rule itself allows the greatest latitude in the matter and enjoins the brethren not to grumble about the colour of their habits, but to be content with whatever can be got most cheaply. In fact there are excellent reasons and ample authorities for both the black habit and the white habit. In any case no one could be so stupid as to think that diversity of colours or customs could make any difference to the salvation of souls. In conclusion, Peter remarks that the real root of all the trouble between the two Orders is the dismay felt by his own black monks at seeing the tide of fashion turn against their venerable institution and the white monks, who are only a new Order, preferred to them everywhere. To this he replies by pleading for mutual tolerance and respect. He implores his black monks to abase themselves before their white-robed brethren for the love of Christ, and he prays that the white monks may put aside any censoriousness and humble themselves before their Cluniac brethren, and in accordance with the Rule they both claim to follow, 'not only to say in word that they are lower and more vile than all, but to believe it in the depths of their hearts'.

This letter from Peter the Venerable impresses one as the letter of a great and magnanimous man to whom all pettiness would be quite foreign and incomprehensible.

In another letter (Benedictine Edition, 264), Peter, after greeting the Abbot of Clairvaux as the great and glorious pillar of the monastic Order, and indeed of the whole Church, goes on to say that, if he were free to order his life according to his pleasure, he would choose to live with Bernard rather than to be a king amongst men. He calls Bernard a fellow citizen of the saints in heaven and once more repeats his great desire to be always with him, or at least to see him often. But as neither of these things is possible, Peter asks whether he might be allowed, as the next best thing, to enjoy Bernard's presence in the person of his beloved secretary, Nicholas. This Nicholas is none other than that notorious secretary of Bernard who, having insinuated himself into the confidence of his abbot and of Peter, finally fled from Clairvaux after grave misconduct, taking with him Bernard's personal seal.

[306]

To Peter the Venerable, Abbot of Cluny

O YOU good man, what have you done? You have praised a sinner, you have numbered a good-for-nothing amongst the blessed! You must now pray that I shall not be led into error. I should be led into error if, in my delight at such great praises, I were to forget the sort of person I am. This almost did happen when I read the letter in which you made me out to be blessed. If words could do that, how happy I would be. Even now I would call myself happy, but by your favour not by my own deserts. Happy to be loved by you and happy in loving you. Although I do not think that even that tit-bit, sweet as it is, can be swallowed whole or even, as they say, admitted to the teeth. Do you wonder why? It is because I can find nothing in myself to deserve such affection, especially from such a man as you. I know that a just man will never wish to be loved more than he deserves. Would that I could imitate as well as I can admire such humility. Would that I could enjoy your company, I do not say always, nor even often, but just once or twice in a year! It could not but be profitable for me to see such an example of all the virtues, such a model of regular observance, such a mirror of sanctity, nor would it be in vain that I should see with the eye of faith how meek and humble you are, which I admit is a thing I have not even yet learned from Christ. But if I go on to do to you what I complain of your doing to me, although I should speak the truth, yet I would violate that rule of truth which says: 'Never do to another what you would not have done to yourself'. And so I will now answer the trifling request with which you concluded your letter. He for whom you have asked is not with me now, but with the Bishop of Auxerre. I am told he is so ill that he cannot come to us without grave inconvenience.

[308]

To the same

To his most reverend father and dear friend Peter, by the grace of God Abbot of Cluny, health and greetings in the source of all true health, from Brother Bernard, styled Abbot of Clairvaux.

WOULD that I were able to express in this letter all that I feel towards you! Then you would certainly see clearly the love for you which God has inscribed upon my heart and engraved upon my very bones. But what need is there for me to commend myself to you in this way? For a long time now we have been united in the closest friendship, and an equal affection has rendered us equals. What could a person of my lowly attainments have in common with a man like you, if you were not so tolerant of my limitations? Thus it has come about that both my lowliness and your magnanimity have been so blended that I could not be lowly without you nor you magnanimous without me. I say this because my son Nicholas, who is your son too, is himself greatly disturbed and has greatly disturbed me by telling me that he noticed that one of my letters to you concluded with bitter words. Believe me who love you that nothing could have come from my heart or left my lips which would have offended your ears. My many occupations are to blame, because when my secretaries have not fully grasped my meaning they are apt to write too sharply, and I do not have time to read through what they have written. Forgive me this time, for whatever I may do with other letters, I shall in future look through my letters to you and trust no one's ears or eyes but my own. The rest will be more fully and more clearly recounted to you by our common son. Harken to him as you would to myself who love you so dearly, not in mere words, but in deed and truth. Greet for me all your holy brethren, and pray them to pray for me.

PETER THE VENERABLE'S REPLY

Peter answers the preceding letter from St. Bernard with the utmost cordiality and affection (Benedictine Edition, 388). He disclaims all the high titles that the saint gives him and retains only that of 'dear friend'. As for the bitter words for which the saint apologized (they were in a letter concerning the business of an English abbot), Peter declares that he was not in the least offended by them, and if he had been the apology of Bernard would have been a more than ample amend. After this Peter refers to the will of one Baro, a Roman subdeacon. He says that although all that he had deposited at Cluny belonged by right to the abbey, yet he is quite willing for Bernard and his brethren to have it. In conclusion he refers to an election at Grenoble to which the Carthusians were objecting. He says that he has entrusted his opinion on the affair to Nicholas and asks Bernard to accept what Nicholas tells him as coming from himself.

[309]

To the same

To his most dear father and lord Peter, by the grace of God Abbot of Cluny, health and greetings from Brother Bernard, styled Abbot of Clairvaux.

WHEN your letter first arrived I was only able to take a short but very affectionate glance at it. I was busy at the time with so many things as you alone know or can know, most loving father. Yet I tore myself away and escaped from the ceaseless questions and petitions of everyone, and shut myself up alone with Nicholas, of whom you are so fond. There I refreshed myself again and again with the charm which emanated from your letter. So fragrant was it with affection that my heart was moved. I was sorry, that, as I was situated, I could not sit down there and then to answer you. My many daily duties were calling me. A great crowd of people from almost every nation under the sun had arrived to see me. I had to attend to them all because for my sins I am born to be embarrassed and consumed with many and manifold cares. In the meantime I am scribbling this short note, but when I have more leisure I will write a careful letter expressing my sentiments more clearly. What you sent us from that will, we assure you in all sincerity, we have received not as a debt but as a gift. I am very glad to hear the truth about the Grenoble affair. I must tell you that my heart glowed at the words of our common son which you in part related to me.[1] I am ready and prepared to do your will wherever I can. At the chapter of abbots at Cîteaux a commemoration was made of you as our special lord, father, and very dear friend, and of all yours, living and dead. The elect of Beauvais greets you as your friend, which he is.

And I Nicholas add my undying affection for you and for all your household.

1. Guy, Prior of the Grande Chartreuse.

[315]

To the Roman Curia, when they elected the Cistercian Abbot of St. Anastasius to be Pope

On the death of Lucius II in 1145, *Bernard Paganelli, formerly a monk of Clairvaux and latterly Abbot of St. Anastasius near Rome (now known as the abbey of Tre Fontane), was elected Pope.*

To his lords and reverend fathers, all the cardinals and bishops in Curia, the greetings of their son.

GOD have mercy on you; what have you done? You have recalled a dead man from the grave and restored him to his fellow men. You have plunged once more into crowds and cares a man who had fled from both. You have made the last first and lo! his final stage is more fraught with danger than his first. A man crucified to the world has been brought back into the world by you, and a man who 'had chosen to lie forgotten in the house of the Lord' you have set up to be the lord of all men. Why have you thwarted the hopes of a needy man, why have you confused the decisions of a poor man, a beggar, a penitent? He was running his course well, what made you block up his path, turn his road, entangle his steps? He has fallen among robbers as though he had been going down from Jerusalem instead of coming up from Jericho. He who had resolutely shaken himself free of the powerful clutches of the devil, the snares of the flesh, the glory of the world, has not been able to escape your hands. Did he leave Pisa so as to receive Rome? Did he, who could not endure the responsibility of being second in charge of one church, covet the lordship of the whole Church?

2. What reason, what counsel, made you, as soon as the late

Pope had died, suddenly rush upon this rustic, lay hands upon him when in hiding from the world, and, knocking away his axe, mattock, or hoe, drag him to the palatine, place him upon a throne, clothe him in purple and fine linen, and gird him with a sword 'ready to take vengeance upon the heathen, to curb nations, to chain kings, and bind princes in fetters'? Had you no other wise and experienced man amongst you who would have been better suited for these things? It certainly seems ridiculous to take a man in rags and make him preside over princes, command bishops, and dispose of kingdoms and empires. Ridiculous or miraculous? Either one or the other. I have no doubts that this could be the work of God 'who does wonderful things as none else', especially when I hear everyone saying that it has been done by the Lord. I have not forgotten the judgements of God in times gone by or what the Scriptures tell us of many men taken from a private and even rustic life by the will of God, to rule over his people. To mention only one, did he not choose David somewhat after the same manner to be his servant, and 'take him away from herding sheep, and bid him leave off following the ewes that were in milk'?

3. And yet I am not happy in my own mind, for his nature is delicate, and his tender diffidence is more accustomed to leisure than to dealing in great affairs. I fear that he may not exercise his apostolate with sufficient firmness. What do you think will be the feelings of a man who from the secrets of contemplation and the sweet solitude of his heart, suddenly finds himself plunged into a vortex of great affairs, like a child suddenly snatched from his mother's arms, like a sheep being led to sacrifice and finding himself in unfamiliar and unwelcome surroundings? Unless the Lord support him with his hand, he must necessarily be overcome and crushed under such an excessive and unaccustomed load, formidable even for a giant, even for the very angels themselves. Nevertheless because it has been done, and many are saying it has been done by the Lord, it must be your concern, dearest friends, to help and comfort with

your fervent support what is clearly the work of your hands. If you have in you any power to console, if there is in you any charity from the Lord, if you have any pity, any compassion, support him in the work to which he has been lifted up by the Lord through you. Whatever things are true, whatever things are seemly, whatever things are of good fame, suggest them to him, persuade him of them, encourage him to do them, and the God of peace will be with you.

[319]

To the Roman People, when they rebelled
against Pope Eugenius

To the nobles, chief citizens, and all the people of Rome, that they may offend no more, but rather do good, from Brother Bernard, styled Abbot of Clairvaux.

ALTHOUGH I am a contemptible and insignificant person, a mere nobody, I am addressing my words to you, the great and famous Roman People. When I consider who I am, to whom I am writing, and at the same time how very different my action could appear to another, I am bowed down by the very burden of it, held back for very shame. But I consider that it is a lesser evil to be in danger of contempt from men than of condemnation by God for keeping silent, for not speaking out the truth, for hiding his justice, when he himself has said: 'Raise thy voice like a trumpet call and tell my people of their transgressions'. It will be something in my favour before God if I can say: 'Thy just dealings are no secret hidden away in my heart; I boast of thy faithful protection, proclaim that mercy, that faithfulness of thine for all to hear it'. Therefore I am not afraid, obscure and timid person though I be, to write from afar to the glorious people of Rome and by a letter from over the mountains to admonish them of their sin and of their danger, in case they should hear me and relent. Who knows if this people who yield not to threat of arms and quail not before the forces of powerful men may not be converted by the prayers of an obscure and poor man. Did it not happen once that the people of Babylon, who had been deceived by wicked judges, at the voice of a mere boy, reconsidered their judgement, so that the life of an innocent person was saved on that day? And so now too 'although I am very young and despised' (young in virtue not in years), God can still give power to my utterance, so that by it the people who have been led astray may reconsider their judgement. This is my answer to those who think that they ought to be indignant at my presumption in writing to you.

2. But if this is not enough, let me add that this matter is one that concerns everyone, it is the common cause of all, great or small. The trouble is in the head, and for this reason there is no member of the body so small or so insignificant as not to be affected by it, not even myself. This very great trouble affects even me although I am the least of all, because what affects the head cannot but affect the body of which I am a member. When the head is suffering does not the tongue cry out for all the members of the body that the head is in pain, and do not all the members of the body confess by means of the tongue that the head is theirs and the pain too? 'For a little, leave me to myself that I may find some comfort in my misery' and not my misery but the misery of the whole Church. 'My head is suffering', are these not the words she is crying out everywhere? What Christian, even though he be the least in the world, does not glory in this head because of those two princes of the world, Peter and Paul, who exalted her by their victory and adorned her with their blood, the one bowing his head on the

cross, the other under the sword? The suffering of the Apostles concerns every Christian, and as 'their utterance fills every land' so their wounds are felt by all.

3. Why, O Romans, why do you offend the princes of the world who are your special patrons? Why do you arouse against you the king of earth and the Lord of heaven, by your intolerable ravings, and by attacking rashly and sacrilegiously the Holy and Apostolic See, which is uniquely exalted by divine and royal privileges; and why do you try to diminish its honour, you who ought to be ready to defend it single handed against the whole world? Thus, foolish Romans, without seeing or understanding what is right, thus do you endeavour to throw over your head and the head of all, in defence of whom you ought rather, if necessary, to sacrifice your own necks. Your fathers subjugated the whole world to the City, but you are coming near to making it ridiculous in the eyes of the whole world. The heir of Peter has been expelled by you from the throne and city of Peter. The cardinals and bishops, ministers of the Lord, have been despoiled by you of their goods and houses. O foolish and senseless people! O people void of brains and heart! Was he not your own head, and were not his eyes your own? What is Rome now but a body without a head,[1] a face with the eyes gouged out, a countenance darkened? Unhappy people, open your eyes and see the desolation which is even now upon you: 'All dim, now and discoloured, the gold that once shone so fair. Alone she dwells in the city, a widow now, once a queen among nations.'

4. But this is only the beginning of evils, I fear there may be worse to come. If you persist in your evil ways, I fear the end may be at hand. 'Come back, maid of Sulem, come back' to your senses. Acknowledge now, late though it be, what great evils you have suffered, and from whom you have suffered it, and still are suffering it. Consider for what reason, for what purpose, by whom and for whose benefit, you have only lately

1. Cf. *Aen.*, 2.255-7.

squandered all the revenues and ornaments of your churches. Whatever gold or silver could be found in the vessels of the altar, on the sacred images themselves, has been torn off and carried away by impious hands. How much of all this have you still got in your purses now? But the beauty of the Lord's house has been irretrievably lost. And now why are you trying to repeat all this mischief, and bring yourself once more on evil days? What hope of gain is luring you on? All that can be said at present is that your latest actions are more reckless than your former, because then not only many of the people, but also some of the clergy and princes of the world, took your part in that schism. But now your hand is against all, and the hand of all is against you. All the world is innocent of your blood, except you yourselves and your children with you. Woe to you, pitiful people, and woe doubly worse than before, not from outside nations, not from the frenzy of the barbarians, not from thousands of armed men, but only from yourselves. Woe to you from your own household and friends, from domestic strife, from cruel wounds self-inflicted, from the torture inflicted on you by your own children.

5. Do you understand now how all are not peaceably disposed towards you in your own household, not all are friends who seem to be so? Even if we had known it before, we are now being taught more plainly by your fate the truth of those words of our Lord: 'A man's own household are his enemies'. Woe to brother from brother in your midst and to children from their parents! Woe to them not from the sword but from treacherous lips and the tongue that utters guile! For how long will you evilly encourage each other to do evil and slay each other with your own tongues, so that you are consuming each other up? Gather together the scattered sheep, return to the meadows, return to your bishop, the shepherd of your souls. Lunatics, return to your senses. I say this not to revile you as an enemy, but to rebuke you as a friend. True friends sometimes rebuke, but flatterers never.

6. I now add entreaties. I entreat you for the love of Christ
to be reconciled to God, to be reconciled to your rulers, I
mean to Peter and Paul whom you have driven from your midst
in the person of Eugenius, their vicar and successor. Be reconciled to the princes of this earth lest perchance the whole
world should take up arms on their behalf against your folly.
Do you not realize that with them against you, you are powerless; with them on your side, you have nothing to fear? Under
their protection you will have no cause to fear the thousand
peoples around you. Be reconciled at the same time to the
thousands of martyrs who are in your midst, but who are
against you on account of the great sin you have committed
and still persist in committing. Be reconciled also to all the
Church of the saints who everywhere are scandalized by what
they hear of you. Otherwise this letter will bear witness against
you and the very Apostles will 'stand forth boldly to meet their
persecutors who thwart all their strivings'. Let us now have an
end to talking. I have proclaimed justice to you, I have foretold your danger, I have not hidden the truth, but I have ex-
horted you to better things. It only remains for me either to be
delighted by your speedy correction or to be inconsolably
saddened by the certainty of your imminent condemnation,
withering away for fear and expectation of what will come
upon your whole city.

[324]

To Pope Eugenius, warning him of the Bishop of Séez

IT is not my habit, as it is of many, to preface anything
I want to say to you, or to approach it in a roundabout way.
So I will come to the point immediately. A deceitful man is

coming to you, in order to deceive you, so I believe. May he not succeed! For this could not happen without danger, very grave danger, to many. As it is always evil to deceive, so it is commonly an evil to be deceived. But it makes a difference who is deceived, and in what. To cheat you, especially in ecclesiastical matters, is all the more dangerous and disgusting because your power and dignity are so great. If, for example, the fox of Séez, by his crafty machinations, is able, as he hopes, cunningly to deceive you so as to be able to return with your authority to the vineyard of the Lord where he did so much harm in so short a time, with what great ferocity will he not rage in the future! Alas, he will devour all that is left of it! He comes to you, a fox, but he will return a lion! And he will no longer use cunning but cruelty against many of the clergy and laity. Therefore we must be on our guard against his guile, so that his violence shall have no opportunity to break out again.

2. Do not let yourself be hoodwinked by the man's sad demeanour, mean clothes, pleading expression, lowly glance, humble words, nor even by his crocodile tears which, I am told, he has taught himself to shed as the occasion demands. All this is just appearances, and you know who it was that said: 'Judge not according to appearances'. The appearances of piety consist in these sort of things, but not always the virtue! These are merely the sheep's clothing, too often, as the Lord tells us, used by wolves so as to be able to slaughter more sheep, who do not hide themselves because they come amongst them disguised. For this reason even some of my own people have written to you on behalf of this man. They have been deceived by his tricks, not paying enough attention to what the Wise Man has so wisely said: 'Here is one that wears the garb of penance for wicked ends, his heart full of guile'. Pay no regard to what he says or to how he bears himself, consider what he has done. From his fruits you shall know him. Many deplorable things are said about him, and if there is one who sees and judges he will have to answer for them. I do not want to tell

you all I have heard of him. One cannot believe everything, on the other hand one cannot discount everything. I will briefly tell you what occurs to me; it will be for you to judge whether I am right or not. I ask myself, why did he avoid his appointed judges? If the reason is that he has some personal complaint about them, they are men above suspicion. If it was because of the inconvenience of the place, it was in his neighbourhood, amongst his own kindred and he could easily have gone to them and explained his business at little expense and small trouble. It only remains to believe that the cunning man fled from a crowd of accusers who could not follow him outside their country for lack of money. I thank his Lordship of Lisieux who, moved by zeal for the house of God, has spared neither himself nor his purse. He is a good brother who desires to raise up seed to his dead brother.[1] Do you also thank him, for he has by his diligence added not a little lustre to your name, since by it the wicked man has been found out and overthrown, and this is to your glory.

[326]

To the Carthusian Prior of Portes

This letter is noteworthy for the final sentence in which the Saint describes and deplores his entanglement in external affairs.

I GATHER from your reply to my letter that you are perturbed because something I wrote to you has given the impression that I am upset. My dear reverend fathers, you have nothing to fear from me who love you sincerely as my friends, and who look up to you as holy men. Perhaps with fatherly affection it was not me whom you feared but for me, because I

1. This was Arnulf, Bishop of Lisieux. Bernard says that he is raising up seed to his dead brother, because he caused some secular canons to observe the rule of St. Augustine which had been given to them by his brother John.

seemed to be disturbed without good reason, or at any rate more than I should have been. It is true that I was distressed, but for you, not with you, and that only very slightly. If even in this I have been rash, without any rashness I will accuse myself of rash judgement and you will forgive me. Pardon me, I pray you, for my nature is such that I am consumed with zeal for your house. I cannot bear to see such holiness as yours tarnished, if there is anything I can do to prevent it. I say tarnished, for God forbid that I should ever believe it could be corrupted. The slightest blemish, not to say disease, in the fair body of your brotherhood saddens me. Clearly it would be a dimming of your lustre for any one of you to take ill a humiliation since a perfect man would take pleasure in it and glory in it. For one who has determined to be perfect any imperfection is a blemish. Therefore this dimming of lustre, this blemish in Brother Noel saddens me. Even if he should be pure before God, what then? He should also watch his behaviour before men.

2. But you say: It was not he that bore it ill, but we who were grieved on his account. It comes to the same thing. Again I will say what I think. I cannot think why you should be grieved on his account unless it is because you feel that what has happened is grievous to him. It is for you to judge whether it is becoming for him to be grieved over such a matter, especially when he is so new to the life. For, if he will pardon my saying so, he was rather like this even before his entry, though whether by his fault only his own conscience can tell. Perhaps this is what was in the mind of the Pope when, as you say, he refused to confirm his election. I expect he forbade the hasty promotion of the new hermit because he was fearful of the tongues of detractors; because he did not want spiteful people to be able to say that this was the fruit that Brother Noel hoped to gather from the desert. But whatever may have been the Pope's intention, whether it was this or something else, you must know that he said nothing to me about it, so no one can say that he

acted under my influence. For my part I am resolved that, so far as I can, I shall at my first opportunity, not only not stand in his way, but with all my strength, with both hands, as they say, draw him where the grace which is in him may best bear fruit for the glory of God. Who will grant me to see learned and holy men as pastors presiding in the Church of God, if not everywhere or even in many places, at least in some? What matter if it is remembered that once when still a youth Brother Noel acted after the fashion of a youth? The old things are passed away and all is made new. He is buried again with Christ by the baptism of the desert, and I shall not rake up again his buried vices.

3. I was very much upset when I heard of the Abbot of Chézy or of Troyes having written harshly to you. When I have the opportunity I shall not fail to tell them what I think as far as is in keeping with the love and friendship I have for them on account of their piety. I thank God that he has not permitted you to be overcome by evil, but has given you the strength to overcome evil by good, instead of returning evil for evil and cursing for cursing. As regards the letters you had written to me in the past against those aforesaid abbots, you may be quite sure that they did not learn about them through any wish or efforts of mine. And now enough of this.

4. It is time for me to remember myself. May my monstrous life, my bitter conscience, move you to pity. I am a sort of modern chimæra,[1] neither cleric nor layman. I have kept the habit of a monk, but I have long ago abandoned the life. I do not wish to tell you what I dare say you have heard from others: what I am doing, what are my purposes, through what dangers I pass in the world, or rather down what precipices I am hurled. If you have not heard, enquire and then, according to what you hear, give your advice and the support of your prayers.

1. *Chimæra:* a triple-bodied monster, lion before, she-goat in the middle and a serpent behind.

To Pope Eugenius

LET others fear your Majesty, so that with trembling lips and fingers and by devious circumlocutions they can hardly come to the point of what they want to say. I have regard only for your honour and advantage and say what I have to say openly and at once; I am not afraid to say what is necessary without any delay or beating about the bush, just as if you were one of ourselves. Therefore I do not hesitate to tell you that you have been deceived and very gravely. Who advised you to thrust ecclesiastical preferment on a man who stands convicted and condemned for ambition? As if he were not anxious enough on his own account to push himself forward! Is this not the man whom Bishop Lambert of holy memory[1] caught red-handed in the most hateful misdeeds perpetrated under the spur of ambition, and degraded with all due solemnity not only from the position he held at the time, but from all prospect of promotion? There is nothing else for you to do but to revoke your decision, and this for the sake of those holy brothers of Corona who are so anxiously calling on you to do so on account of the holy and learned bishop who was the prime mover in this matter, as well as for the sake of conscience, no one else's conscience but yours. It only remains for me to satisfy my own conscience by quoting to you those words, 'Be angry and sin not'. You will sin if you are not angry with the man who gave you this deceitful advice, and inveigled from you such an unworthy decision.

1. Bishop of Angoulême in succession to Gerard. The Benedictine monastery of Corona was in his diocese.

[339]

To the same

This is a good example of the Saint's powers of invective.

A SERPENT has deceived me! A double-faced cunning wretch, void of all righteousness, afraid of an interview, an enemy of his own conscience, battening on the injury of his brethren, has without my knowledge obtained letters of recommendation from me through the Bishop of Beauvais. For what would I not do for this man? If you do not wish my conscience to be even further burdened, see that this cunning villain gains nothing and is not able to use any letter of mine for persecuting innocent people. Although even this would not satisfy me if his evil swindler and greedy extortioner were not made to pay the penalty of his misdeeds.

To Count Theobald

…n of the age, unwillingly tolerated by the Church, …en of the nobility to be invested with the revenues …me rich benefices. But the Saint, ahead of his times in this as in so much else, strongly opposed this abuse and refused to be a party of it even for the sake of the son of his old friend and most generous benefactor, Count Theobald.

YOU know that I care for you, but how much I do so God knows better than you. I am quite sure that you too are fond of me, but for the sake of God. Therefore if I should offend God, you would have no reason for your affection since

then God would not be with me. Why should a great prince like you care for an insignificant creature like me, unless you believed that God were with me? So perhaps it would not be to your advantage for me to offend God. But I would certainly offend God were I to do what you want me to do. For I know quite well that ecclesiastical honours and preferments are due to those who are able and willing to administer them worthily for the honour of God. So to obtain them by my influence for your young son would not be just to you or yours and would be dangerous for myself. It is not lawful for anyone, even for an adult, to hold benefices in many churches, except by dispensation on account of some great need of the Church or because of some outstanding advantage. Therefore if you feel this too hard a saying and are still determined to carry out your plan, I beg you to excuse me from having any part in it. I am sure that you would be able to obtain what you want by your own influence and that of your friends. And so you would achieve your purpose without my sinning. Certainly I wish your William well, but before all I would that he should stand well with God. Hence I am unwilling that he should do anything against the will of God lest he should lose God. But if anyone should wish differently, I would not be a party to it lest I too should lose God. When he wants something that he can have without offending God, then I shall prove myself a friend and, if necessary, do all I can to help him. To one who, like you, loves righteousness, there is no need for me to labour to excuse righteousness. Please make my excuses to the countess in accordance with what I have written.

[351]

To Count Henry, the Son of Theobald, Count of Champagne

No matter how deeply involved the Saint might have been in high matters of state, yet he did not consider the plight of a poor Abbot who had lost his pigs beneath his attention. There are countless examples amongst his letters of the Saint's concern for the small affairs of humble people.

THE Abbot of Châtillon, a good man, when he set out for Rome left all his property under my protection. And now the servants of Simon, men of Belfort, have taken off his pigs. I assure you I would rather have had my own pigs stolen. The King of kings has set you up as a prince upon earth so that by his power and for his sake you may encourage the good, restrain the evil, defend the poor, and give justice to those who suffer injuries. If you do this you will be fulfilling the functions of your state and can have every reason to hope that God will increase and strengthen your principality. But if you fail to do that it is much to be feared that the very honour and power which you seem to have may be taken away from you, and may God forbid such a thing!

[353]

To Pope Eugenius, on behalf of the Monks of Miroir

The rancour between the Cluniac monks and the Cistercians took a more concrete shape after Innocent II had recognized the services of the Abbot of Clairvaux during the schism by

*exempting all Cistercian houses from paying tithe, thereby de-
priving the Cluniacs of one-tenth of their revenue. It came to
a head in the case of Gigny, a Cluniac priory in Burgundy. The
monks of Gigny organized an attack on the Cistercian abbey
of Miroir and inflicted damage amounting to some thousands
of pounds in our money. The Pope ordered that the monks of
Gigny should make full compensation for all the damage that
had been done. A conference was held under the auspices of
the Abbot of Cluny to assess the damage and arrange for the
payment, but no satisfactory conclusion was arrived at and
the matter remained unsettled at the death of St. Bernard.*

IN the hope of reaching a peaceful settlement I met the
monks of Gigny at Cluny. We worked hard for peace, but
nothing came of our endeavours except the ruin of our hopes.
We repeated the instructions you gave in your letter about the
payment of compensation and the restitution of what had been
taken away, but all to no purpose. The damage was very great
for, not to go into details, one whole abbey was destroyed and
the cost of rebuilding it is estimated at not less than thirty thousand *solidi*. They thought that this was too much for them to
pay. Since we had lost so much I was prepared to forgo full
compensation, but the sum they offered was so trivial that the
venerable Abbot of Cluny, whose efforts on behalf of peace
have been more kind than successful, did not think it worth
our while to accept it. And so no agreement was reached because the compensation they offered was so absurdly small.
They said that certain evil-minded persons amongst them had
done this thing and that they should see to it, that it was no concern of theirs. This is an absurd excuse. It is notorious in the
whole neighbourhood that the outrage was committed by the
men of the monastery, that some of the monks were present at
the time, and that all consented to it. Up to the present I have
not heard of any one of them being opposed to it. The abbot
himself has openly refuted and condemned this sort of shuffling

by declaring that a monastery is entitled to require full compensation for any damages that it may suffer from another. We await the last word in this matter from you, for it has been more than clearly proved that it can only be settled with a strong hand.

[357]

To a certain layman

I HAVE never met you, but I have heard of you. You have the reputation of being a wise man and you enjoy a respected position in the world. But my dear son Peter, to whom you seem to be well known and related by blood, has asked me to write to you or, I should say, to write back to you. For you have written to him, and I could wish that your letter had been creditable to yourself and profitable for him. This is not the case, for you have had the audacity to try and dissuade a soldier of Christ from the service of his Lord. I tell you, there is one who will see and judge this. Are not your own sins enough for you that you must saddle yourself with the sins of another by doing your best to entice a repentant young man back to his follies and thus, in your hard and unrepentant heart, to lay up wrath for yourself on that day of wrath? As though the devil were not tempting Peter enough without the help of you who are supposed to be a Christian and his friend and leader. You have behaved towards him like another serpent, but he has not yielded to you like another Eve. He was shaken but not overthrown by what you wrote, for he is founded upon a firm rock.

2. I shall not return evil for evil, on the contrary I shall try to overcome evil with good by praying for you, by desiring better dispositions for you, and by trying to impart them with my letter. First of all, so that you may be in very truth as wise

as people say you are, I send you to the Wise Man saying: 'Suffer him to do good who may, and thou thyself, when thou mayest, do good'. You have the time to do good, but for how long will you have it? How much of life is there left to you, especially now that you are an old man? 'For what is life but a vapour which appeareth for a little while, and afterwards shall vanish away?' If you are truly wise then that curse will not come upon you: 'Never yet did I see a fool secure in his possessions but I prophesied disaster, there and then, for his fair prospects'. The truly wise man did well to call the falsely wise fools, for the wisdom of this world is foolishness with God. 'Ah, if you would but take thought, learn your lesson, and pay heed to your final end'. If only you were wise in the things of God, if only you had a true estimation of the things of this world and paid more heed to the depths beneath you, surely then you would dread what is beneath you, crave for the heights above you, and scorn what lies to your hand! My mind, or rather my soul, suggests much that I might say to you. But until I know from your answer how you have taken what I have already said, I will refrain from adding anything more. I do not wish to become burdensome to one with whom I hope to be on friendly terms in future, and whom I would gladly help to salvation if he would permit me. Although she has done nothing to deserve it, I greet your dear wife in Christ.

[365]

To the Countess de Blois

The Countess de Blois was the wife of Theobald the Great, Count of Champagne. This is perhaps one of the most human and charming of all the Saint's letters, and yet another indication of how very far he was from the morose ideal set forth by some of his more modern and less saintly admirers.

I AM sorry your son[1] has behaved badly towards you. I deplore as much the conduct of the son as the wrongs of his mother. Yet, after all, such conduct is excusable in a young son. Youth is ever prone to such faults and is itself an excuse for them. Do you not realize that 'all the thoughts and imaginations of a man's heart are bent towards evil from youth'? You may be sure that the merits and alms of his father will bring about a change for the better in him. You must offer more and more vows and prayers to God for him, because, even though at the moment his conduct towards you is not what it should be, yet nevertheless a mother ought not and cannot lose her maternal affection for her children. 'Can a mother ever forget the son she bore in her womb?' asks the Prophet, and he adds: 'even if she were to forget, I will not be forgetful of thee'. The young man has so many excellent qualities that we must offer prayers and tears to the Lord, that God may enable him (as I am sure he will) to emulate the goodness of his father. He must be treated with gentleness and kindly forbearance, because by such treatment he will be more encouraged to do good than if he were exasperated by nagging and scolding. I am sure that by these means we will soon be able to rejoice over a happy change in him. There is nothing I desire more than that he should change for the better. I wish I could find his conduct towards others as irreproachable as I have always found it towards myself, for I have never known him anything but most ready and willing to do all I wished. May God reward him for this! But, as you have asked me to do, I am always remonstrating with him about his conduct towards you, and I shall continue to do so.

1. This was probably Henry, who succeeded his father in 1151.

To Hugh, a novice, who afterwards became Abbot of Bonneval

This Hugh was, apparently, the nephew of St. Hugh, Bishop of Grenoble. This very fine letter of encouragement would be suitable for any novice of any age time.

To his very dear son in Christ, Hugh, 'a new creature in Christ', that he may take courage in the Lord, from Brother Bernard, styled Abbot of Clairvaux.

WHEN I heard the good news of your conversion, my heart was filled with joy. It is a cause of joy for men and angels. Already it is a festal day in heaven, a day resounding with songs of praise and thanksgiving. A noble youth, gently nurtured, has conquered the evil one, scorned the world, sacrificed his body, renounced the affection of his parents, and, taking to himself wings, leaped over the snares of riches. Whence such wisdom, my son? Not even among the ancients of Babylon was such wisdom to be found. They were those who, according to or rather against the teaching of the Apostle, 'wished to become rich and fall into temptation, the devil's snare for them'. But the wisdom of my Hugh is of heaven and not of this world: 'I give thee praise, Father, that thou hast hidden all this from the wise and revealed it to a child'. Do you also, my son, thank our Redeemer for his gift to you, and 'keep the innocence of a child, with the thoughts of grown men'. Do not let the roughness of our life frighten your tender years. Remember that the rougher the thistle, the softer the cloth.[1] The sweetness of Christ will take the bitterness from the prophet's

1. A reference to the practice of beating new cloth with thistles to make it soft.

broth. If you feel the stings of temptation, lift your eyes to the
serpent on the staff, and draw life from the wounds of Christ.
He will be your mother, and you will be his son. The nails
which cleave his hands and feet, must also pass through yours.

2. But 'a man's household are his own enemies'. These are
they who love not you but the satisfaction they derive from
you. But let them hear from you those words: 'If you really
love me, you would be glad that I am on my way to my Father'.
And now hear what blessed Jerome says: 'If your mother
should lie prostrate at the door, if she should bare her breasts,
the breasts that gave you suck, if your nephew should be hang-
ing by his neck, yet with dry eyes fixed upon the Cross go
ahead and tread over your prostrate mother and father. It is the
height of piety to be cruel for Christ's sake.'[1] Do not be moved
by the tears of demented parents who weep because from being a child of wrath you have become a child of God. Why
have these unhappy people sentiments so harsh? What cruel
love, what mistaken affection is theirs! Bad company, it is said,
corrupts noble minds. And so I advise you, my son, to avoid as
far as you can idle talking with guests, it only fills the ears
without filling the mind. Learn to pray, to lift up your heart to
God, your eyes in supplication to heaven. It were an impious
thing to believe that God could ever close his heart to you or
be deaf to your cry and sighs. For the rest, remember always
and in everything to obey the counsels of your spiritual fathers
as well as the commandments of the Divine Majesty. Do this
and you shall live; do this and a rich blessing shall come upon
you so that for every single thing you have left you will receive a hundredfold in return, even during this life. Do not believe anyone who tries to persuade you that you have been
overhasty and would have done better to have waited until
you were older. Believe rather him who said: 'It is well thou
shouldst learn to bear the yoke, now in thy youth'. Farewell
and persevere, for only perseverance is crowned.

1. *Ep Heliod.*, 1.

To Malachy, Archbishop of Ireland

To the venerable lord and most blessed father, Malachy, by the grace of God Archbishop of Ireland, and Apostolic Legate, that he may find favour before God, from Bernard, Abbot of Clairvaux.

AMONGST all the many worries and troubles by which I am distracted, your brethren from a distant land, your letter, and your gift of a staff are my comfort. Your letter shows me your good-will, your staff supports my weak body, and your brothers serve God humbly. I have accepted all, all have given me pleasure, and all work together for my good. With regard to your wish that I should send you two of the brothers to prepare a place, I have discussed it with the brethren and we are agreed that it would not be well for them to be separated from us until Christ is more fully formed in them, until they are better equipped to fight for the Lord. When they have been instructed in the school of the Holy Ghost, when they are clothed with strength from on high, then they will return to their father to sing the songs of the Lord no longer in a strange land but in their own.

2. Do you, in the meantime, with the wisdom given you by the Lord look for and prepare a site similar to what you have seen here, far removed from the turmoil of the world. The time is not far distant when I shall be able with God's grace to send you men fashioned anew in Christ. Blessed for ever be the name of the Lord by whose gift it has come about that we have sons in common whom your teaching has planted, my exhortations have watered, and to whom God has given increase. I beg you to preach the word of the Lord so as to 'make known to his people the salvation that is to release them from their sins'. As you are both archbishop and apostolic legate you have a

twofold duty in this matter. For the rest because 'we are be-trayed, all of us, into many faults', and moving much amongst men of the world we collect much of the world's dust, I com-mend myself to the prayers of yourself and your friends, so that Christ, the source of all pity, may deign to wash me clean in the waters of his mercy, since he said to Peter: 'If I do not wash thee, it means that thou hast no companionship with me'. Indeed I not only beg this of you as a favour, but ask for it in return for my prayers to God on your behalf, if the prayers of a sinner like myself can avail anything. Farewell in the Lord.

[384]

To the same

To Malachy, by the grace of God bishop and legate of the Apostolic See, whatever the devotion and prayers of a poor sinner can avail, from Bernard, styled Abbot of Clairvaux.

I HAVE done what you commanded, if not as it should have been done, at any rate as it could have been done at the time. The calls on me have grown so many that I have been scarcely able to accomplish the little that I have done. I have sent you these few seeds that you see before you. They may suffice for the sowing of a small part of that field where Isaac had gone to meditate when Rebecca was brought to him by the servant of Abraham, to be happily united to him for ever after. Scorn not this seed that I have sent you, for in it I find fulfilled in our day those words of the Prophet: 'Except the Lord of hosts had left us seed, we had been as Sodom, and we should have been as Gomorrah'. I have sowed and now it is for you to water, then God will give the increase. I greet the saints who are with you and humbly commend myself to your prayers and theirs.

To the same

To his most loving father and most reverend lord, Malachy, by the grace of God bishop and legate of the Holy and Apostolic See, the greetings and, for what they are worth, the prayers of Brother Bernard, Abbot of Clairvaux.

HOW agreeable are your words, how pleasant the thought of you, lord and father! You command all the affection, and all the devotion of which I am capable. There is no need for many words where such affection flourishes. I am sure that the Spirit of God bears testimony to your spirit that I am all yours, little though that be. Do not, most loving and longed-for father, do not forget the poor man who clings to you with such affection, never forget your needy friend. I do not commend myself to you as though our friendship were something new, for it is my boast in the Lord that for a long time now my insignificant person has found favour in your eyes. Yet I pray that this affection which is no new growth may yet grow anew every day. I commend to you my sons, who are yours too, and I do so all the more earnestly for their being so far away from me. You know how, after God, I put all my trust in you by entrusting them to you, because it seemed wrong to refuse your prayers. Do all you can to open your heart to them and cherish them. Never on any pretext let your care and ardour for them flag or fade, never allow to perish what your hand has planted.

2. I have learned from your letters and from those of my brethren that the house flourishes exceedingly both in temporal and in spiritual things. With my whole heart I render thanks to God for this, and my congratulations to you. But because there is still need for vigilance in a new country amongst a people little accustomed to the monastic life and unfamiliar

with it,[1] I beg you in the Lord not to remove your care from them until the work you have so well begun has been perfectly finished. Concerning the brethren who have returned, I would have been well contented for them to have remained with you. But perhaps those natives of your country who are little disciplined and who found it hard to obey observances that were strange to them, may have been in some measure the occasion of their return.

3. I have sent back to you my very dear son Christian, having instructed him as well as I could in the observance of our Order, and I hope that in future he will be more careful about them. Do not be surprised that I have not been able to send many with him, for I could not find many suitable men who were willing to go, and I was loath to oblige them to do so against their will. My dear brother Robert acceded to my request this time like an obedient son. It will be your business to help him in the buildings and other things necessary for the well-being of your house. I would also suggest that you persuade those religious who you are hoping will be useful to the new monastery that they should unite with their Order, for this would be very advantageous to the house, and you would be better obeyed. Farewell, and always remember me in Christ.

[386]

To the Brethren in Ireland, on the passing
of Blessed Malachy

St. Malachy died on November 2nd, 1148. He had been an intimate friend of St. Bernard since first meeting him when he stopped at Clairvaux on his way to Rome in the year 1139.

1. In spite of partisan historians, it cannot be denied that the religious position in Ireland at this time was not healthy. See St. Bernard's *Life of S. Malachy.*

To his brother religious in Ireland, and especially to those houses founded by Bishop Malachy of blessed memory, the consolation of the Holy Spirit, from Brother Bernard, styled Abbot of Clairvaux.

IF we had here an abiding city we might rightly shed many tears at the loss of such a fellow citizen as Malachy;[1] and if we look, as we should, for the one that is to come, the loss of such a valuable leader will still be an occasion for sorrow, yet nevertheless in this case knowledge should moderate our feelings and sure hope set a limit to our grief. It ought to be no matter for wonder if our affection wrings a groan from our hearts, if our sense of bereavement expresses itself in tears, yet there should be measure in our grief, we should, in fact, find some consolation for it in the contemplation, not of what we can see, but of what we cannot see, for we see only what passes, what endures we cannot see. We must be glad for the sake of this holy soul, otherwise he would accuse us in the words of our Lord to the Apostles: 'If you really loved me you would be glad to hear that I am on my way to my Father'. The spirit of our father has gone ahead of us to the 'Father of a world of spirits'. We would prove ourselves not only wanting in charity but also ungrateful for all that we have received through him, were we not glad for his sake that he has passed from his many labours to everlasting repose, from the dangers of the world to the safety of heaven, from the world to the Father. It is an act of filial piety to grieve for the death of Malachy, but it were an act of even greater filial piety to rejoice with him in the life that he has found. Has he not found life? Surely he has, and a blessed life: 'In the eyes of fools he seemed to die, but all is well with him'.

2. Even considerations of our own advantage suggest that

1. *Si habemus hic manentem civitatem, copiosissimis jure lacrymis plangeremus*. . . . Eales: 'If we had here a continuing city, we should *not* have to shed abundant tears . . .'

we should rejoice and be glad that we have such a powerful patron in the court of heaven, a faithful advocate whose deep love will not permit him to forget us, and whose well tried holiness will obtain for him the favour of God. Who would dare to believe that the holy Malachy loves his sons less now or is less able to help them than he was? There is no doubt that since God loved him before he died he now enjoys a deeper and more sure experience of God's love; and that since he loved his own, he loved them to the end. May it be far from us, O holy soul, to consider your prayers less helpful to us now that you are offering them to the Divine Majesty with even greater eagerness, now that you are no longer living by faith but reigning by vision! Far may it be from us to believe that your charity is in any way less active that it was, now that you sit at the very fount of charity and are able to draw deep draughts of it instead of the drops for which you used to thirst. Charity is strong and cannot yield to death, it is even stronger than death. When he lay dying he remembered you and lovingly commended you to God, and he begged even me, a person of no consequence, always to remember you. For this reason I thought it well to write and tell you that I am ready with all my heart to give you such help as I can both in spiritual matters, if my incompetence in such things can achieve anything through the prayers of our blessed father, and in material matters if any opportunity should arise.

3. And also, dear sons, I feel the deepest compassion for the Irish Church in her great bereavement, and my sympathy for you is all the greater for my realization of the debt I owe you. The Lord has highly honoured us by favouring our place with the blessed death of Malachy and enriching it with the treasure of his precious body. Do not take it ill that he should have his tomb with us, since God out of his abundant mercy has so ordained it that you should have him while he lived and we when he was dead. For both you and us he was a common father, and still is, for this was the wish he expressed to us on his

death-bed. Wherefore we embrace you all with deep affection as our true brothers for the sake of this great father of ours, just as we are inspired to regard you as such by the very spiritual relationship by which we are united.

4. I exhort you, my brethren, to follow carefully in the footsteps of our father, and all the more zealously for knowing from daily experience his holy way of life. You will prove yourselves his true sons by manfully keeping his teaching; and as you saw in him and received from him a pattern of how you ought to live, live by that pattern, and make more of it than ever: 'Wise sons are the pride of their father'. Even I have been stirred from my sloth and imbued with reverence by the pattern of perfection he set before me. May he so draw me after him that I may run willingly and eagerly in the fragrance of his virtues, while the memory of them is still fresh. May Christ have you all in his safe keeping praying as you are for us!

[388]

To the Brethren of St. Anastasius

To his very dear sons in Christ, the brethren of St. Anastasius, greetings and prayers from Brother Bernard, styled Abbot of Clairvaux.

HEAVEN is my witness how greatly I love you all in Jesus Christ, and how great would be my desire to see you were such a thing possible, not only on your own account but also on my own. It would be an enormous joy and comfort for me to embrace you, my sons, my joy, and my crown. This is not yet possible for me, but I firmly trust in God's mercy that the day will come when I shall be able to see you, and then my heart will be glad and my gladness no man shall take from me. In the meantime it is certainly a great joy and consolation for

me to hear of you from my dear brother-abbot, Bernard. I
congratulate you on the satisfaction you have given him by
your discipline and zeal in the matter of obedience and poverty;
without doubt your reward for this will be great in heaven. I
beg and implore you, dearest brothers, so to act, so to stand
firm in the Lord, as to be always careful for the observance of
the Order that the Order may always be careful for you. Be
eager always to preserve unity in the bonds of peace, having
towards each other, but especially towards your superiors, the
humble charity 'that is the bond that makes us perfect'. Seek
humility before all things and peace above all things for the
sake of the indwelling Spirit of God which rests only on the
peaceful and humble.

2. But there is one thing your venerable abbot has asked me
about which does not seem to me at all good. And I believe that
I have the Spirit of God and know the will of God in this matter. I fully realize that you live in an unhealthy region[1] and that
many of you are sick, but remember him who said: 'I delight to
boast of the weaknesses that humiliate me, so that the strength
of Christ may enshrine itself in me', and 'When I am weakest
then I am strongest of all'. I have the very greatest sympathy
for bodily sickness, but I consider that sickness of the soul is
much more to be feared and avoided. It is not at all in keeping
with your profession to seek for bodily medicines, and they are
not really conducive to health. The use of common herbs, such
as are used by the poor, can sometimes be tolerated, and such is
our custom. But to buy special kinds of medicines, to seek out
doctors and swallow their nostrums, this does not become religious, is contrary to simplicity, and is especially inconsistent
with the decency and simplicity of our Order. We know that
'those who live the life of nature cannot be acceptable to God'

1. The monastery of St. Anastasius was situated in the Campagna outside
Rome. To within living memory this district has been riddled with malaria.
St. Bernard's attitude towards medicine was probably wise in the state of
medical knowledge at that time. Less wise was the selection of such an
unhealthy region for a monastery.

and for us who 'have received no spirit of worldly wisdom, but the spirit that comes from God' the proper medicine is humility and the most suitable prayer is 'purge me of my sin, the guilt which I freely acknowledge'. This is the health you must try to obtain, seek out, and preserve, dearest brothers, because 'vain is the help of man'.

[389]

To Archbishop Theobald, on behalf of
John of Salisbury

So far from being an opponent of sound learning as some of his more modern admirers have imagined, the Saint was not only one of the most learned men of his age but also one of the most fervent patrons of scholars as this letter shows as well as the letter to the Bishop of Rochester (Let. 271.) on behalf of Robert Pullen.

YOU do me a signal favour and honour me very much when you favour my friends for my sake. Yet I seek not honour from any man, but the kingdom of God and the justice thereof. I am sending your Highness John, the bearer of this letter. He is a friend of mine and of my friends, and I beg that he may benefit from the friendship for which I count on you. He has a good reputation amongst good men, not less for his life than for his learning. I have not learned this from those who exaggerate and use words lightly, but from my own sons whose words I believe as my own eyes. I had already commended him to you in person, but now that I am absent I do so much more and with all the more confidence for having learned from reliable witnesses about his life and habits. If I have any influence with you, and I know that I have much, provide for

him that he may have the means to live decently and honourably, and I beg you to do this without delay for he has nowhere
to turn. In the meantime provide for his needs, I beg you, and
let me thus experience, most loving father, those depths of affection which you retain in your heart for me.

[390]

To Hildegarde, Abbess of Mont St. Rupert

*Hildegarde was a well-known visionary, favoured with several
rather surprising revelations. Her prophecies were more widely
known than generally understood. But she enjoyed the favour
of Pope Eugenius and several distinguished churchmen. In a
letter to St. Bernard she congratulated him on his preaching of
the Crusade and declared that she saw him 'as a man in the
sun'. But in the following reply to one of her letters, the Abbot
of Clairvaux seems to word himself with a certain circumspec-
tion.*

To his beloved daughter in Christ, Hildegarde, whatever the
prayers of a sinner can avail, from Brother Bernard, styled
Abbot of Clairvaux.

THAT others should believe me a better person than
I know myself to be, is due more to human stupidity than any
special merits of my own. I hasten to reply to your sweet and
kindly letter, although the multitude of my affairs obliges me to
do so more briefly than I could wish. I congratulate you on the
grace of God that is in you and admonish you to regard it as a
gift and respond to it with all humility and devotion in the sure
knowledge that 'God flouts the scornful, and gives the humble
man his grace'. This is what I beg and implore you to do. How
could I presume to teach or advise you who are favoured with

hidden knowledge and in whom 'the influence of Christ's anointing still lives so that you have no need of teaching', for you are said to be able to search the secrets of heaven and to discern by the light of the Holy Spirit things that are beyond the knowledge of man. It is rather for me to beg that you may not forget me before God, or those who are united to me in spiritual fellowship. I am sure that when your spirit is united to God you could help and benefit us much, for 'when a just man prays fervently, there is great virtue in his prayer'. We pray without ceasing for you that you may be strengthened in all good, instructed in interior things, and guided to what endures, so that those who put their trust in God may not fall by losing faith in you, but may rather derive strength so as to make ever greater progress in good, from the sight of your own progress in the graces which you are known to have received from God.

[391]

To the English People

The manuscript of this letter in the Bibliothèque Nationale, Paris (fonds latin, MS. 14845, fol. 257), has been known for some years but, to the best of our belief, it has never before been published or translated.

I ADDRESS myself to you, the people of England, in the cause of Christ, in whom lies your salvation. I say this so that the warrant of the Lord and my zeal in his interests may excuse my hardihood in addressing you. I am a person of small account, but my desire for you in Christ is not small. This is my reason and motive for writing, this is why I make bold to address you all by letter. I would have preferred to do so by word of mouth had I but the strength to come to you as I desire.

2. Now is the acceptable time, now is the day of abundant salvation. The earth is shaken because the Lord of heaven is losing his land, the land in which he appeared to men, in which he lived amongst men for more than thirty years; the land made glorious by his miracles, holy by his blood; the land in which the flowers of his resurrection first blossomed. And now, for our sins, the enemy of the Cross has begun to lift his sacrilegious head there, and to devastate with the sword that blessed land, that land of promise. Alas, if there should be none to withstand him, he will soon invade the very city of the living God, over-turn the arsenal of our redemption, and defile the holy places which have been adorned by the blood of the immaculate lamb. They have cast their greedy eyes especially on the holy sanctu-aries of our Christian Religion, and they long particularly to violate that couch on which, for our sakes, the Lord of our life fell asleep in death.

3. What are you doing, you mighty men of valour? What are you doing, you servants of the Cross? Will you thus cast holy things to dogs, pearls before swine? How great a number of sinners have here confessed with tears and obtained pardon for their sins since the time when these holy precincts were cleansed of pagan filth by the swords of our fathers! The evil one sees this and is enraged, he gnashes his teeth and withers away in fury. He stirs up his vessels of wrath so that if they do but once lay hands upon these holy places there shall be no sign or trace of piety left. Such a catastrophe would be a source of appalling grief for all time, but it would also be a source of confusion and endless shame for our generation. What think you, my brethren? Is the hand of the Lord shortened and is he now powerless to work salvation, so that he must call upon us, petty worms of the earth, to save and restore to him his herit-age? Could he not send more than twelve legions of angels, or even just say the word and save his land? Most certainly he has the power to do this whenever he wishes, but I tell you that God is trying you. 'He looks down from heaven at the race of

men, to find one soul that reflects, and makes God its aim', one soul that sorrows for him. For God has pity on his people and on those who have grievously fallen away and has prepared for them a means of salvation. Consider with what care he plans our salvation, and be amazed. Look, sinners, at the depths of his pity, and take courage. He does not want your death but rather that you should turn to him and live. So he seeks not to overthrow you but to help you. When Almighty God so treats murderers, thieves, adulterers, perjurers, and such like, as persons able to find righteousness in his service, what is it but an act of exquisite courtesy all God's own? Do not hesitate. God is good, and were he intent on your punishment he would not have asked of you this present service or indeed have accepted it even had you offered it. Again I say consider the Almighty's goodness and pay heed to his plans of mercy. He puts himself under obligation to you, or rather feigns to do so, so that he can help you to satisfy your obligations towards himself. He puts himself in your debt so that, in return for your taking up arms in his cause, he can reward you with pardon for your sins and everlasting glory. I call blessed the generation that can seize an opportunity of such rich indulgence as this, blessed to be alive in this year of jubilee, this year of God's choice. The blessing is spread throughout the whole world, and all the world is flocking to receive this badge of immortality.

4. Your land is well known to be rich in young and vigorous men. The world is full of their praises, and the renown of their courage is on the lips of all. Gird yourselves therefore like men and take up arms with joy and with zeal for your Christian name, in order to 'take vengeance on the heathen, and curb the nations'. For how long will your men continue to shed Christian blood; for how long will they continue to fight amongst themselves? You attack each other, you slay each other and by each other you are slain. What is this savage craving of yours? Put a stop to it now, for it is not fighting but foolery. Thus to risk both soul and body is not brave but shocking, is not strength

but folly. But now, O mighty soldiers, O men of war, you have a cause for which you can fight without danger to your souls; a cause in which to conquer is glorious and for which to die is gain.

5. But to those of you who are merchants, men quick to seek a bargain, let me point out the advantages of this great opportunity. Do not miss them. Take up the sign of the Cross and you will find indulgence for all the sins which you humbly confess. The cost is small, the reward is great. Venture with devotion and the gain will be God's kingdom. They do well therefore who have taken up this heavenly sign, and they also will do well, and profit themselves, who hasten to take up what will prove to be for them a sign of salvation.

6. For the rest, not I but the Apostle warns you, brethren, not to believe every spirit. I have heard with great joy of the zeal for God's glory which burns in your midst, but your zeal needs the timely restraint of knowledge. The Jews are not to be persecuted, killed or even put to flight. Ask anyone who knows the Sacred Scriptures what he finds foretold of the Jews in the psalm. 'Not for their destruction do I pray', it says. The Jews are for us the living words of Scripture, for they remind us always of what our Lord suffered. They are dispersed all over the world so that by expiating their crime they may be everywhere the living witnesses of our redemption. Hence the same psalm adds, 'only let thy power disperse them'. And so it is: dispersed they are. Under Christian princes they endure a hard captivity, but 'they only wait for the time of their deliverance'. Finally we are told by the Apostle that when the time is ripe all Israel shall be saved. But those who die before will remain in death. I will not mention those Christian money lenders, if they can be called Christian, who, where there are no Jews, act, I grieve to say, in a manner worse than any Jew. If the Jews are utterly wiped out, what will become of our hope for their promised salvation, their eventual conversion? If the pagans were similarly subjugated to us then, in my opinion, we should

wait for them rather than seek them out with swords. But as they have now begun to attack us, it is necessary for those of us who do not carry a sword in vain to repel them with force. It is an act of Christian piety both 'to vanquish the proud' and also 'to spare the subjected',[1] especially those for whom we have a law and a promise, and whose flesh was shared by Christ whose name be for ever blessed.

The above letter was also sent 'To the lords and very dear fathers, the archbishops, bishops, and all the clergy and people of Eastern France and Bavaria, that they may abound in the spirit of strength, from Bernard, styled Abbot of Clairvaux' (*Benedictine Edition*, 363).

[411]

To Suger, Abbot of St. Denis

A letter to comfort Abbot Suger on his death-bed.

To his dear and intimate friend Suger, by the grace of God Abbot of St. Denis, Brother Bernard sends glory from within and grace from on high.

FEAR not, man of God, to put off the earthy man which is holding you down to the earth, and which would bring you down even to the regions under the earth. It is this which troubles, burdens, and aggrieves you. But why trouble about your clothing of flesh, when you are about to put on the garb of immortality in heaven? It is ready for you, but it will not be given to you already clothed; it will clothe you, but not while you are still clothed in the flesh. Wait patiently, and be glad to be found naked and unclothed. God himself wishes

1. *Aeneid*, 6, 853.

man to be clothed, but not while he is still clothed in the flesh. The man of God will not return to God, until what he has of the earth has gone back to the earth. These two, the man of God and the earthy man, are at variance one with the other, and there will be no peace for you until they are separated; and if there should be peace, it would not be the peace of God, nor would it be peace with God. You are not one of those who say: 'Peace, when there is no peace'. The peace which passes all understanding is awaiting you, and the righteous are waiting for this peace to be given you, and the joy of the Lord awaits you.

2. And I, dear friend, am torn by the desire to see you, that I may receive a dying man's blessing. But no man can arrange his life just as he wishes, and so I cannot dare to promise what I am not sure of being able to perform; yet I will try my best to do what I am not yet able to see my way to doing. Perhaps I shall come, perhaps I shall not. But whatever happens I, who have loved you from the first, shall love you without end. I say with all confidence that I can never lose one whom I have loved unto the end: one to whom my soul cleaves so firmly that it can never be separated, does not go away but only goes before. Be mindful of me when you come to where I shall follow you, so that I may be permitted soon to come after you and come to you. In the meantime be sure that I shall never lose the dear memory of you, although to my sorrow I lose your dear presence. Yet God can keep you with us in answer to our prayers, he can still preserve you for those who need you, of this there can be no doubt.

[424]

To Eskil, Archbishop of Lund

Eskil was one of St. Bernard's most devoted admirers, and the admiration was mutual. We are told that when Eskil, at great trouble and expense, came to Clairvaux with the express purpose of meeting the man of God, the monks were no less edified by the bishop than the bishop was edified by the monks. He wished ardently to join the community but was not able to satisfy this wish until the end of his life.

To his most loving father and lord Eskil, by the grace of God Archbishop of Lund, greetings in the Lord, from Brother Bernard, styled Abbot of Clairvaux.

YOUR letter and greetings, or rather your expressions of affection, were most welcome because of the special love you and I have for each other. Your troubles are, for this reason, my own; I do not have to make them so. I cannot but grieve for your grief, dear father, or hear of your worries and troubles but with worry and trouble. Whatever provokes you touches me and wrings my heart, and whatever oppresses you weighs on me too. I believe I owe you and you owe me all the favour and affection that absent friends can bestow on one another. I am undaunted, but I am not untruthful: it is your condescension that makes me bold. How, but for this, could I ever dare to presume to much? How, otherwise, could a small person like myself ever dare to hope for so much from a great man like you? I cannot repay you for your affection, but I have one, whose mercy endures for ever, who will repay for me. I speak of the Lord in whom and for whom you love me with such devotion and bind me to you with such affection. Blessed be your holy angel who put this in your heart, and blessed be God who disposed you to it. I am proud of the privilege of your affection, and I have been much refreshed from the riches of your heart by our most dear brother, your son William. I am refreshed by your messenger, by your letter, and by all who pass from you to me or by way of me.

2. Would that I had the power from on high to say all this to you and not write it, so that I might open my heart to you by word of mouth rather than by the written word. Certainly the living word is more welcome than the written word, and the tongue more eloquent than the pen; for the eyes of the speaker lend credence to his words, and the expression of the face conveys affection better than the pen.[1] But, being absent from you, this is beyond my power and so I must satisfy myself with the second best alternative of a letter. I saw your messenger with great pleasure, and I have done all I could to further your business with the Pope. About that secret wish that burns in your heart,[2] the bearer of this letter, your William, will tell you what I think; your William, I say, and especially yours in the heart of Christ. Attend to what he says on this matter as you would to myself. My daily cares are calling me, a crowd of visitors oblige me to break off this letter before I have finished. But although all this may make my letter brief, it cannot lessen my affection. It can control my actions but not my heart. This is all yours to command as you wish for as long as I am alive, my very dear friend worthy of all honour and respect.

[430]

To Abbot Guy and the Brethren of Montier-Ramey

This letter concerns the Office in honour of St. Victor which the Abbot of Clairvaux composed at the request of the community of Montier-Ramey. It is of interest because it contains

1. St. Bernard was a Burgundian.
2. Eskil's desire to enter Clairvaux.

St. Bernard's views on liturgical worship. The Office is pub-lished amongst the works of St. Bernard.

To the venerable Guy, Abbot of Montier-Ramey, and the holy brethren of his community, that they may serve the Lord in holiness, from Bernard their servant.

YOU, my dear Abbot Guy, and your brethren are ask-ing me to compose for you something which can be solemnly recited or sung by you on the feast of St. Victor whose relics repose in your midst. I hesitate, but you press me; I try to ex-cuse myself, but you urge me on. You will take no refusal, and you ignore my only too well justified diffidence. You add the requests of others to your own, as if anyone would be more likely to persuade me than you. But even you must understand that in a matter like this, it is not your affection for me that you should consider, but the sort of position I hold in the Church. The sublime nature of the task you have set demands that you should require the services, not of a friend, but of someone learned and worthy: of a man whose great authority, holy life, mature style, would imbue his work and accord bet-ter with the holiness of it.

2. Shall the writings of one so insignificant amongst the Christian peoples as myself be read aloud in the churches? What capacity or what eloquence do I possess that from me, of all people, joyous and pleasing prayers and hymns should be required? Shall I begin anew to praise upon earth one who is deemed praiseworthy and praised in heaven itself? To try and add to the praises sung in heaven were a depredation rather than an augmentation. Not that men should deny their praises to those who are glorified by the angels, but in their festivals anything that savours of novelty or frivolity would be out of place. Such occasions require something venerable and beyond question orthodox, something redolent with holy gravity that

would edify the people. But if you want to hear something new, and if the occasion demands it, then let something be chosen that would both please and profit the hearers by the dignity of its diction and the authority of the author. Furthermore, the sense of the words should be unmistakable, and they should shine with truth, tell of righteousness, incite to humility, and inculcate justice; they should bring truth to the minds of the hearers, devotion to their affections, the Cross to their vices, and discipline to their senses. If there is to be singing, the melody should be grave and not flippant or uncouth. It should be sweet but not frivolous; it should both enchant the ears and move the heart; it should lighten sad hearts and soften angry passions; and it should never obscure but enhance the sense of the words. Not a little spiritual profit is lost when minds are distracted from the sense of the words by the frivolity of the melody, when more is conveyed by the modulations of the voice than by the variations of the meaning.

3. This is what should be heard in churches and the sort of man the composer should be. Am I such a person, or is what I have composed like this? In the words of the Lord, I have bestirred myself to give you what I could out of my poverty, at your entreaties, at your persistence; if not because of your friendship, at any rate because of your importunity. I have given, not what you wanted, but what I could, according to my powers if not according to your desires. I have written two sermons on the life of the saint in my own words but based upon the ancient accounts you sent me. I have tried to avoid obscure brevity on one hand and wearisome prolixity on the other. As regards the singing, I have composed a hymn, but I have kept the sense clear at the expense of the metre. I have arranged twelve responsories with twenty-seven antiphons in their places, and I have added one responsory which I have assigned to first vespers, likewise two short ones to be sung, according to your custom, one at Lauds and one at Vespers on

the day itself. And for all this I demand payment, I am after a reward. I have done my best and, whether you are pleased with it or not, you must reward me with your prayers.

[434]

To Baldwin, Bishop of Noyon

This letter is remarkable for its quiet humour. Evidently, as we can gather from the end of the letter, this was considered a characteristic of the saint. It is to be regretted that so many of his letters have perished, and that these were, most probably, his personal familiar letters.

To the lord Baldwin, Bishop of Noyon, something better than he deserves, from Brother Bernard, styled Abbot of Clairvaux.

I AM sending you the small boy who is bringing this letter to eat your bread, that I may find out how mean you are from the sort of welcome you give him. But you have no cause for tears or lamentations, he has a small stomach and will be content with little. I shall be grateful if he returns wiser rather than stouter. The tone of this letter will have to serve as my seal because it is not to hand, neither is your Godfrey.

[469]

To Arnold of Chartres, Abbot of Bonneval

I HAVE received your charitable gift in the spirit of charity, if not of pleasure. What room can there be in me for pleasure when suffering claims me completely for her own? The only sort of pleasure I have is in eating nothing. So that suffering may never be absent from me, even sleep has left me. Weakness of stomach is the whole of my trouble. I take a little liquid food frequently during the day and night, so as to keep up my strength, but I cannot take anything solid. This little that I do take causes me great suffering, but I fear that it might be worse if I took nothing at all. If I sometimes take a little more than usual, it is only with the greatest discomfort. My feet and legs are swollen as though I had dropsy. But in the midst of all this, so as to conceal nothing from an anxious friend, according to the inward man (I speak as one without knowledge of such things) I have a ready spirit in a weak body. Pray our Saviour, who wills not the death of a sinner, that he will not put off my timely departure, but that he may watch over me in my passing. Support, I beg you, with your prayers a poor wretch destitute of all virtue, so that the enemy who lies in wait for me may find no place where he can grip me with his teeth and wound me. I have written this with my own hand so that when you see the familiar writing you may recognize how well I love you. But I would have preferred to have answered one of your letters than to have been the one to write first.